A MONUMENT
TO
ST. AUGUSTINE

A MONUMENT
TO
SAINT AUGUSTINE

ESSAYS ON SOME ASPECTS OF HIS THOUGHT
WRITTEN IN COMMEMORATION
OF HIS 15th CENTENARY

By

M. C. D'ARCY, S. J.

MAURICE BLONDEL

CHRISTOPHER DAWSON

ETIENNE GILSON

JACQUES MARITAIN

C. C. MARTINDALE, S. J.

ERICH PRZYWARA, S. J.

JOHN-BAPTIST REEVES, O.P.

B. ROLAND-GOSSELIN

E. I. WATKIN

WIPF & STOCK · Eugene, Oregon

Wipf and Stock Publishers
199 W 8th Ave, Suite 3
Eugene, OR 97401

A Monument to Saint Augustine
Essays on Some Aspects of His Thought Written in
Commemoration of His 15th Centenary

By D'Arcy, M. C., Blondel, Maurice, et al.

ISBN 13: 978-1-5326-1358-6
Publication date 3/31/2017
Previously published by The Camelot Press Ltd, 1930.

NIHIL OBSTAT : EDUARDUS D. MAHONEY
CENSOR DEPUTATUS.
IMPRIMATUR : EDM: CAN: SURMONT
VIC. GEN.
WESTMONASTERII, DIE 4A AUGUSTI 1930.

CONTENTS

COMPILER'S NOTE

When this volume was first planned it was thought that it would be possible to review within its limits the main directions in which St. Augustine's thought flowed and came to make itself felt at selected points in history. But it was later realized that a single volume could not possibly do justice to its subject if it pretended to anything beyond superficial treatment. Thus the compiler was left with the problem of making a selection of the available material. He had the alternative of sinking disconnected shafts or quarrying in quarters more or less contiguous. He chose the latter in the belief that a collection of essays could be formed at once unified within itself and approaching the special needs and interests of its readers – who might thus read it, indeed, as written : in personal sympathy, in commemoration.

So it happens that here is a monument which attempts to be worthy and appropriate while acknowledging that it is by no means complete. It is dedicated to the more general aspects of St. Augustine's thought : to St. Augustine the Philosopher, the Sociologist and the Man of Letters, not to St. Augustine the Doctor of Grace and the Ecclesiologist. Indeed the latter aspects are so important and have given rise to such a vast specialized literature that it is necessary to devote a separate volume to them, which is already in course of preparation. The present volume rightly comes first as it attempts to evaluate the general influence which St. Augustine has had in Western thought and culture and his meaning for us at the present day.

Finally, the compiler would like to acknowledge a debt of gratitude to Fr. John-Baptist Reeves, O.P., and to Mr. Christopher Dawson for their help at every stage of his work, which otherwise could never have been accomplished.

T. F. B.

EPINICIUM AUGUSTINI [1]

De profundis tenebrarum
Mundo lumen exit clarum,
   Et scintillat hodie.

Olim quidem vas erroris
Augustinus, vas honoris
   Datus est Ecclesiæ.

Verbo Dei dum obedit,
Statim credit et accedit
   Ad baptismi gratiam.

Quam imprimis tuebatur
Verbis, scriptis execratur
   Erroris fallaciam.

Firmans fidem, formans mores,
Legis sacræ perversores
   Verbi necat gladio.

Obmutescit Fortunatus,
Cedunt Manes et Donatus
   Tantæ lucis radio.

Mundus marcens et inanis,
Et doctrinis tritus vanis,
   Per pestem hæreticam.

Multum cœpit fructum ferre,
Dum in fines orbis terræ
   Fidem sparsit unicam.

[1] Sequence from a Mass in honour of St. Augustine by Lancillotto Cornelio, O.S.A. *Sancti Augustini Vita*, Antwerp, 1616.

Clericali vitæ formam
Conquadravit iuxta normam
  Cœtus apostolici.

Sui quippe nihil habebant
Tanquam suum : sed vivebant
  In communi clerici.

Sic multorum pro salute
Diu vivens in virtute,
  Dormivit cum patribus.

In extremis nil legavit,
Qui nil suum æstimavit,
Immo totum reputavit
  Commune cum fratribus.

Salve gemma Confessorum,
Lingua Christi, vox cælorum,
Scriba vitæ, lux Doctorum,
  Præsul beatissime.

Qui te Patrem venerantur
Te ductore consequantur
Vitam in qua glorientur
  Cum sanctorum agmine. Amen.

CHRISTOPHER DAWSON

ST. AUGUSTINE AND HIS AGE

" *The world itself now bears witness to its approaching end by the evidence of its failing powers. There is not so much rain in winter for fertilizing the seeds, nor in summer is there so much warmth for ripening them. The springtime is no longer so mild, nor the autumn so rich in fruit. Less marble is quarried from the exhausted mountains, and the dwindling supplies of gold and silver show that the mines are worked out and the impoverished veins of metal diminish from day to day. The peasant is failing and disappearing from the fields, the sailor at sea, the soldier in the camp, uprightness in the forum, justice in the court, concord in friendships, skill in the arts, discipline in morals. Can anything that is old preserve the same powers that it had in the prime and vigour of its youth? It is inevitable that whatever is tending downwards to decay and approaches its end must decrease in strength, like the setting sun and the waning moon, and the dying tree and the failing stream. This is the sentence passed on the world ; this is God's law : that all that has risen should fall and that all that has grown should wax old, and that strong things should become weak and great things should become small, and that when they have been weakened and diminished they should come to an end.*"

ST. CYPRIAN, *Ad Demetrianum*, c. iii.

I. THE DYING WORLD

St. Augustine has often been regarded as standing outside his own age – as the inaugurator of a new world and the first mediæval man, while others, on the contrary, have seen in him rather the heir of the old classical culture and one of the last representatives of antiquity. There is an element of truth in both these views, but for all that he belongs neither to the mediæval nor to the classical world. He is essentially a man of his own age – that strange age of the Christian Empire which has been so despised by the historians, but which nevertheless marks one of the vital moments in the history of the world. It witnessed the fall of Rome, the passing of that great order which had controlled the fortunes of the world for five centuries and more, and the laying of the foundations of a new world. And Augustine was no mere passive spectator of the crisis. He was, to a far greater degree than any emperor or general or barbarian war-lord, a maker of history and a builder of the bridge which was to lead from the old world to the new.

Unfortunately, although there is no lack of historical evidence, the real importance of this period is seldom appreciated. Ever since the Renaissance the teaching of ancient history has been treated as part of the study of the classics and consequently comes to an end with the age of the Antonines, while the teaching of modern history is equally bound up with the nationalist idea and begins with the rise of the existing European peoples. Consequently there is a gap of some five hundred years from the third to the seventh century in the knowledge of the ordinary educated person. It lasts from the collapse of the old Empire in the third century A.D. to the break-up of the reconstituted

Eastern Empire in the seventh century under the stress of the Mohammedan invasions. This is the period of the Christian Empire, the Empire of Constantine and Justinian, the age of the Fathers and of the great councils. It deserves to be studied as a whole and for its own sake, instead of piecemeal and from conflicting points of view. Hitherto the secular historians have confined themselves to one side of the evidence and the ecclesiastical historians to the other, without paying much attention to each other's results. We have to go back to the days of Tillemont to find an historian who is equally competent in both fields. The modern historians of the period have shown themselves notably unsympathetic to its religious achievements. The greatest of them – Gibbon and the late Professor Bury – were free-thinkers with a strong bias against Christianity, while the remainder, from the days of Finlay and Burckhardt and Gregorovius to Seeck and Stein and Rostovtzeff in our time, all write from a secularist point of view. This is peculiarly unfortunate, not only because by far the larger part of the historical evidence has a religious character, but still more because the whole historical development becomes inexplicable when viewed from a purely secular standpoint. To neglect or despise the religious achievement of the age is as fatal to any true understanding of it as a complete disregard of the economic factor would be in the case of nineteenth-century Europe. For the real interest and importance of that age are essentially religious. It marks the failure of the greatest experiment in secular civilization that the world had ever seen, and the return of society to spiritual principles. It was at once an age of material loss and of spiritual recovery, when amidst the ruins of a bankrupt order men strove slowly and painfully to rebuild the house of life on eternal foundations.

This vital revolution owes nothing to the coming of the new peoples. It was already accomplished while the Roman

Empire was intact and the Eternal City was still inviolate. Yet it was this change rather than the material collapse of the Roman state which marks the real break between the ancient classical civilization and that of the Byzantine and mediæval world.

Rome had won her world empire by her genius for military and political organization, but her positive contribution to culture was comparatively small. She was rather an agent in the expansion of culture than its creator. Her part was that of the soldier and engineer who cleared the way and built the roads for the advance of civilization. The cosmopolitan culture which became common to the whole Roman Empire was itself mainly the creation of the Hellenic genius. It had its origins in the life of the Greek city-state and had already acquired the character of a world civilization in the great states of the Hellenistic world. Alexander the Great and his successors had made it their mission to spread this civilization throughout the lands that they had conquered. All over the East, from the Mediterranean and the Black Sea to the Oxus and the Indus, countless cities sprang up which in their constitution, their social life, and their buildings were modelled on the pattern of the Greek city. And each of these cities became a centre of diffusion for Western culture. The peasants no doubt continued to live their own life and served their new masters as they had served so many conquerors in the past, but the upper and middle classes were by degrees drawn into the privileged society and were either completely Hellenized or at least acquired a superficial veneer of Greek manners and culture. A single type of urban civilization gradually came to prevail throughout the Hellenistic world.

Rome in her turn took on this inheritance from the great Hellenistic monarchies and carried on their work. But she did so in a strictly practical and utilitarian spirit. At first, indeed, her attitude was entirely selfish, and she organized

BA

the world only to exploit it. Roman capitalists, money-lenders, slave-dealers and tax-gatherers descended on the East like a swarm of locusts and sucked the life out of the dependent communities. Every Roman, from the aristocratic capitalist like Brutus or Lucullus down to the meanest agent of the great financial corporations, had his share in the plunder.[1] The age of the Republic culminated in an orgy of economic exploitation which ruined the prosperity of the subject peoples and brought Rome herself to the verge of destruction.

The crisis was averted by the foundation of the Empire. Julius Cæsar and Augustus put an end to the misrule of the capitalist oligarchy and the tyranny of military adventurers and returned to the Hellenistic ideal of an enlightened monarchy. The provinces recovered their prosperity, and alike in the Hellenistic East and the Latin West there was a fresh expansion of urban civilization. For two centuries the ancient world enjoyed an age of continuous material progress.

Everywhere from Britain to Arabia and from Morocco to Armenia wealth and prosperity were spreading, new cities were being founded, and the more backward peoples were adopting a higher form of civilization. And nowhere was this process more striking than in Africa, where even to-day the stately ruins of so many Roman cities still remain to impress the modern tourist with their evidence of vanished civilization. Even a comparatively remote and unimportant town like Timgad, in North Africa, possesses public buildings and monuments finer than those of many a modern city of vastly superior wealth and population. It had its theatres and amphitheatres in which free spectacles were provided for the entertainment of the people. It had porticoes and basilicas

---

[1] It is a characteristic that Brutus, who was regarded in later times as a model of republican virtue, quarrelled with Cicero because the latter was forced to reduce the interest on Brutus's loans to the impoverished cities of Cilicia from forty-eight per cent. to a beggarly twelve per cent. !

where the citizens could attend to public business or idle away their leisure time. It had baths and gymnasia, libraries and lecture halls, and temples which were not, like our churches, destined solely for religious worship, but were the centre of civic ceremonial and public festivities. There has probably never been an age in which the opportunities for living an enjoyable and civilized existence were so widely diffused. For the ancient city was not, like the average modern town, a factory or a place of business ; it existed for the enjoyment of its citizens and it was the centre of an active communal life, lived in public and at the public expense.

This was most strikingly exemplified at Rome itself, where the Greek democratic principle of the right of the citizen to be fed and amused at the expense of the state had been carried to its extreme conclusions. These rights were the only remaining privilege of the Roman democracy, which had completely lost all share in the government of the Empire, but, so far from disappearing with the loss of political rights, they continued to expand down to the last period of the Empire. The corn dole had been limited by Augustus to some 200,000 citizens, but even so it involved a vast organization, the traces of which are to be seen in the remains of the great public corn *dépôts* at Ostia, and the setting aside for the use of the capital of the chief corn-growing areas of the Mediterranean world – Egypt and Sicily. Moreover, in the course of time the free distribution of other articles such as oil, wine and bacon were added to the corn dole. Gifts of money had been common even in republican times, and during the reign of Augustus no less than six distributions of between £2 and £3 10s. per head were made to between 200,000 and 320,000 persons.

No less important was the amusement of the people. The games of the circus and the amphitheatre involved enormous expenditure and occupied a considerable part of the year. Apart from the special festivals, which might last as long as a hundred days on end, the regular games took up sixty-six days a year in the time of Augustus, and had increased to a hundred and seventy-five days by the fourth century.

Finally, vast sums of public money were absorbed by the public buildings. To some extent this expenditure served ends of real value, above all in the case of the great aqueducts which ensured to Rome a better water supply than that of most modern capitals. For the most part, however, it was entirely unproductive. The Colosseum – which has stood for eighteen centuries as a symbol of the material power of imperial Rome – was created to serve the brutal amusements of the Roman populace. The imperial palaces and fora, with their temples and libraries and porticoes, provided a sumptuous background for the social life of the Court and the capital. But the most characteristic monuments of the imperial period are the thermæ, which continued to increase in size and splendour down to the age of Diocletian and Constantine. They were not mere public baths in our sense of the word, but true palaces for the people, of vast size, containing baths and gymnasia, lecture-rooms and libraries, and adorned with the masterpieces of Greek and Hellenistic art. Public building on such a scale far surpassed anything that the modern world has yet seen. Imperial Rome became a city of gold[1] and marble, a worthy incarnation of the *Dea Roma* whom her subjects worshipped. And the same ideal was pursued by all the cities of the Empire according to their capacity. Each tried to surpass its neighbour in the splendour of its public buildings and the number of its games and festivals. Not only millionaires, like Herodes Atticus,

[1] She was literally a " golden city," for the growing scarcity of precious metal which characterized the later Empire is attributed by historians in part to the enormous quantities of gold which were used to gild the roofs and domes of the temples and public buildings of Rome.

but every citizen of moderate wealth, used his money unstintingly in the service of his native city, either by building baths, theatres and porticoes, or by providing public spectacles or endowments for educational and charitable purposes.

All this testifies to a high level of material culture and to an admirable development of public spirit on the part of the citizen class, but from the moral and spiritual point of view it was less satisfactory. All the vast development of material prosperity and external display had no spiritual purpose behind it. Its ultimate end was the satisfaction of corporate selfishness. The religious element in ancient culture, which had been the inspiration of civic patriotism in the fifth and sixth centuries B.C., had almost disappeared from the cosmopolitan civilization of the imperial age. The temples and the gods remained, but they had lost their spiritual significance and had become little more than an ornamental appendage to public life and an occasion for civic ceremonial. For the educated, the only real religion was philosophy – a philosophy which provided high moral ideals for the *élite*, but which was incapable of influencing the mass of society.

The true religion of society was not the philosophic paganism of men like Marcus Aurelius or St. Augustine's correspondent, Maximus of Madaura, but the cult of material pleasure and success. Christianity had more to fear from Trimalchio than from Julian, and the real Antichrist was not Apollo, but Belial, "the prince of this world." And this is fully recognized by the majority of Christian writers from the time of St. Paul down to the fifth century. St. Augustine himself, in a well-known chapter of *The City of God*, reveals the naked materialism which lay behind the opposition of pagan society to Christianity, and shows that it was as irreconcilable with the old Roman traditions as with Christian teaching. Its ideal was not civic virtue and patriotism, but to have a good time and bigger and better shows. " They do not trouble," he writes, " about the moral degradation of the Empire ; all that they ask is that it should be prosperous and secure. ' What concerns us,' they say, ' is that everyone should be able to increase his wealth so that he can afford a lavish expenditure and can keep the weaker in subjection. Let the poor serve the rich for the sake of their bellies and so that they can live in idleness under their protection, and let the rich use the poor as dependants and to enhance their prestige. . . . Let the laws protect the rights of property and leave men's morals alone. Let there be plenty of public prostitutes for whosoever wants them, above all for those who cannot afford to keep mistresses of their own. Let there be gorgeous palaces and sumptuous banquets, where anybody can play and drink and gorge himself and be dissipated by day or night, as much as he pleases or is able. Let the noise of dancing be everywhere, and let the theatres resound with lewd merriment and with every kind of cruel and vicious pleasure. Let the man who dislikes these pleasures be regarded as a public enemy, and if he tries to interfere with them, let the mob be free to hound him to death. But as for the rulers who devote themselves to giving the people a good time, let them be treated as gods and worshipped accordingly. Only let them take care that neither war nor plague nor any other calamity may interfere with this reign of prosperity.' "[1]

This indictment of the spirit of hedonism and materialism which dominated Roman society runs through all the writings of the Fathers and is supported by many non-Christian writers. Even allowing for the exaggerations of the moralist, there can be little doubt of its substantial truth. Nor was this spirit confined to great cities such as Rome and Antioch and Carthage ; it was also characteristic of

[1] Condensed from *De Civitate Dei*, II, xx ; cf. *Ep.* cxxxviii, 3, 14.

provincial society, as St. Jerome testifies in a characteristic sentence[1] about his own countrymen. It is a mistake to suppose that the age of the Empire was a religious one because it was marked by so many new religious movements. The mystery religions and the tendency towards mysticism and asceticism are a proof of the religious bankruptcy of society which drove the religious-minded to seek spiritual life outside the life of the city and of society in an esoteric ideal of individual salvation. Even Stoicism, the one sect of the time which inculcated a disinterested ideal of social duty, was fundamentally an unsocial and individualistic creed. The reigning culture had become almost completely secularized, and the religious and the social instincts were becoming opposed to one another.

The one exception to this tendency is to be found in the Jewish tradition, and that was the one religious tradition which had preserved its independence in face of the cosmopolitan Hellenistic culture. The attempt of the Seleucid kings to Hellenize Judæa had led to the great national rising of the Maccabean period, which was nothing less than a crusade against Hellenism, and though the Roman Empire succeeded in breaking down the material resistance of the nation, it could not overcome their spiritual opposition. The Jews remained a people apart, and refused to submit to the dominant culture or to share in the life of the city. The primitive Church inherited this tradition. The Christians claimed, no less than the Jews, to be a people apart – " a chosen race, a royal priesthood, a holy nation." But this claim no longer involved any political aspirations. Throughout the centuries of persecution the Christians remained faithful to the teachings of St. Peter and St. Paul and submitted to the imperial government as a power ordained of God. St. Clement's noble prayer on behalf of

---

[1] " *In mea enim patria, rusticitatis vernacula, deus venter est et de die vivitur, sanctior est ille qui ditior est.*"—*Ep.* vii, 5.

princes and rulers would not be out of place in the altered circumstances of a Christian society.

But this political loyalty to the Empire as a state only throws into stronger relief the irreconcilable hostility of Christianity to the imperial culture. The Church was to a great extent an alternative and a substitute for the communal life of the city-state. It appealed to all those elements which failed to find satisfaction in the material prosperity of the dominant culture – the unprivileged classes, the poor and the oppressed, the subject oriental populations, and above all those who were dissatisfied with the materialism and sensuality of pagan society and who felt the need for a living religion on which to base their lives.

Consequently it was inevitable that Christianity should come into conflict with the pagan government and society. To the ordinary man the Christian was an anti-social atheist, " an enemy of the human race," who cut himself off from everything that made life worth living. To the authorities he was a centre of passive disaffection, a disloyal subject who would not take his share of the public service or pay homage to the emperor. The Christian, on his part, regarded the official worship of the emperor as a supreme act of blasphemy – the deification of material power and the setting up of the creature in place of the Creator. So long as the Empire confined itself to its secular function as the guardian of peace and order, the Church was ready to recognize it as the representative of God, but as soon as it claimed an exclusive allegiance and attempted to dominate the souls as well as the bodies of its subjects, the Church condemned it as the representative of Antichrist. Thus the denunciations of the Apocalypse are as integral a part of the Christian attitude to the Empire as St. Paul's doctrine of loyal submission. To St. John the official cultus of the Emperor, as organized in the province of Asia, is the worship of the Beast, and Rome herself, the *Dea Roma* of the state religion, is the great harlot enthroned upon the waters, drunken with the blood of the saints and the blood of the martyrs of Jesus. It is, however, important to notice that Rome is not described as a conquering military power, but as the centre of a luxurious cosmopolitan culture, the great market in which all the merchants of the earth congregate. It is the triumphant materialism of Rome, not her military and political oppression, which is denounced in the Apocalypse.

Nothing can give a more vivid impression of the failure of material civilization to satisfy the needs of the human soul than St. John's vision of the arraignment of the great heathen world power before the eternal justice by the souls of its innocent victims. Ancient civilization had set itself in opposition to the religious spirit and had alienated the deepest forces in the mind of the age, and thereby its ultimate doom was sealed. There is a remarkable passage in one of the sermons of St. Gregory in which he looks back from the disorder and misery of the age in which he lived to the material prosperity of the world in which the martyrs had suffered. In his own days the world seemed dying. " Everywhere death, everywhere mourning, everywhere desolation." In the age of Trajan, on the contrary, " there was long life and health, material prosperity, growth of population and the tranquillity of daily peace, yet while the world was still flourishing in itself, in their hearts it had already withered."[1] *In cordibus aruerat* – that was the innermost secret of the fall of ancient civilization. It had lost its roots in the human soul and was growing more and more empty and sterile. The vital centre of the society of the future was to be found, not in the city-state, but in the Christian *ecclesia*.

Are we, then, to conclude with Renan that the rise of Christianity was the real cause of the decline of the Empire

[1] St. Gregory, *Hom.* xxviii.

— that " Christianity was a vampire which sucked the life-blood of ancient society and produced that state of general enervation against which patriotic emperors struggled in vain " ?[1] Certainly the victory of Christianity does mark a most profound and vital aspect of the decline of the old culture, but it does not follow that it was directly responsible for it. The cosmopolitan urban culture of the later Empire broke down through its own inherent weaknesses, and even before the victory of Christianity it had already failed to justify itself on sociological and economic grounds.

In spite of its apparent prosperity and its brilliant outward appearance, the vast development of city life under the Empire was out of all proportion to its real strength. It was an elaborate superstructure built on relatively weak and unstable foundations. For the urban civilization of the imperial age was essentially the civilization of a leisured class, a society of consumers, which rested on a foundation of slave labour and rural serfdom. The vast civic expenditure on public buildings and public games was unproductive and entailed an increasing drain on the economic resources of the Empire. And at the same time the process of urbanization led to a similar exhaustion of human resources. For the citizen class was extremely sterile and had to be constantly recruited by new elements usually drawn from the class of freedmen. Moreover, neither the upper nor the lower classes of the city provided suitable military material, and the Empire came to rely more and more on the rural population, especially the natives of the recently conquered and less civilized provinces, for its supply of troops. [2]

The Roman Empire and the process of urbanization which accompanied it were, in fact, a vast system of exploitation which organized the resources of the provinces and concentrated them in the hands of a privileged class. The system

[1] Renan : *Marc-Aurèle*, p. 589.
[2] Cf. Rostovtzeff : *Social and Economic History of the Roman Empire* (1926), pp. 332-3.

worked well so long as the Empire was expanding, for there was no lack of new territory to urbanize and new masses of cheap slave labour with which to cultivate it. But the close of the period of external expansion and internal peace at the end of the second century put an end to this state of things and the Empire was left with diminishing resources to face the growing menace of external invasion and internal disruption. In spite of its apparent wealth and splendour, the urban society of the Empire had no reserve forces either of men or of money, and it was unable to face the crisis. The wealthy provincial bourgeoisie, which had been the backbone of the Empire in the second century, was financially ruined and lost its hold on the government. Power passed to the soldiery who belonged by origin to the peasant class and had no sympathy with the civic tradition.[1]

Thus the third century witnessed a social and constitutional revolution of the most far-reaching kind. The great break in the history of the ancient world – the end of the old society and the inauguration of a new order – took place not in the age of St. Augustine, when the barbarians conquered the western provinces and the unity of the Empire was destroyed, but more than a century earlier, in the age of military anarchy which followed the fall of the house of Severus. When the Illyrian soldier-emperors succeeded in stemming the tide of anarchy and beating back the enemies of Rome, the Empire which they re-established was no longer the same state. The old civic society was moribund, and neither the Senate, nor the Italian citizen body, nor the provincial city-states, were any longer strong enough to form a satisfactory basis of government and administration. Only the army and the imperial power itself had survived as living forces. But the emperor was not only the first magistrate

---

[1] According to Rostovtzeff (*op. cit.*, ch. xi), the motive force of this revolution is to be found in the class conflict between the peasant soldiery and the urban bourgeoisie, which he compares to the class conflict of bourgeois and proletariat in our own times.

of the Roman republic, he was also the representative of the great Hellenistic monarchies which had themselves inherited the absolutist traditions of the oriental state. In the East, and above all in Egypt, the organization of society was entirely different from that of the Græco-Roman world. Instead of a free citizen class, based on slave labour, practically the whole population consisted either of serfs or officials and priests. The institutions of the city-state, private property and slavery hardly existed. The whole economic life of Egypt was directly controlled by the state, and every class was bound to its special task. It was, in fact, a great system of state socialism, in which the state was the one landowner and organized the manufacture and distribution of goods by means of state monopolies and state factories and warehouses.

It was from this source that the new principles were derived on which Diocletian and his successors based their work of reorganization. The imperial office itself acquired the characteristics of an oriental kingdom. The emperor ceased to be primarily the *princeps* of the Roman state and the commander-in-chief of the Roman armies and became a sacred monarch surrounded by the ceremonial and solemn ritual of an oriental Court. " The Sacred Palace " became the centre of government and the apex of a vast official hierarchy. The Empire was no longer a federation of city-states, each of which was a self-governing unit, but a centralized bureaucratic state which controlled the life of its members down to the minutest detail. Society was based on the principle of compulsory state service, and every class and occupation was subjected to state regulation and tended to become a fixed hereditary caste. The trades which were most essential to the public service, especially those connected with the food supply, were organized as hereditary guilds which were corporately responsible for the fulfilment of their obligations. The same principle was applied even more strictly to the land, on which the state depended in the last resort alike for its food supply and its revenue. Consequently the government did all in its power to prevent land going out of cultivation. The peasant, whether a slave or a freeman, was bound to his holding and was forbidden to abandon its cultivation or to migrate elsewhere. If a holding became derelict, and no owner could be found, the neighbouring land-holders were jointly responsible for its cultivation and taxes. In the same way, the members of the citizen class became corporately liable for the payment of taxes on the whole city territory, and were bound to their *curia* – their town council – just as the peasant was bound to his land, so that a citizen who attempted to escape his financial burdens by entering the army or migrating elsewhere was liable to be arrested and sent back to his *curia*, like a runaway slave.

Under these conditions the old civic ideal of the leisured classes passed away and was replaced by that of the servile state. The urban aristocracy lost its economic prosperity and its social prestige, and its place was taken by the members of the official hierarchy and by the great landowners who stood outside the *curia* and who were strong enough to hold their own against the exactions of the taxgatherers and the oppression of the bureaucracy. Society tended more and more to return to an agrarian foundation, and the city-state was no longer the vital centre of the whole social structure, as it had been during the eight classical centuries of Mediterranean culture.

But this social revolution involved no less fundamental changes in the relations of the Empire to religion. The old official cultus was essentially bound up with the institutions of the city-state, and now that these had lost their vitality the state was in danger of being left without any religious foundation. The new unitary state required a religion of a more universal character than the polytheistic cults of the city-state possessed, and, as a matter of fact, we observe throughout the third century a tendency towards a vague semi-philosophic monotheism in pagan society.[1] This tendency finds expression in the worship of the sun, which was adopted by Aurelian and his successors as the tutelary deity of the Empire. No doubt it owed much to Syrian and Persian influences, but we see in the writings of Julian[2] how easily it adapted itself to the ideals of contemporary philosophic speculation and how well suited it was to serve as a principle of inspiration in the religious life of the age and as the official cult of the new orientalized monarchy.

Nevertheless, this solution was not destined to prevail. For Constantine, instead of contenting himself with the vague solar monotheism which had been the religion of his house, made an abrupt break with tradition and found a new religious basis for the Empire in an alliance with the outlawed and persecuted Christian Church. It was an act of extraordinary courage, and it is not altogether surprising that many historians, from the time of Gibbon to Ferdinand Lot in our day, should regard it as an act of madness which endangered the stability of the Empire by sacrificing the interests of the most loyal and influential part of the citizens in order to conciliate an unpatriotic minority. Yet it is possible that Constantine, even as a statesman, was more far-sighted than his critics. The Church was the one living creative force in the social and spiritual life of the age. It brought to society just those elements of freedom, private initiative and co-operative action of which the Empire itself stood most in need.

The life had gone out of the civic organization, and citizenship meant little more than the obligation to pay taxes. The citizenship of the future was to be found in the Church. It

---

[1] Cf. especially the hymn of the army of Licinius to the *Summus Deus* which has been preserved by Lactantius : *De mort. persecut.* xlvi, 6.

[2] *Oratio* iv.

was a far wider citizenship than that of the old city-state, since it was open to all, even to the slave, and the poor enjoyed a specially privileged position. They were the *plebs Christi*, the people of Christ, and the wealth of the Church was in a very real sense " the patrimony of the poor." In the same way the functions of the city magistrates as the representatives and protectors of the people passed to the magistrates of the new society – the Christian bishop. While the former had become mere puppets in the hands of the bureaucracy, the latter was the one independent power in the society of the later Empire. The choice of the bishop was the last right which the people preserved, and we know from countless instances how eagerly they availed themselves of it. A man who had the gift of leadership and who was trusted by the people was liable to be elected, whether he wished it or not. In the case of St. Ambrose we see a high secular official, who was not even baptized, being chosen bishop of the most important see in North Italy by popular acclamation and ordained in spite of his personal wishes. Even more strange is the case of Synesius, a Neo-platonist and a man of letters who was chosen bishop of Ptolemais in Lybia mainly on account of his patriotism and as a bold defender of the rights of his fellow-citizens.[1]

The Christian bishop was, in fact, the dominant figure in the life of the time. His position was something entirely new, for which no precedent can be found in the old religion of the city-state or in the priesthoods of the oriental mystery religions. Not only did he possess enormous religious prestige as the head of the Christian Church, but he was the leader of the people in social matters also. He occupied the position of a popular tribune, whose duty it was to defend the poor and the oppressed and to see that the strong did not

---

[1] In the case of St. Augustine's successor we have an instance of a more regular and ecclesiastical type of election, and the report of the proceedings which has been preserved in St. Augustine's letters (ccxiii) shows how closely the procedure resembled that of a civic assembly.

abuse their power. He alone stood between the people and the oppression of the bureaucracy. He was not afraid to withstand an unjust law or to excommunicate an oppressive governor, and the life and correspondence of St. Ambrose or St. Basil or Synesius or St. Augustine himself shows how frequently a bishop was called upon to intervene between the government and the people, and how fearlessly he performed his duty. On one occasion it is recorded that the prætorian prefect was so offended by St. Basil's freedom of speech that he declared that he had never in his life been spoken to in such a manner. " No doubt," replied St. Basil, " you have never met a bishop."

In the same way, it was the bishop rather than the city magistrate who inherited the civic tradition of popular oratory. While the Forum and the Agora were silent, the Churches resounded to the applause and exclamations of crowds who were still swayed by the voice of the orator. In St. John Chrysostom's homilies *On the Statues*, delivered to the people of Antioch when the fate of their city hung in the balance, we hear the last echo of the great Hellenic tradition of oratory which goes back to the golden age of Athenian democracy. And if the sermons of St. Augustine lack the classical grace of his great Syrian contemporary, they are no less interesting as examples of genuine popular oratory adapted to the simpler and less refined tastes of an ordinary provincial audience.

The Church was also taking the place of the state as the organizer of charity and of the support of the poor. Every church had its *matriculum*, or list of persons in receipt of regular relief, and enormous sums were spent in every kind of charitable work. All over the Empire, hospitals, orphanages and hostels for travellers were being built and endowed ; so that the basilica was often the centre of a whole quarter which lived by and for the church. Thus the Church stands out in this dark age as the one hope of humanity both spiritually and materially. It saved the individual from being entirely crushed under the pressure of the servile state and it opened to him a new world of social and spiritual activity in which the free personality had room to develop itself.

Hence, when the final collapse of the imperial government in the West took place the bishop remained the natural leader of the Roman population. He was the representative of the old secular culture as well as of the new spiritual society, and it was through him, above all, that the continuity of Western civilization was preserved.

> *Comme aux jours de scandales*
> *Un vieil évêque en sa ville assiégée*
> *Par des Alains, des Goths ou des Vandales*
>
> . . . . . .
>
> *Son esprit las porte un double fardeau*
> *Derrière lui sur le mur noir et froid*
> *La vieille louve allaite les jumeaux*
>
> *Et devant lui Jésus meurt sur la croix.*[1]

In the fourth century, however, these diverse traditions were still far from being completely reconciled with one another. There were, in fact, three distinct elements – and even three distinct societies – in the culture of the later Empire.

There was the new religious society of the Christian Church, with its tradition of independent spiritual authority ; there was the city-state, with its Hellenistic traditions of intellectual and material culture ; and there was the Empire itself, which more and more was coming to represent the oriental tradition of sacred monarchy and bureaucratic collectivism. The Church no longer held itself entirely aloof

[1] R. Salomé : *Notre Pays*, p. 52.

CA

from secular society, but it had not yet succeeded in Christianizing it. The civic culture remained pagan in spirit and, to a great extent, in outward form. But while the Church remained hostile to the paganism and immorality of civic life, as seen above all in the public shows and the games of the amphitheatre, she could not refuse to recognize the value of the classical tradition in its intellectual aspects. The Fathers were, almost without exception, men who had passed through the schools of rhetoric and whose minds were steeped in classical literature. St. Basil and St. Gregory Nazianzen had studied at the university of Athens, the centre of pagan culture ; St. John Chrysostom was the most brilliant pupil of Libanius, the greatest heathen professor of his time ; St. Augustine was himself a professional teacher of rhetoric ; while St. Jerome is, of all his generation, the most typical representative of the rhetorical tradition in all its strength and weakness.

Consequently the patristic culture is a blend of Christian and classical elements. The writings of St. Ambrose are as full of reminiscences of the classics as those of a Renaissance scholar. The two Apollinarii, St. Gregory Nazianzen, Paulinus and Prudentius did their best to create a Christian literature based upon classical models. It is true that in the case of St. Augustine we see a gradual evolution from the Christian humanism of Cassiacum to the anti-Pelagian severity of his later years. But it is easy to exaggerate the change, since he continued to realize the educational value of classical literature and to acknowledge his sympathy with the Platonic tradition. Nor must we attach too much importance to the famous vision in which St. Jerome was condemned as " a Ciceronian and not a Christian." After all, as he himself observed, when Rufinus taxed him with inconsistency, it was only a dream, and in spite of his visionary experience he ultimately returned to his Plato and Cicero.

This fusion of the old culture with the new religion was

of incalculable importance for the future of Europe. Although the secular culture of the ancient city passed away
with the city itself, the patristic culture lived on in the
Church. The course of studies which St. Augustine had described in his treatise *On Christian Doctrine* became the programme of the monastic schools, and bore fruit in men like
Bede and Alcuin. Thanks to the work of the Fathers and of
their age, the mediæval world never entirely lost touch with
the tradition of ancient civilization

In the same way the relations between the Church and
the imperial order were becoming more intimate in this
period. Although the Church condemned the cruelty and
the oppression of the weak which were so prevalent during
the later Empire, she was wholly favourable to the principles of authority and hierarchy on which the imperial
order was based. The ideal of a world state which should
secure universal peace and the reign of law was thoroughly
in harmony with Christian principles ; indeed, the political
unity of the world empire seemed to be the natural counterpart of the spiritual unity of the Catholic Church. Hence we
find a new attitude to the Empire in the Christian literature
of the fifth century – an appreciation of the positive services
which Rome had rendered to the cause of humanity and a
realization of the common unity of Roman civilization –
Romania, to use Orosius's expression – as something
greater and more permanent than even the political structure of the imperial state. At the beginning of the fifth
century the Spaniard Prudentius already anticipates Dante's
belief in the providential mission of the Roman Empire as
a preparation for the world religion of Christianity. " In all
parts of the world," he writes, " men live to-day as members
of the same city and children of the same hearth. Justice,
the forum, commerce, the arts and marriage unite the
inhabitants of the most distant shores ; from the mingling of
so many different bloods, a single race is born. Such is the

fruit of the victories and triumphs of the Roman Empire : thus has the road been prepared for the coming of Christ."[1]

But this new far-seeing spirit of Christian patriotism was confined to a small aristocratic circle, to men of letters like Prudentius and Paulinus of Nola. The average man who felt the heavy hand of the taxgatherer and the quartermaster could not take so wide a view. The pessimism and defeatism of Salvian is no doubt inspired by moral preoccupations, but he also expresses the criticism and discontent which were widespread in the society of the time. The Church, as the representative of the poor and the oppressed, could not be a whole-hearted supporter of the existing order. In the west, at least, the adherents of the old religion still claimed to be the true representatives of the national Roman tradition, and attributed all the misfortunes of the Empire to its abandonment of the service of the gods. It was natural that patriotic Romans, like Symmachus, should feel that the destinies of Rome were inseparably bound up with the religion of Numa and Augustus. To them the new religion, like the new capital, was an oriental *parvenu*, fit only for slaves and foreigners. A true Roman, they felt, could not abandon the temples and altars which had become doubly sacred from their glorious past.

In fact, even at the end of the fourth century the situation of Christianity in the west was still not altogether secure. Many of the highest positions in the Empire were in the hands of pagans, and the prætorian prefect, Flavian Nicomachus, took advantage of the revolt of Arbogast and Eugenius in 392–394 to reinstitute pagan worship and to reconsecrate the city by a solemn lustral purification. Moreover, the events which followed the victory of Theodorius

---

[1] Prudentius : *Contra Symmachum*, 582–91. Cf. *Peristephanon*, II, 419 *seq.* The same idea appears in the anonymous *De Vocatione Gentium*, II, xvi, and is developed at greater length by St. Leo, *Sermo* lxxxii. It had, however, already appeared in the East, though in a less specifically Roman form, in the writing of Eusebius (esp. *Theophany*, III, i–ii) and in the Apology of Melito of Sardis.

only served to justify the criticism of the pagans. The reign of the miserable Honorius witnessed a continuous series of disasters, and if, as Claudian hoped, the conservative party could have found an able leader in the person of Stilicho, it is possible that there might have been yet another pagan reaction.

But this was not to be. Stilicho fell, and his fall was followed by that of Rome itself. To pagan and Christian alike it seemed the end of all things—in St. Jerome's words, " the light of the world was put out and the head of the Empire was cut off." It is true that Alaric's raid on Rome was not in itself decisive ; it was an episode in a long-drawn-out tragedy. Every year the tide of barbarism rose higher and fresh territories were overwhelmed. It is the tendency of modern historians to minimize the importance of the invasions, but it is difficult to exaggerate the horror and suffering which they involved. It was not war as we understand it, but brigandage on a vast scale exercised upon an unwarlike and almost defenceless population. It meant the sack of cities, the massacre and enslavement of the population and the devastation of the open country. In Macedonia the Roman envoys to Attila in 448 found the once populous city of Naissus empty save for the dead, and they were forced to camp outside. In Africa, if a city refused to surrender, the Vandals would drive their captives up to the walls and slaughter them in masses so that the stench of their corpses should render the defences untenable.

" The mind shudders," wrote St. Jerome, " when dwelling on the ruin of our day. For twenty years and more, Roman blood has been flowing ceaselessly over the broad countries between Constantinople and the Julian Alps, where the Goths, the Huns and the Vandals spread ruin and death. . . . How many Roman nobles have been their prey ! How many matrons and maidens have fallen victims to their lust ! Bishops live in prison, priests and clerics fall by the sword, churches are plundered, Christ's altars are turned into feeding-troughs, the remains of the martyrs are thrown out of their coffins. On every side sorrow, on every side lamentation, everywhere the image of death."[1]

And this was in 396, when the storm was only beginning. It was to last, not for decades, but for generations, until the very memory of peace was gone. It was no ordinary political catastrophe, but " a day of the Lord " such as the Hebrew prophets describe, a judgement of the nations in which a whole civilization and social order which had failed to justify their existence were rooted up and thrown into the fire.

.   .   .   .

It was in this age of ruin and distress that St. Augustine lived and worked. To the materialist, nothing could be more futile than the spectacle of Augustine busying himself with the reunion of the African Church and the refutation of the Pelagians, while civilization was falling to pieces about his ears. It would seem like the activity of an ant which works on while its nest is being destroyed. But St. Augustine saw things otherwise. To him the ruin of civilization and the destruction of the Empire were not very important things. He looked beyond the aimless and bloody chaos of history to the world of eternal realities from which the world of sense derives all the significance which it possesses. His thoughts were fixed, not on the fate of the city of Rome or the city of Hippo, nor on the struggle of Roman and barbarian, but on those other cities which have their foundations in heaven and in hell, and on the warfare between " the world-rulers of the dark æon " and the princes of light. And, in fact, though the age of St. Augustine ended in ruin and though the Church of Africa, in the service of which he spent his life, was destined to be blotted out as completely as if it had never been, he was justified in his faith. The spirit of Augustine

[1] *Ep.* lx ; cf. *Ep.* cxxiii, written in 409 on the destruction of Gaul.

continued to live and bear fruit long after Christian Africa had ceased to exist. It entered into the tradition of the Western Church and moulded the thought of Western Christendom so that our very civilization bears the imprint of his genius. However far we have travelled since the fifth century and however much we have learnt from other teachers, the work of St. Augustine still remains an inalienable part of our spiritual heritage.

But you are come to Mount Sion, and to the city of the living God, the heavenly Jerusalem, and to the company of many thousands of angels, and to the assembly of the first-born, who are written in the heavens, and to God the Judge of all, and to the spirits of the just made perfect. . . .

HEBREWS xii, 22–3.

II. THE CITY OF GOD

St. Augustine's work of *The City of God* was inspired by the circumstances described in the last chapter. It was, like all his books, a *livre de circonstance*, written with a definitely controversial aim in response to a particular need. But during the fourteen years – from 412 to 426 – during which he was engaged upon it, the work developed from a controversial pamphlet into a vast synthesis which embraces the history of the whole human race and its destinies in time and eternity. It is the one great work of Christian antiquity which professedly deals with the relation of the state and of human society in general to Christian principles ; and consequently it has had an incalculable influence on the development of European thought. Alike to Orosius and to Charlemagne, to Gregory I and Gregory VII, to St. Thomas and Bossuet, it remained the classical expression of Christian political thought and of the Christian attitude to history. And in modern times it has not lost its importance. It is the only one among the writings of the Fathers which the secular historian never altogether neglects, and throughout the nineteenth century it was generally regarded as justifying the right of St. Augustine to be treated as the founder of the philosophy of history.

Of late years, however, there had been a tendency, especially in Germany, to challenge this claim and to criticize St. Augustine's method as fundamentally anti-historical, since it interprets history according to a rigid theological scheme and regards the whole process of human development as predetermined by timeless and changeless transcendental principles.[1] Certainly *The City of God* is not a

[1] E.g. H. Grundmann : *Studien über Joachim von Floris* (1927), pp. 74–5 ; cf. also H. Scholz : *Glaube und Unglaube in der Weltgeschichte* (1911).

philosophical theory of history in the sense of rational induction from historical facts. He does not discover anything from history, but merely sees in history the working out of universal principles. But we may well question whether Hegel or any of the nineteenth-century philosophers of history did otherwise. They did not derive their theories from history, but read their philosophy into history.

What St. Augustine does give us is a synthesis of universal history in the light of Christian principles. His theory of history is strictly deduced from his theory of human nature, which, in turn, follows necessarily from his theology of creation and grace. It is not a rational theory in so far as it begins and ends in revealed dogma ; but it is rational in the strict logic of its procedure and it involves a definitely rational and philosophic theory of the nature of society and law and of the relation of social life to ethics.

Herein consists its originality, since it unites in a coherent system two distinct intellectual traditions which had hitherto proved irreconcilable. The Hellenic world possessed a theory of society and a political philosophy, but it had never arrived at a philosophy of history. The Greek mind tended towards cosmological rather than historical speculation. In the Greek view of things, Time had little significance or value. It was the bare " number of movement," an unintelligible element which intruded itself into reality in consequence of the impermanence and instability of sensible things. Consequently it could possess no ultimate or spiritual meaning. It is intelligible only in so far as it is regular – that is to say, tending to a recurrent identity. And this element of recurrence is due to the influence of the heavenly bodies, those eternal and divine existences whose movement imparts to this lower world all that it has of order and intelligibility.

Consequently, in so far as human history consists of unique and individual events it is unworthy of science and philosophy.

Its value is to be found only in that aspect of it which is independent of time – in the ideal character of the hero, the ideal wisdom of the sage, and the ideal order of the good commonwealth. The only spiritual meaning that history possesses is to be found in the examples that it gives of moral virtue or political wisdom or their opposites. Like Greek art, Greek history created a series of classical types which were transmitted as a permanent possession to later antiquity. Certainly Greece had its philosophical historians, such as Thucydides and, above all, Polybius, but to them also the power which governs history is an external necessity – Nemesis or Tyche – which lessens rather than increases the intrinsic importance of human affairs.

The Christian, on the other hand, possessed no philosophy of society or politics, but he had a theory of history. The time element, in his view of the world, was all-important. The idea, so shocking to the Hellenic mind or to that of the modern rationalist, that God intervenes in history and that a small and uncultured Semitic people had been made the vehicle of an absolute divine purpose, was to him the very centre and basis of his faith. Instead of the theogonies and mythologies which were the characteristic forms of expression in Greek and oriental religion, Christianity from the first based its teaching on a *sacred history*.[1]

Moreover, this history was not merely a record of past events ; it was conceived as the revelation of a divine plan which embraced all ages and peoples. As the Hebrew prophets had already taught that the changes of secular history, the rise and fall of kingdoms and nations, were designed to serve God's ultimate purpose in the salvation of Israel and the establishment of His Kingdom, so the New Testament teaches that the whole Jewish dispensation was itself a stage in the divine plan, and that the barrier between Jew and Gentile was now to be removed so that humanity might be

[1] Cf. for example, the speech of Stephen in *Acts* vii.

united in an organic spiritual unity.[1] The coming of Christ
is the turning-point of history. It marks " the fullness of
times,"[2] the coming of age of humanity and the fulfilment of
the cosmic purpose. Henceforward mankind had entered on
a new phase. The old things had passed away and all things
were become new.

Consequently the existing order of things had no finality
for the Christian. The kingdoms of the world were judged
and their ultimate doom was sealed. The building had been
condemned and the mine which was to destroy it was laid,
though the exact moment of the explosion was uncertain.
The Christian had to keep his eyes fixed on the future like a
servant who waits for the return of his master. He had to
detach himself from the present order and prepare himself
for the coming of the Kingdom.

Now from the modern point of view this may seem to
destroy the meaning of history no less effectively than the
Hellenic view of the insignificance of time. As Newman
writes, " When once the Christ had come . . . nothing remained but to gather in His Saints. No higher Priest could
come, no truer doctrine. The Light and Life of men had
appeared and had suffered and had risen again ; and nothing
more was left to do. Earth had had its most solemn event,
and seen its most august sight ; and therefore it was the last
time. And hence, though time intervene between Christ's
first and second coming, it is not *recognized* (as I may say) in
the Gospel Scheme, but is, as it were, an accident. . . . When
He says that He will come soon, ' soon ' is not a word of time
but of natural order. This present state of things, ' the
present distress,' as St. Paul calls it, is ever *close upon* the next
world and resolves itself into it."[3]

---

[1] *Eph.* ii.

[2] St. Paul uses two expressions (*Gal.* iv, 4 and *Eph.* i, 10) : $\pi\lambda\acute{\eta}\rho\omega\mu\alpha$ $\tauο\hat{υ}$
$\chiρ\acute{ο}\nuου$ – the fullness of time in respect to man's age, and $\pi\lambda\acute{\eta}\rho\omega\mu\alpha$ $\tau\hat{\omega}\nu$ $\kappa\alpha\iota\rho\hat{\omega}\nu$
– the completion of the cycle of seasons. Cf. Prat : *Théologie de S. Paul* (second
edition), II, 151.

[3] *Parochial Sermons*, VI, xvii.

ST. AUGUSTINE AND HIS AGE 47

But on the other hand, although the kingdom for which the Christian hoped was a spiritual and eternal one, it was not a kind of abstract Nirvana, it was a real kingdom which was to be the crown and culmination of history and the realization of the destiny of the human race. Indeed, it was often conceived in a temporal and earthly form ; for the majority of the early Fathers interpreted the Apocalypse in a literal sense and believed that Christ would reign with His saints on earth for a thousand years before the final judgement.[1] So vivid and intense was this expectation that the new Jerusalem seemed already hovering over the earth in readiness for its descent, and Tertullian records how the soldiers of Severus's army had seen its walls on the horizon, shining in the light of dawn, for forty days, as they marched through Palestine. Such a state of mind might easily lead, as it did in the case of Tertullian, to the visionary fanaticism of Montanism. But even in its excesses it was less dangerous to orthodoxy than the spiritualistic theosophy of the Gnostics, which dissolved the whole historical basis of Christianity, and consequently it was defended by apologists, such as Justin Martyr and Irenæus, as a bulwark of the concrete reality of the Christian hope.

Moreover, all Christians, whether they were millenniarists or not, believed that they already possessed a pledge and foretaste of the future kingdom in the Church. They were not, like the other religious bodies of the time, a group of individuals united by common beliefs and a common worship, they were a true people. All the wealth of historical associations and social emotion which were contained in the Old Testament had been separated from its national and racial limitations and transferred to the new international spiritual community. Thereby the Church acquired many of the characteristics of a political society ; that is to say,

---

[1] Tixeront : *Histoire des Dogmes* I, 217 ff. On millenniarism at Rome in the third century cf. d'Alès : *La Théologie de S. Hippolyte*, v.

Christians possessed a real social tradition of their own and a kind of patriotism which was distinct from that of the secular state in which they lived.

This social dualism is one of the most striking characteristics of early Christianity. Indeed, it is characteristic of Christianity in general ; for the idea of the two societies and the twofold citizenship is found nowhere else in the same form. It entered deeply into St. Augustine's thought and supplied the fundamental theme of *The City of God*. In fact, St. Augustine's idea of the two cities is no new discovery but a direct inheritance from tradition. In its early Christian form, however, this dualism was much simpler and more concrete than it afterwards became. The mediæval problem of the co-existence of the two societies and the two authorities within the unity of the Christian people was yet to arise. Instead there was the abrupt contrast of two opposing orders – the Kingdom of God and the kingdom of this world – the present age and the age to come. The Empire was the society of the past, and the Church was the society of the future, and, though they met and mingled physically, there was no spiritual contact between them. It is true, as we have seen, that the Christian recognized the powers of this world as ordained by God and observed a strict but passive obedience to the Empire. But this loyalty to the state was purely external. It simply meant, as St. Augustine says, that the Church during her commixture with Babylon must recognize the external order of the earthly state which was to the advantage of both – *utamur et nos sua pace.*[1]

Hence there could be no bond of spiritual fellowship or common citizenship between the members of the two societies. In his relations with the state and secular society the Christian felt himself to be an alien – *peregrinus* ; his true citizenship was in the Kingdom of Heaven. Tertullian writes,

[1] *De Civitate Dei*, XIX, xxvi. " That the peace of God's enemies is useful to the piety of His friends as long as their earthly pilgrimage lasts." Cf. also *ibid.*, xvii.

" Your citizenship, your magistracies and the very name of your *curia* is the Church of Christ. . . . We are called away even from dwelling in this Babylon of the Apocalypse, how much more from sharing in its pomps ? . . . For you are an alien in this world, and a citizen of the city of Jerusalem that is above."[1]

It is true that Tertullian was a rigorist, but in this respect, at any rate, his attitude does not differ essentially from that of St. Cyprian or of the earlier tradition in general. There was, however, a growing tendency in the third century for Christians to enter into closer relations with the outer world and to assimilate Greek thought and culture. This culminated in Origen's synthesis of Christianity and Hellenism, which had a profound influence, not only on theology, but also on the social and political attitude of Christians. Porphyry remarks that " though Origen was a Christian in his manner of life, he was a Hellene in his religious thought and surreptitiously introduced Greek ideas into alien myths."

This is, of course, the exaggeration of a hostile critic ; nevertheless it is impossible to deny that Origen is completely Greek in his attitude to history and cosmology. He broke entirely, not only with the millenniarist tradition, but also with the concrete realism of Christian eschatology, and substituted in its place the cosmological speculations of later Greek philosophy. The Kingdom of God was conceived by him in a metaphysical sense as the realm of spiritual reality – the supersensuous and intelligible world. The historical facts of Christian revelation consequently tended to lose their unique value and became the symbols of higher immaterial realities – a kind of Christian *Mythos*. In place of the *sacred history* of humanity from the Fall to the Redemption we have a vast cosmic drama like that of the Gnostic systems, in which the heavenly spirits fall from their immaterial bliss into the bondage of matter, or into the form of demons.

[1] *De Corona*, xiii.

D A

Salvation consists not in the redemption of the body, but in the liberation of the soul from the bondage of matter and its gradual return through the seven planetary heavens to its original home. Consequently there is no longer any real unity in the human race, since it consists of a number of individual spirits which have become men, so to speak, accidentally, in consequence of their own faults in a previous state of existence.

No doubt these ideas are not the centre of Origen's faith. They are counterbalanced by his orthodoxy of intention and his desire to adhere to Catholic tradition. Nevertheless, they inevitably produced a new attitude to the Church and a new view of its relation to humanity. The traditional conception of the Church as an objective society, the new Israel, and the forerunner of the Kingdom of God fell into the background as compared with a more intellectualist view of the Church as the teacher of an esoteric doctrine or *gnosis* which leads the human soul from time to eternity. Here again Origen is the representative of the Græco-oriental ideals which found their full expression in the mystery religions.

The result of this change of emphasis was to reduce the opposition which had previously existed between the Church and secular society. Unlike the earlier Fathers, Origen was quite prepared to admit the possibility of a general conversion of the Empire, and in his work against Celsus he paints a glowing picture of the advantages that the Empire would enjoy if it was united in one great " City of God " under the Christian faith. But Origen's City of God, unlike Augustine's, has perhaps more affinity with the world state of the Stoics than with the divine Kingdom of Jewish and Christian prophecy. It found its fulfilment in the Christian Empire of Constantine and his successors, as we can see from the writings of Eusebius of Cæsarea, the greatest representative of the tradition of Origen in the following age.

Eusebius goes further than any of the other Fathers in his rejection of millenniarism and of the old realistic eschatology. For him prophecy finds an adequate fulfilment in the historical circumstances of his own age. The Messianic Kingdom of Isaiah is the Christian Empire, and Constantine himself is the new David, while the new Jerusalem which St. John saw descending from heaven like a bride adorned for her husband means to Eusebius nothing more than the building of the Church of the Holy Sepulchre at Constantine's orders.[1]

Such a standpoint leaves no room for the old Christian and Jewish social dualism. The emperor is not only the leader of the Christian people, his monarchy is the earthly counterpart and reflection of the rule of the Divine Word. As the Word reigns in heaven, so Constantine reigns on earth, purging it from idolatry and error and preparing men's minds to receive the truth. The kingdoms of this world have become the Kingdom of God and of His Christ, and nothing more remains to do this side of eternity.[2]

It is not enough to dismiss all this as mere flattery on the part of a courtier prelate. The Eusebian ideal of monarchy has a great philosophical and historical tradition behind it. It goes back, on the one hand, to the Hellenistic theory of kingship, as represented by Dio Chrysostom, and, on the other, to the oriental tradition of sacred monarchy which is as old as civilization itself. It is true that it is not specifically Christian and it is entirely irreconcilable with the strictly religious attitude of men like Athanasius, who were prepared to sacrifice the unity of the Empire to a theological principle. Nevertheless, it was ultimately destined to triumph, at least in the East, for it finds its fulfilment in the Byzantine

[1] *Life of Constantine*, III, xxxiii. So too he applies the passage in *Dan.* vii, 17. ("And the saints of the Most High shall receive the Kingdom") to Dalmatius and Hanibalianus, who were made Cæsars by Constantine (*Oration on the Tricennalia of Constantine*, iii.).

[2] Eusebius develops the parallel at great length in his *Oration on the Tricennalia of Constantine*, ii–x.

Church-State indissolubly united under the rule of an Orthodox emperor.

In the West, however, Christian thought followed an entirely different course of development. At the time when Origen was creating a speculative theology and a philosophy of religion, the attention of the Western Church was concentrated on the concrete problems of its corporate life. From an intellectual point of view the controversies on discipline and Church order which occupied the Western mind seem barren and uninteresting in comparison with the great doctrinal issues which were being debated in the East. But historically they are the proof of a strong social tradition and of an autonomous and vigorous corporate life.

Nowhere was this tradition so strong as in Africa ; indeed, so far as its literary and intellectual expression is concerned, Africa was actually the creator of the Western tradition. By far the larger part of Latin Christian literature is African in origin, and the rest of the Latin West produced no writers, save Ambrose and Jerome, who are worthy to be compared with the great African doctors. This, no doubt, was largely due to the fact that Africa possessed a more strongly marked national character than any other Western province. The old Libyo-Phœnicean population had been submerged by the tide of Roman culture, but it still subsisted, and during the later Empire it began to reassert its national individuality in the same way as did the subject nationalities of the Eastern provinces. And, as in Syria and Egypt, this revival of national feeling found an outlet through religious channels. It did not go so far as to create a new vernacular Christian literature, as was the case in Syria, for the old Punic tongue survived mainly among the peasants and the uneducated classes,[1] but though it expressed itself in a Latin medium, its content was far more

---

[1] Although the emperor Severus, according to his biographer, found it easier to express himself in Punic than in Latin.

original and characteristic than that of the Syriac or Coptic literatures.

This is already apparent in the work of Tertullian, perhaps the most original genius whom the Church of Africa ever produced. After the smooth commonplaces of Fronto or the florid preciosity of Apuleius the rhetoric of Tertullian is at once exhilarating and terrific.[1] It is as though one were to go out of a literary *salon* into a thunderstorm. His work is marked by a spirit of fierce and indomitable hostility to the whole tradition of pagan civilization, both social and intellectual. He has no desire to minimize the opposition between the Church and the Empire, for all his hopes are fixed on the passing of the present order and the coming of the Kingdom of the Saints. Similarly he has no sympathy with the conciliatory attitude of the Alexandrian School towards Greek philosophy. " What has Athens to do with Jerusalem ? " he writes. " What concord is there between the Academy and the Church ? " . . . " Our instruction comes from the Porch of Solomon who taught that the Lord should be sought in simplicity of heart. Away with all attempts to produce a mottled Christianity of Stoic, Platonic and dialectic composition. We want no curious disputation after possessing Christ Jesus. . . ."[2]

This uncompromising spirit remained characteristic of the African Church, so that Carthage became the antithesis of Alexandria in the development of Christian thought. It remained a stronghold of the old realistic eschatology and of millenniarist ideas, which were held not only by Tertullian, but by Arnobius and Lactantius and Commodian. The work of the latter, especially, shows how the apocalyptic ideas of the Christians might become charged with a feeling of hostility to the injustice of the social order and to the

---

[1] It is true that Tertullian's style is no less artificial than that of Apuleius, by whom he was perhaps influenced, but the general effect that it produces is utterly different.

[2] *De Præscriptione*, vii. (Homes's trans.).

Roman Empire itself. In his strangely barbaric verses, which, nevertheless, sometimes possess a certain rugged grandeur, Commodian inveighs against the luxury and oppression of the rich and exults over the approaching doom of the heathen world-power.

> *Tollatur imperium, quod fuit inique repletum,*
> *Quod per tributa mala diu macerabat omnes*
>
> .   .   .   .
>
> *Haec quidem gaudebat, sed tota terra gemebat ;*
> *Vix tamen advenit illi retributio digna,*
> *Luget in æternum quæ se jactabat æterna.*[1]

And the same intransigent spirit shows itself in the cult of martyrdom, which attained an extraordinarily high development in Africa, especially among the lower classes. Cultivated pagans saw in the martyrs the rivals and substitutes of the old gods and regarded their cult as typical of the barbarous anti-Roman or anti-Hellenic spirit of the new religion. Maximus, the old pagan scholar of Madaura, protested to St. Augustine that he could not bear to see Romans leaving their ancestral temples to worship at the tombs of low-born criminals with vile Punic names, such as Mygdo and Lucitas and Namphanio " and others in an endless list with names abhorred both by gods and men." And he concludes : " It almost seems to me at this time as if a second battle of Actium had begun in which Egyptian monsters, doomed soon to perish, dare to raise their weapons against the gods of the Romans."[2]

In fact the conversion of the Empire had not altered the fierce and uncompromising spirit of African Christianity.

---

[1] *Carmen apologeticum*, 889–90 and 921–3. " May the Empire be destroyed which was filled with injustice and which long afflicted the world with heavy taxes. . . . Rome rejoiced while the whole earth groaned. Yet at last due retribution falls upon her. She who boasted herself eternal shall mourn eternally."

[2] *Ep.* xvi.

On the contrary, the peace of the Church was in Africa merely the occasion of fresh wars. The Donatist movement had its origin, like so many other schisms, in a local dispute on the question of the position of those who had lapsed or compromised their loyalty under the stress of persecution. But the intervention of the Roman state changed what might have been an unimportant local schism into a movement of almost national importance, and roused the native fanaticism of the African spirit. To the Donatists the Catholic Church was " the Church of the traitors,"[1] which had sold its birthright and leagued itself " with the princes of this world for the slaughter of the saints." They themselves claimed to be the true representatives of the glorious tradition of the old African Church, for they also were persecuted by the world, they also were a martyr Church, the faithful remnant of the saints.

The African Church had been called by Christ to share in His passion, and the persecution of the Donatists was the first act of the final struggle of the forces of evil against the Kingdom of God. " *Sicut enim in Africa factum est,*" writes Tyconius, " *ita fieri oportet in toto mundo, revelari Antichristum sicut et nobis ex parte revelatum est.*" " *Ex Africa manifestabitur omnis ecclesia.*"[2]

But the Donatist movement was not only a spiritual protest against any compromise with the world ; it also roused all the forces of social discontent and national fanaticism. The wild peasant bands of the Circumcellions, who roamed the country, with their war-cry of " *Deo laudes,*" were primarily religious fanatics who sought an opportunity of martyrdom. But they were also champions of the poor and

[1] *Traditores* – primarily those who had delivered (*tradere*) the sacred books to the authorities during the persecution of Diocletian, but the word also has the evil association of our " traitor."
[2] From the *Commentary on the Apocalypse* of Beatus in Monceaux. *Hist. Litt. de l'Afrique Chrétienne,* V, p. 288, notes 2 and 3 : " For as it has been done in Africa, so it must be done in the whole world and Antichrist must be revealed, as has been revealed to us in part." " Out of Africa all the Church shall be revealed."

the oppressed, who forced the landlords to enfranchise their slaves and free their debtors, and who, when they met a rich man driving in his chariot, would make him yield his place to his footman, as a literal fulfilment of the words of the Magnificat, *deposuit potentes de sede et exaltavit humiles.* In fact, we have in Donatism a typical example of the results of an exclusive insistence on the apocalyptic and anti-secular aspects of Christianity, a tendency which was destined to reappear at a later period in the excesses of the Taborites, the Anabaptists and some of the Puritan sects.

The existence of this movement, so powerful, so self-confident, and so uncompromising, had a profound effect on Augustine's life and thought. The situation of the Church in Africa was essentially different from anything which existed elsewhere. The Catholics were not, as in many of the eastern provinces, the dominant element in society, nor were they, as in other parts of the West, the acknowledged representatives of the new faith against paganism. In numbers they were probably equal to the Donatists, but intellectually they were the weaker party, since with the exception of Optatus of Milevis the whole literary tradition of African Christianity had been in the hands of the Donatists ; indeed, from the schism to the time of Optatus, a space of more than fifty years, not a single literary representative of the Catholic cause had appeared.

Hence during the thirty years of his ecclesiastical life St. Augustine had to fight a continuous battle, not only against the paganism and unbelief of the open enemies of Christianity, but also against the fanaticism and sectarianism of his fellow-Christians. The extinction of the Donatist schism was the work to which before all others his later life was dedicated, and it inevitably affected his views of the nature of the Church and its relation to the secular power. The Catholics had been in alliance with the state since the time of Constantine, and relied upon the help of the secular arm both for their own protection and for the suppression of the schismatics. Consequently, Augustine could no longer maintain the attitude of hostile independence towards the state which marked the African spirit, and which the Donatists still preserved. Nevertheless, he was himself a true African. Indeed, we may say that he was an African first and a Roman afterwards, since, in spite of his genuine loyalty towards the Empire, he shows none of the specifically Roman patriotism which marks Ambrose or Prudentius. Rome is to him always " the second Babylon,"[1] the supreme example of human pride and ambition, and he seems to take a bitter pleasure in recounting the crimes and misfortunes of her history.[2] On the other hand, he often shows his African patriotism, notably in his reply to the letter of Maximus of Madaura to which I have already referred, where he defends the Punic language from the charge of barbarism.[3]

It is true that there is nothing provincial about Augustine's mind, for he had assimilated classical culture and especially Greek thought to a greater extent than any other Western Father. But for all that he remained an African, the last and greatest representative of the tradition of Tertullian and Cyprian, and when he took up the task of defending Christianity against the attacks of the pagans, he was carrying on not only their work, but also their spirit and their thought. If we compare *The City of God* with the works of the great Greek apologists, the *Contra Celsum* of Origen, the *Contra Gentes* of Athanasius and the *Præparatio Evangelica* of Eusebius, we are at once struck by the contrast of his method. He does

---

[1] *De Civitate Dei*, XVIII, ii, xxii.

[2] E.g. the passage on Rome after Cannæ in *De Civitate Dei*, III, xix.

[3] " Surely, considering that you are an African and that we are both settled in Africa, you could not have so forgotten yourself when writing to Africans as to think that Punic names were a fit theme for censure. . . . And if the Punic language is rejected by you, you virtually deny what has been admitted by most learned men, that many things have been wisely preserved from oblivion in books written in the Punic tongue. Nay, you ought even to be ashamed of having been born in the country in which the cradle of this language is still warm." *Ep.* xvii. (trans. J. G. Cunningham). Julian of Eclanum after sneers at St. Augustine as " a Punic Aristotle " and " *philosophaster Pænosum.*"

not base his treatment of the subject on philosophic and metaphysical arguments, as the Greek Fathers had done, but on the eschatological and social dualism, which, as we have seen, was characteristic of the earliest Christian teaching and to which the African tradition, as a whole, had proved so faithful.

Moreover, the particular form in which Augustine expresses this dualism, and which supplies the central unifying idea of the whole work, was itself derived from an African source, namely from Tyconius, the most original Donatist writer of the fourth century.[1] Tyconius represents the African tradition in its purest and most uncontaminated form. He owes nothing to classical culture or to philosophic ideas ; his inspiration is entirely Biblical and Hebraic. Indeed, his interpretation of the Bible resembles that of the Jewish Midrash far more than the ordinary type of patristic exegesis. It is a proof of the two-sidedness of Augustine's genius that he could appreciate the obscure and tortuous originality of Tyconius as well as the limpid classicism of Cicero. He was deeply influenced by Tyconius, not only in his interpretation of scripture,[2] but also in his theology and in his attitude to history ; above all, in his central doctrine of the Two Cities. In his commentary on the Apocalypse, Tyconius had written, " Behold two cities, the City of God and the City of the Devil. . . . Of them, one desires to serve the world, and the other to serve Christ ; one seeks to reign in this world, the other to fly from this world. One is afflicted, and the other rejoices ; one smites, and the other is smitten ; one slays, and the other is slain ; the one in order to be the more justified thereby, the other to fill up the measure of its iniquities. And each of them strive together the one that

---

[1] Strictly speaking, Tyconius was not a Donatist, but an " Afro-Catholic," since he believed not that the Donatists were the only true Church but that they formed part of the Catholic Church, although they were not in communion with it.

[2] Cf. especially Augustine's incorporation of the " Rules " of Tyconius in his *De Doctrina Christiana*.

it may receive damnation, the other that it may acquire salvation."[1]

This idea had entered deeply into Augustine's thought from the first. He was already meditating on it at Tagaste in 390 ; in 400 he makes use of it in his treatise *On Catechizing the Unlearned*, and finally, in *The City of God*, he makes it the subject of his greatest work. In his mind, however, the idea had acquired a more profound significance than that which Tyconius had given it. To the latter, the Two Cities were apocalyptic symbols derived from the imagery of the Bible and bound up with his realistic eschatological ideas. To Augustine, on the other hand, they had acquired a philosophic meaning and had been related to a rational theory of sociology. He taught that every human society finds its constituent principle in a common will – a will to life, a will to enjoyment, above all, a will to peace. He defines a people as a " multitude of rational creatures associated in a common agreement as to the things which it loves."[1] Hence, in order to see what a people is like we must consider the objects of its love. If the society is associated in a love of that which is good, it will be a good society ; if the objects of its love are evil, it will be bad. And thus the moral law of individual and social life are the same, since both to the city and to the individual we can apply the same principle – *non faciunt bonos vel malos mores nisi boni vel mali amores.*

And thus the sociology of St. Augustine is based on the same psychological principle which pervades his whole thought – the principle of the all-importance of the will and the sovereignty of love. The power of love has the same importance in the spiritual world as the force of gravity possesses in the physical world.[3] As a man's love moves him,

---

[1] Beatus, *Comm. in Apocalypsin*, ed. Florez, pp. 506–7.
[2] *De Civitate Dei*, XIX, xxiv.
[3] Following the Aristotelian theory according to which every substance naturally tends to its " proper place " – τόπος οἰκεῖος ; cf. Augustine, *Confessions*, XIII, i, x ; *De Civitate Dei*, XI, xxviii.

so must he go, and so must he become ; *pondus meum amor meus, eo feror quocumque feror.*

And though the desires of men appear to be infinite they are in reality reducible to one. All men desire happiness, all seek after peace ; and all their lusts and hates and hopes and fears are directed to that final end. The only essential difference consists in the nature of the peace and happiness that are desired, for, by the very fact of his spiritual autonomy, man has the power to choose his own good ; either to find his peace in subordinating his will to the divine order, or to refer all things to the satisfaction of his own desires and to make himself the centre of his universe – " a darkened image of the divine Omnipotence." It is here and here only that the root of dualism is to be found : in the opposition between the " natural man " who lives for himself and desires only a material felicity and a temporal peace, and the spiritual man who lives for God and seeks a spiritual beatitude and a peace which is eternal. The two tendencies of will produce two kinds of men and two types of society, and so we finally come to the great generalization on which St. Augustine's work is founded. " Two lives built two Cities – the earthly, which is built up by the love of self to the contempt of God, and the heavenly, which is built up by the love of God to the contempt of self." [1]

From this generalization springs the whole Augustinian theory of history, since the two cities " have been running their course mingling one with the other through all the changes of times from the beginning of the human race, and shall so move on together until the end of the world, when they are destined to be separated at the last judgement." [2]

In the latter part of *The City of God* (books xv to xviii) St. Augustine gives a brief synopsis of world history from this point of view. On the one hand he follows the course

[1] *De Civitate Dei*, XIV, xxviii.
[2] *De Catechizandis Rudibus*, XXI, xxxvii ; cf. ibid., XIX, xxxi and *De Civitate Dei*, XIV, i, xxviii, XV, i, ii.

of the earthly city – the mystical Babylon – through the ages, and finds its completest manifestation in the two world empires of Assyria and Rome " to which all the other Kingdoms are but appendices." On the other hand, he traces the development of the heavenly City : from its beginnings with the patriarchs, through the history of Israel and the holy city of the first Jerusalem, down to its final earthly manifestation in the Catholic Church.

The rigid simplification of history which such a sketch demands necessarily emphasizes the uncompromising severity of St. Augustine's thought. At first sight he seems, no less than Tertullian or Commodian, to condemn the state and all secular civilization as founded on human pride and selfishness, and to find the only good society in the Church and the Kingdom of the Saints. And in a sense this conclusion does follow from the Augustinian doctrine of man. The human race has been vitiated at its source. It has become a waste product – a *massa damnata*. The process of redemption consists in grafting a new humanity on to the old stock, and in building a new world out of the *débris* of the old. Consequently, in the social life of unregenerate humanity St. Augustine sees a flood of infectious and hereditary evil against which the unassisted power of the individual will struggles in vain. " Woe to thee," he cries, " thou river of human custom ! Who shall stop thy course ? How long will it be before thou art dried up ? How long wilt thou roll the sons of Eve into that great and fearful ocean which even they who have ascended the wood (of the Cross) can scarcely cross ? "[1]

This view of human nature and of the social burden of evil finds still further confirmation in the spectacle of universal history. St. Augustine, no less than St. Cyprian,[2] sees the kingdoms of the world founded in injustice and prospering by bloodshed and oppression. He did not share the patriotic

---

[1] *Confessions*, I, xxv.   [2] Cf. especially St. Cyprian's *Epistle to Donatus*.

optimism of writers like Eusebius and Prudentius, for he realized, more keenly perhaps than any other ancient writer, at what a cost of human suffering the benefits of the imperial unity had been purchased. " The imperial city," he writes, " endeavours to communicate her language to all the lands she has subdued to procure a fuller society and a greater abundance of interpreters on both sides. It is true, but how many lives has this cost ! and suppose that done, the worst is not past, for . . . the wider extension of her empire produced still greater wars. . . . Wherefore he that does but consider with compassion all these extremes of sorrow and bloodshed must needs say that this is a mystery. But he that endures them without a sorrowful emotion or thought thereof, is far more wretched to imagine he has the bliss of a god when he has lost the natural feelings of a man."[1]

In the same way the vaunted blessings of Roman law are only secured by an infinity of acts of injustice to individuals by the torture of innocent witnesses and the condemnation of the guiltless. The magistrate would think it wrong not to discharge the duties of his office, " but he never holds it a sin to torture innocent witnesses, and when he has made them their own accusers, to put them to death as guilty."[2] Consequently the consideration of history leads Augustine to reject the political idealism of the philosophers and to dispute Cicero's thesis that the state rests essentially on justice. If this were the case, he argues, Rome itself would be no state ; in fact, since true justice is not to be found in any earthly kingdom, the only true state will be the City of God.[3] Accordingly, in order to avoid this extreme conclusion he eliminates all moral elements from his definition of the state, and describes it, in the passage to which I have already referred, as based on a common will, whether the object of that will be good or bad.[4]

---

[1] *De Civitate Dei*, XIX, vii (trans. J. Healey).   [2] *De Civitate Dei*, XIX, vi.
[3] *De Civitate Dei*, II, xxi.   [4] Cf. above, p. 59.

The drastic realism of this definition has proved shocking to several modern writers on Augustine. Indeed, so distinguished a student of political thought as Dr. A. J. Carlyle is unwilling to admit that St. Augustine really meant what he said,[1] and he cites the famous passage in book iv, chapter 4, " Set justice aside and what are kingdoms but great robberies,"[2] to show that the quality of justice is essential to any real state. The actual tendency of the passage, however, appears to be quite the contrary. St. Augustine is arguing that there is no difference between the conqueror and the robber except the scale of their operations, for, he continues, " What is banditry but a little kingdom ? " and he approves the reply of the pirate to Alexander the Great, " Because I do it, with a little ship, I am called a robber, and you, because you do it with a great fleet, are called an emperor."

In reality there is nothing inconsistent or morally discreditable about St. Augustine's views. They follow necessarily from his doctrine of original sin ; indeed, they are implicit in the whole Christian social tradition and they frequently find expression in later Christian literature. The famous passage in the letter of Pope Gregory VII to Hermann of Metz, which has been regarded by many modern writers as showing his belief of the diabolic origin of the state, is simply an assertion of the same point of view ; while Newman, who in this, as in so many other respects, is a faithful follower of the patristic tradition, affirms the same principle in the most uncompromising terms. " Earthly kingdoms," he says, " are founded, not in justice, but in injustice. They are created by the sword, by robbery, cruelty, perjury, craft and fraud. There never was a kingdom, except Christ's, which was not conceived and born, nurtured and educated, in sin. There never was a state, but was committed

---

[1] " If he did," he writes, " I cannot but feel that it was a deplorable error for a great Christian teacher." *Social and Political Ideas of Some Great Mediæval Thinkers*, ed. F. J. C. Hearnshaw, p. 51.
[2] *Remota justitia quid regna nisi magna latrocinia ?*

to acts and maxims, which is its crime to maintain and its ruin to abandon. What monarchy is there but began in invasion or usurpation? What revolution has been effected without self-will, violence, or hypocrisy? What popular government but is blown about by every wind, as if it had no conscience and no responsibilities? What dominion of the few but is selfish and unscrupulous? Where is military strength without the passion for war? Where is trade without the love of filthy lucre, which is the root of all evil?"[1]

But from this condemnation of the actual reign of injustice in human society it does not follow that either Newman or Augustine intended to suggest that the state belonged to a non-moral sphere and that men in their social relations might follow a different law to that which governed their moral life as individuals. On the contrary, St. Augustine frequently insists that it is Christianity which makes good citizens, and that the one remedy for the ills of society is to be found in the same power which heals the moral weakness of the individual soul. " Here also is security for the welfare and renown of a commonwealth ; for no state is perfectly established and preserved otherwise than on the foundations and by the bond of faith and of firm concord, when the highest and truest good, namely God, is loved by all, and men love each other in Him without dissimulation because they love one another for His sake."[2]

Moreover, though St. Augustine emphasizes so strongly the moral dualism which is inherent in the Christian theory of life, he differs from the earlier representatives of the African school in his intense realization of a universal reasonable order which binds all nature together and which governs alike the stars in their courses and the rise and fall of kingdoms. This belief is one of the fundamental elements in Augustine's thought. It dominated his mind in the first days

[1] From " Sanctity the Token of the Christian Empire " in *Sermons on Subjects of the Day*, p. 273 (first edition).
[2] *Ep.* cxxxvii, 5, 18 (trans. Cunningham) ; cf. *Ep.* cxxxviii, 15 and 17.

of his conversion, when he composed the treatise *De Ordine*, and it was preserved unimpaired to the last. It finds typical expression in the following passage in *The City of God* : " The true God from Whom is all being, beauty, form and number, weight and measure ; He from Whom all nature, mean and excellent, all seeds of forms, all forms of seeds, all motions both of forms and seeds, derive and have being ; . . . He (I say) having left neither heaven nor earth, nor angel nor man, no, nor the most base and contemptible creature, neither the bird's feather, nor the herb's flower, nor the tree's leaf, without the true harmony of their parts, and peaceful concord of composition ; it is in no way credible that He would leave the kingdoms of men and their bondages and freedoms loose and uncomprised in the laws of His eternal providence."[1]

Here Augustine is nearer to Origen than Tertullian ; in fact this fundamental concept of the Universal Law – *lex æterna* – is derived from purely Hellenic sources. It is the characteristically Greek idea of cosmic order which pervades the whole Hellenic tradition from Heraclitus and Pythagoras to the later Stoics and neo-Platonists, and which had reached Augustine by way of Cicero and Plotinus.[2] This Hellenic influence is to be seen above all in Augustine's profound sense of the æsthetic beauty of order and in his doctrine that even the evil and suffering of the world find their æsthetic justification in the universal harmony of creation, an idea which had already found classic expression in the great lines of Cleanthes's Hymn to Zeus :

" Thou knowest how to make even that which is uneven and to order what is disordered, and unlovely things are lovely to Thee. For so Thou bringest together all things in one, the good with the bad, that there results from all one reasonable order abiding for ever."

---

[1] *De Civitate Dei*, V, xi (trans. J. Healey).

[2] Cf. P. A. Schubert, *Augustins Lex Æterna Lehre nach Inhalt und Quellen* (1924).

EA

Thus St. Augustine was able to view history from a much wider standpoint than that of Tertullian or the Donatists. He can admit that the Earthly City also has its place in the universal order, and that the social virtues of the worldly, which from a religious point of view are often nothing but " splendid vices," yet possess a real value in their own order, and bear their appropriate fruits in social life. And in the same way he believes that the disorder and confusion of history are only apparent, and that God orders all events in His Providence in a universal harmony which the created mind cannot grasp.

This philosophic universalism is not confined to Augustine's conception of the order of nature ; it also affects his eschatology and his doctrine of the Church. Above all, it determined his treatment of the central theme of his great work – *The City of God* – and entirely alienated him from the realistic literalism of the old apocalyptic tradition. To Augustine, the City of God is not the concrete millennial kingdom of the older apologists, nor is it the visible hierarchical Church. It is a transcendent and timeless reality, a society of which " the King is Truth, the law is Love and the duration is Eternity."[1] It is older than the world, since its first and truest citizens are the angels. It is as wide as humanity, since " in all successive ages Christ is the same Son of God, co-eternal with the Father, and the unchangeable Wisdom by Whom universal nature was called into existence and by participation in Whom every rational soul is made blessed." Consequently, " from the beginning of the human race whosoever believed in Him and in any way knew Him, and lived in a pious and just manner according to His precepts, was undoubtedly saved by Him in whatsoever time and place he may have lived."[2]

Thus the City of God is co-extensive with the spiritual creation in so far as it has not been vitiated by sin. It is, in

---

[1] *Ep.* cxxxviii, 3, 17.   [2] *Ep.* cii, 2, 11 and 12.

fact, nothing less than the spiritual unity of the whole universe, as planned by the Divine Providence, and the ultimate goal of creation.

These conceptions are quite irreconcilable with the old millenniarist belief which was still so strong in the West, and which Augustine himself had formerly accepted. They led him to adopt Tyconius's interpretation of the crucial passage in the Apocalypse, according to which the earthly reign of Christ is nothing else but the life of the Church militant : an explanation which henceforth gained general acceptance in the West. Moreover, he went further than Tyconius himself and the great majority of earlier writers by abandoning all attempts to give the data of prophecy an exact chronological interpretation with regard to the future, and by discouraging the prevalent assumption of the imminence of the end of the world.[1]

Thus St. Augustine influenced Christian eschatology in the West no less decisively than Origen had done in the East almost two centuries earlier, and to some extent their influences tended in the same direction. To Augustine, as to Origen, the ideal of the Kingdom of God acquired a metaphysical form, and became identified with the ultimate timeless reality of spiritual being. The Augustinian City of God bears a certain resemblance to the neo-Platonic concept of the Intelligible World – κόσμος νοητὸς : indeed, the Christian Platonists of later times, who were equally devoted to Augustine and Plotinus, deliberately make a conflation of the two ideas. Thus John Norris of Bemerton writes of his " Ideal World " : " Thou art that Glorious Jerusalem, whose foundations are upon the Holy Hills, the everlasting Mountains, even the Eternal Essences and Immutable Ideas of Things. . . . Here are τὰ ὄντα – the Things that are and that

---

[1] *Ep.* cxcix. In another passage he even goes so far as to entertain the hypothesis of the world being still in existence 500,000 years hence (*De Civitate Dei*, XII, xii) ; elsewhere, however, he speaks of the world having reached old age (e.g. *Sermo* xxxi. 8 ; *Ep.* cxxxvii, 16).

truly and chiefly are *quæ vere summeque sunt*, as St. Austin speaks and that because they necessarily and immutably are, and cannot either not be or be otherwise. Here live, flourish and shine those bright and unperishing Realities whereof the Things of this World are but the Image, the Reflection, the Shadow, the Echo."[1]

This Platonic idealism did indeed leave a deep imprint on St. Augustine's thought. Nevertheless, he never went so far in this direction as Origen had done, for his Platonism did not destroy his sense of the reality and importance of the historical process. To Origen, on the contrary, the temporal process had no finality. There was an infinite succession of worlds through which the immortal soul pursued its endless course. Since " the soul is immortal and eternal, it is possible that, in the many and endless periods of duration in the immeasurable and different worlds, it may descend from the highest good to the lowest evil, or be restored from the lowest evil to the highest good."[2] This is not precisely the classical Hellenic doctrine, since, as I have pointed out elsewhere,[3] Origen expressly rejects the theory of the Return of All Things as irreconcilable with a belief in free will. It has a much closer resemblance to the Hindu doctrine of *samsara* – the endless chain of existences, which are the fruit of the soul's own acts. But although this theory allows for the freedom of the will, it is destructive of the organic unity of humanity and of the significance of its social destinies to an even greater extent than the purely Hellenic doctrine. Consequently, St. Augustine rejected it no less firmly than the theory of cyclic recurrence. He admits that the idea of a perpetual return is a natural consequence of the belief in the eternity of the world, but if we once accept the doctrine of Creation, as Origen himself did, there is no further need

---

[1] J. Norris, *An Essay Towards the Theory of the Ideal or Intelligible World*, I, 430–6 (1701).
[2] Origen : *De Principiis*, III, i, 21 (trans. I. Crombie).
[3] *Progress and Religion*, p. 156.

for the theory of "the circumrotation of souls," or for the belief that nothing new or final can take place in time. Humanity has had an absolute beginning and travels to an absolute goal. There can be no return. That which is begun in time is consummated in eternity.[1] Hence time is not a perpetually revolving image of eternity; it is an irreversible process moving in a definite direction.

This recognition of the uniqueness and irreversibility of the temporal process – this "explosion of the perpetual cycles" – is one of the most remarkable achievements of St. Augustine's thought. It is true that the change of attitude was implicit in Christianity itself, since the whole Christian revelation rests on temporal events which nevertheless possess an absolute significance and an eternal value. As St. Augustine says, Christ is the straight way by which the mind escapes from the circular maze of pagan thought.[2] But although this change had been realized by faith and religious experience, it still awaited philosophic analysis and definition. This it received from St. Augustine, who was not only founder of the Christian philosophy of history, but was actually the first man in the world to discover the meaning of time.

His subtle and profound mind found a peculiar attraction in the contemplation of the mystery of time which is so essentially bound up with the mystery of created being.[3] He was intensely sensitive to the pathos of mutability – *omnis quippe iste ordo pulcherrima rerum valde bonarum modis suis peractis transiturus est ; et mane quippe in eis factum est et vespera*[4] – but he felt that the very possibility of this act of contemplation showed that the mind in some sense transcended the

[1] *De Civitate Dei*, XII, xi-xx, XXI, xvii.
[2] "*Viam rectam sequentes, quae nobis est Cristus, eo duce et salvatore a vano et inepto impiorum circumitu iter fidei mentemque avertamus*" *De Civitate Dei*, XII, xx.
[3] Cf. *De Civitate Dei*, XII, xv, xi, vi.
[4] *Confessions*, XIII, xxxv. "For all this most fair order of things truly good will pass away when its measures are accomplished, and they have their morning and their evening."

process which it contemplated. Consequently he could not rest satisfied with the naïve objectivism of Greek science which identified time with the movement of the heavenly bodies. [1] If the movement of bodies is the only measure of time, how can we speak of past and future ? A movement which has passed has ceased to exist, and a movement which is to come has not begun to exist. There remains only the present of the passing moment, a moving point in nothingness. Therefore, he concludes, the measure of time is not to be found in things, but in the soul – time is spiritual extension – *distentio animæ.*

Thus the past is the soul's remembrance, the future is its expectation, and the present is its attention. The future, which does not exist, cannot be long ; what we mean by a long future is a long expectation of the future, and a long past means a long memory of the past. " It is, then, in thee; my soul, that I measure time. . . . The impression which things make upon thee as they pass and which remains when they have passed away is what I measure. I measure this which is present, and not the things which have passed away that it might be. Therefore this is time (*tempora*) or else I must say that I do not measure time at all." [2]

Finally, he compares the time-process with the recitation of a poem which a man knows by heart. Before it is begun the recitation exists only in anticipation ; when it is finished it is all in the memory ; but while it is in progress, it exists, like time, in three dimensions – " the life of this my action is extended into the memory, on account of what I have said, and into expectation, on account of what I am about to say ; yet my attention remains present and it is through this that what was future is transposed and becomes past." And what is true of the poem holds good equally of each line and syllable of it, and of the wider action of which it forms part, and also of the life of man which is composed

[1] *Confessions*, XI, xxiii.   [2] *Ibid.*, XI, xxvii.

of a series of such actions, and of the whole world of man which is the sum of individual lives.[1]

Now this new theory of time which St. Augustine originated also renders possible a new conception of history. If man is not the slave and creature of time, but its master and creator, then history also becomes a creative process. It does not repeat itself meaninglessly ; it grows into organic unity with the growth of human experience. The past does not die ; it becomes incorporated in humanity. And hence progress is possible, since the life of society and of humanity itself possesses continuity and the capacity for spiritual growth no less than the life of the individual.

How far St. Augustine realized all this may indeed be questioned. Many modern writers do, in fact, deny that he conceived of the possibility of progress or that he had any real historical sense. They argue, as I said before, that *The City of God* conceives humanity as divided between two static eternal orders whose eternal lot is predestined from the beginning. But this criticism is, I think, due to a misconception of the Augustinian attitude to history. It is true that Augustine did not consider the problem of secular progress, but then secular history, in Augustine's view, was essentially unprogressive. It was the spectacle of humanity perpetually engaged in chasing its own tail. The true history of the human race is to be found in the process of enlightenment and salvation by which human nature is liberated and restored to spiritual freedom. Nor did Augustine view this process in an abstract and unhistorical way. For he constantly insists on the organic unity of the history of humanity, which passes through a regular succession of ages, like the life of an individual man ;[2] and he shows how " the epochs of the world are linked together in a wonderful way " by the gradual development of the divine plan.[3] For God, who is " the unchangeable Governor as He is the unchangeable

___
[1] *Confessions.*, xxviii.   [2] E.g. *De Vera Religione*, XXVII, l.   [3] *Ep.* cxxxvii, 15.

Creator of mutable things, orders all events in His providence until the beauty of the completed course of time, of which the component parts are the dispensations adapted to each successive age, shall be finished, like the grand melody of some ineffably wise master of song."[1]

It is true, as we have already seen, that in *The City of God* St. Augustine always emphasizes the eternal and transcendent character of the Heavenly City in contrast to the mutability and evil of earthly life. It is impossible to identify the City of God with the Church as some writers have done, since in the Heavenly City there is no room for evil or imperfection, no admixture of sinners with the saints. But, on the other hand, it is an even more serious error to separate the two concepts completely and to conclude that St. Augustine assigned no absolute and transcendent value to the hierarchical Church. Certainly the Church is not the eternal City of God, but it is its organ and representative in the world. It is the point at which the transcendent spiritual order inserts itself into the sensible world, the one bridge by which the creature can pass from Time to Eternity. St. Augustine's point of view is, in fact, precisely the same as that which Newman so often expresses, though their terminology is somewhat different. Like Augustine, Newman emphasizes the spiritual and eternal character of the City of God and regards the visible Church as its earthly manifestation. " The unseen world through God's secret power and mercy encroaches upon this ; and the Church that is seen is just that portion of it by which it encroaches, it is like the islands in the sea, which are in truth but the tops of the everlasting hills, high and vast and deeply rooted, which a deluge covers."[2]

And neither in the case of St. Augustine nor in that of Newman does this emphasizing of the transcendence and

[1] *Ep.* cxxxviii, 5 (trans. Cunningham).
[2] "The Communion of Saints " in *Parochial Sermons* (first edition), IV, p. 201.

spirituality of the City of God lead to any depreciation of the hierarchical Church. The latter describes the Christian Church as an Imperial power – " not a mere creed or philosophy but a *counter kingdom*." " It occupied ground ; it claimed to rule over those whom hitherto this world's governments ruled over without rival ; and it is only in proportion as things that are are brought into this kingdom and made subservient to it ; it is only as kings and princes, nobles and rulers, men of business and men of letters, the craftsman and the trader and the labourer humble themselves to Christ's Church and (in the language of the prophet Isaiah) ' bow down to her with their faces toward the earth and lick up the dust of her feet,' that the world becomes living and spiritual, and a fit object of love and a resting-place for Christians."[1]

The late Dr. Figgis, in his admirable lectures : *The Political Aspects of St. Augustine's " City of God,"* has referred to this sermon of Newman as showing how far later Western tradition carried " the political way of thinking about the Church, which had been inaugurated by St. Augustine. But here again Newman's teaching really represents, not the views of his own time nor even those of the Middle Ages, but a deliberate revival of the patristic Augustinian doctrines. We have seen how primitive Christianity, and the early Western tradition in particular, showed an intense social realism in their eschatology and in their conception of the Church and the Kingdom of God. St. Augustine definitely abandoned the millenniarist tradition and adopted a thoroughly spiritual eschatology. But he preserved the traditional social realism in his attitude to the Church : indeed, he reinforced it by his identification of the Church with the millennial kingdom of the Apocalypse. *Ecclesia et nunc est regnum Christi regnumque cœlorum.*[2] Consequently it is in the Church that

---

[1] *Sermons Bearing on Subjects of the Day* (first edition), pp. 257 and 120.
[2] *De Civitate Dei*, XX, x.

the prophecies of the kingdom find their fulfilment, and even
those which seem to refer to the last Judgement may really
be applied to " that advent of the Saviour by which He is
coming through all the present time in His Church, that is
to say in His members, gradually and little by little, for it
is all His Body."[1]

" *O beata ecclesia*," he writes, " *quodam tempore audisti, quodam
tempore vidisti. . . . Omnia enim quæ modo complentur antea pro-
phetata sunt. Erige oculos ergo, et diffunde per mundum : vide jam
hereditatem usque ad terminos orbis terræ. Vide jam impleri quod
dictum est : Adorabunt eum omnes reges terræ, omnes gentes serviunt
illi.*"[2]

The grain of mustard-seed has grown until it is greater
than all the herbs, and the great ones of this world have
taken refuge under its branches. The yoke of Christ is on
the neck of kings, and we have seen the head of the greatest
empire that the world has known laying aside his crown and
kneeling before the tomb of the Fisherman.[3]

Hence Augustine bases his claim to make use of the secular
power against the Donatists, not on the rights of the state to
intervene in religious matters, but on the right of the Church
to make use of the powers of this world which God has subdued to Christ according to His prophecy : " All the kings
of the earth shall adore Him and all nations shall serve Him "
– " *et ideo hac Ecclesiæ potestate utimur, quam ei Dominus et pro-
misit et dedit.*"[4]

To   some – notably   to   Reuter   and   Harnack – this

[1] *De Civitate Dei*, XX, v.
[2] *Enarrationes in Psalmos*, LXVII, vii. " O blessed Church, once thou hast
heard, now thou hast seen. For what the Church has heard in promises, she
now sees manifested. For all things that were formerly prophesied, are now
fulfilled. Lift up thine eyes and look abroad over the world. Behold now thine
inheritance even to the ends of the earth. See now fulfilled what was spoken :
' All the kings of the earth shall worship Him, all nations shall do Him service.' "
[3] *Sermo* xliv, 2 ; *Ep.* ccxxxii, 3. We may observe that the same facts on which
Eusebius rests his glorification of the Emperor are used by Augustine to exalt
the Church.
[4] *Ep.* cv, 5, 6 ; cf. *Ep.* xxxv, 3. " And, therefore, we are making use of this
power which the Lord both promised and gave to the Church."

exaltation of the visible Church has seemed fundamentally inconsistent with the Augustinian doctrine of grace. It is indeed difficult to understand Augustine's theology if we approach it from the standpoint of the principles of the Reformation. But if we ignore modern developments, and study Augustine's doctrine of grace and the Church from a purely Augustinian standpoint, its unity and consistency are manifest.

St. Augustine never separates the moral from the social life. The dynamic force of both the individual and the society is found in the will, and the object of their will determines the moral character of their life. And as the corruption of the will by original sin in Adam becomes a social evil by an hereditary transmission through the flesh which unites fallen humanity in the common slavery of concupiscence, so too the restoration of the will by grace in Christ is a social good which is transmitted sacramentally by the action of the Spirit and unites regenerate humanity in a free spiritual society under the law of charity. The grace of Christ is only found in " the society of Christ." " Whence," says he, " should the City of God originally begin or progressively develop or ultimately attain its end, unless the life of the saints was a social one ? "[1] Thus the Church is actually the new humanity in process of formation, and its earthly history is that of the building of the City of God which has its completion in eternity, " *Adhuc ædificatur templum Dei.*"[2] " *Vos tanquam lapides vivi coædificamini in templum Dei.*"[3] Hence, in spite of all the imperfections of the earthly Church, it is nevertheless the most perfect society that this world can know. Indeed, it is the only true society, because it is the only society which has its source in a spiritual will. The kingdoms of the earth seek after the goods of the earth ; the Church, and the Church alone, seeks spiritual goods and a peace which is eternal.

Such a doctrine may seem to leave little room for the

---

[1] *De Civitate Dei*, XIX, v. [2] *Sermo* clxiii, 3. [3] *Ibid.*, clvi, 12, 13.

claims of the state. In fact, it is difficult to deny that the state does occupy a very subordinate position in St. Augustine's view. At its worst it is a hostile power, the incarnation of injustice and self-will. At its best, it is a perfectly legitimate and necessary society, but one which is limited to temporary and partial ends, and it is bound to subordinate itself to the greater and more universal spiritual society in which even its own members find their real citizenship. In fact, the state bears much the same relation to the Church that a Friendly Society or a guild bears to the state : it fulfils a useful function and has a right to the loyalty of its members, but it can never claim to be the equal of the larger society or to act as a substitute for it.

It is on the ground of these conceptions that St. Augustine has so often been regarded as the originator of the mediæval theocratic ideal, and even (by Reuter) as " the founder of Roman Catholicism."[1] And indeed is it to him more than any other individual that we owe the characteristically Western ideal of the Church as a dynamic social power in contrast to the static and metaphysical conceptions which dominated Byzantine Christianity. But it does not necessarily follow that the influence of St. Augustine tended to weaken the moral authority of the state or to deprive ordinary social life of spiritual significance. If we consider the matter, not from the narrow standpoint of the juristic relations of Church and state, but as St. Augustine himself did, from the point of view of the relative importance of the spiritual and material element in life, we shall see that his doctrine really made for moral freedom and responsibility. Under the Roman Empire, as in the sacred monarchies of the oriental type, the state is exalted as a superhuman power against which the individual personality had no rights and the individual will had no power. In the East, even Christianity

---

[1] Cf. C. H. Turner in the *Cambridge Mediæval History*, I, 173 : " St. Augustine's theory of the *Civitas Dei* was, in germ, that of the mediæval papacy, without the name of Rome."

proved powerless to change this tradition, and alike in the Byzantine Empire and in Russia the Church consecrated anew the old oriental ideal of an omnipotent sacred state and a passive people. In the West, however, St. Augustine broke decisively with this tradition by depriving the state of its aura of divinity and seeking the principle of social order in the human will. In this way the Augustinian theory, for all its otherworldliness, first made possible the ideal of a social order resting upon the free personality and a common effort towards moral ends. And thus the Western ideals of freedom and progress and social justice owe more than we realize to the profound thought of the great African who was himself indifferent to secular progress and to the transitory fortunes of the earthly state, " for he looked for a city that has foundations whose builder and maker is God."

C. C. MARTINDALE, S.J.

A SKETCH OF THE LIFE AND
CHARACTER OF ST. AUGUSTINE

A SKETCH OF THE LIFE AND CHARACTER OF ST. AUGUSTINE

Anyone who professes to estimate the character of a many-sided man runs every risk of subjectivism – not only because he may see in his subject what he likes seeing, but because even if he says nothing false, he may altogether fail to see, and so omit, what is true and valuable. Such a writer's duty then, is to obey at all points the evidence, to pray that he may not be misusing it unawares, and to disclaim any intention of dogmatizing, or of imposing his impressions on his readers.

I think that the evidence for an estimate of the " character " of St. Augustine is almost equally distributed throughout his works ; for, in such matters one must look out for unconscious self-revelation far rather than deliberate attempts at self-explanation – rather as many of St. Paul's most significant dogmatic assertions are not made as such at all, but almost without his noticing them, and in illustration of something else. Hence I think that you see St. Augustine's " character " unexpectedly in casual sentences in his sermons, as when he remarks that the church is very cold. But it would be idle to pretend that the *Confessions* are not our main evidence. Forthwith, we cannot disregard a generation-worth of theory that the *Confessions* are bad evidence at least so far as past history goes, and, therefore, useless for forming an idea of the evolution, at any rate, of Augustine's character, or of the crisis of his conversion. For the *Confessions* were written in 397–400 ; while his three books *Against the Academics, On the Happy Life, On Order,* and his two books of *Soliloquies,* were all written immediately or very soon after his conversion, about the autumn of 396 or in January 397.

Now the *Confessions* and this set of philosophical treatises or dialogues are thought, by some, to be so different among themselves as to clash and even to contradict one another. The *Confessions* are said to display a man absorbed in the emotional and mystical experience of conversion, enthralled by the *Psalms*, passionately " religious." The other books are felt to display Augustine as perfectly serene, taking a holiday in a very comfortable country house with his mother and some friends, discussing Virgil and neo-Platonism – and with so much sympathy for its doctrines that the extreme form which the new theory has taken is, that Augustine had not been converted to Christianity at all, but to neo-Platonism, and that even his baptism was a sort of philosophical technicality. Few have the courage to accuse him of conscious insincerity, and of twisting facts in order to write an edifying book. But they argue that he had had plenty of time to forget what really happened, and that his mind had meanwhile recast itself ; that he " telescoped " his memories and antedated his real conversion ; and that in the throes of the emotion of writing the *Confessions* he emotionalized the distant facts.

I believe that the *Confessions* and the philosophical books alike provide valid evidence for judging St. Augustine.

In any case, Augustine had an astounding memory, and in the *Confessions* he shows this in a thousand ways ; and as for his conversion-period, he records a detail such as that at Cassiciacum he had a toothache so appalling that he could not talk, and asked his friends, by means of a request written on waxed tablets, to pray that it might get better. They prayed ; and the pain fled so abruptly that he was frightened out of his wits – " I had not experienced anything like that in all my years ! " God was the God of every kind of rescue – He saved from poor human toothache, as from eternal loss.

Moreover, he had his *Soliloquies* and other treatises before him as he wrote the *Confessions*. He had ceased to like them much ; but he was perfectly aware of what they contained, and of what he was like when he wrote them. I am sure that in such circumstances he could not have invented and proclaimed an Augustine such as he *saw* was not the real one. He could not have created a mythical *Confessions*-Augustine when the *Soliloquies*-Augustine was before his eyes.

Further, the " treatises " themselves not only contain emphatic assertions that Augustine prayed much, prayed " with many tears " – " I prayed to God, weeping almost daily " (I find a naïve charm in that "almost" !) – and emphatic assertions such as : " I have decided to desert Christ's authority absolutely at no point," but they were in part, at any rate, rather artificialized. He admits that he repeats the actual words of Alypius, and his own (for they were taken down in shorthand) ; as for the other speakers, he " arranged " their remarks – and, after all, everyone was conscious that a set discussion, in traditional form, was proceeding, and everyone spoke as they felt people in such circumstances ought to speak – except his mother, who was once and again rather shocked. Indeed, if anyone was " not yet Christian," it was Alypius, who thought it " undignified " that Christ's name should be brought into such discussions. Augustine, who rebuked this, can none the less have gone so far as he could to satisfy the æsthetic preferences of his friend.

It might, then, be urged that neither those several treatises nor the *Confessions* provide good evidence, for both were intended for publication, both were "arranged " in view of an audience meant to be " moved," affected. The argument might apply in some measure to the treatises : but even there Augustine was feeling : " This, which actually occurred, was actually said, *ought* to move and affect you." St. John in his *Apocalypse*, even St. Paul (to some degree) in his *Letter to the Romans*, put his writing into a recognizable " form." But they had not the slightest idea of suggesting that what they were saying was not true. As for the *Confessions*, you have to remember that the Latin, let alone the African, felt not the slightest difficulty about exhibiting his emotions. Even now, the " I " element in a Southern writer's book is apt to appear quite indecent to the heavily masked Northerner. Augustine was perfectly aware that everyone would read the *Confessions*, and indeed would have been sorry if they did not : but he assumed that they would be quite sure that they were truthful – so much so that the whole of the *Confessions* is an outpouring of his soul to God – God is the immediate audience ; and only now and again does the author look aside (and down) towards his human hearers. This *public spontaneity* is alien to our sentiment, and must not be judged, as probable or improbable, according to it.

All the same, you might still ask whether Augustine could have been both the man of the treatises and the man of the *Confessions*. Certainly he could. Again, remember that we are discussing an African of an intensely active intellect, as well as of an extremely passionate nature. (Everyone knows that Augustine was like that ; so I am not anticipating too much.) Now while an Englishman, perhaps, could have remained for days at a time in a sort of sentimental dream, no man on earth could have remained even one day at Augustine's fever-heat of spiritual illumination and ardour. There would have been hours, at any rate, of daze. And when, after some time, the country house at Cassiciacum was put by Verecundus at Augustine's disposal, still less would he have been able to spend the whole of a single day in ecstatic joy or tearful penitence. Why, you must have seen " even an English " convert divide his time between passionate piety and enthusiastic argument. You may even be nervous when you watch his " fervour," and have to try not to find his controversial zeal grow tedious. Such an one prays, and he argues. In the treatises, Augustine bequeathed a record of his arguments ; in the *Confessions*, of what may widely be called his prayer. Naturally, in each sort of document he concentrated on that about which the document was written – naturally, since he reacted keenly to whatever he was thinking about, he paid little attention to his " prayer-life " when writing against the Academics ; little enough to the Academics when writing of God's overbrimming graces. Each omits what neither could wholly have related. I see, then, Augustine, at Cassiciacum, spending part of his day in the care of his friend's estate ; part – out of doors or (when it rained) in the bathing-hall – in vigorous, light-hearted disputation ; part, at night or in the early morning, praying, weeping, thanking, exulting in his faith. The two accounts of those early days of Christian life are perfectly compatible so far as psychology goes ; and of both I will make use.

I believe that the theory of the " two Augustines " will soon prove to have occupied but a brief period in Augustinian study.

(i)

The practice of pursuing the roots of character into childhood has established itself, and is legitimate, and especially justified in the case of Augustine, who never hesitated to do so himself. Augustine, so tormented by the mystery of human origin, anxious as to whether his life within his mother's womb might not already have succeeded to some secret pre-existence, would, I think, have entered very readily into modern suggestions concerned with the formative importance – even mental – of that hidden time. But he was never psycho-analysed ! He insists that he remembers no more of his infancy than of his ante-natal existence. What we are certain of is that his father was of honourable estate and sensitive about the good upbringing of his boy, but almost poor ; this clash between ideals and position may have accounted for some of his testiness. A fractious father and a gentle mother always affect a child ;

besides, Patritius was not a Christian ; Monica[1] was devout.
Yet the child was not baptized, though the preliminary
ceremonies of baptism – Christ's cross ; Christ's salt – were
given to him, and these made a true impression on his
imagination, destined to be so active.

Tagaste, the little town where he was born, November
13th, 354, was semi-Donatist; none the less, at school he met
" men who prayed." Augustine collected from them –
though they but corroborated Monica – the impression of
God as a Great Someone, invisible, yet able to help if
asked. The little boy, when he could hardly talk, prayed
hard not to be whipped. He was clever ; his memory already
showed itself as good ; but he was easily distracted, both by
curiosity and by games – he says he was always playing ball
when he should have been learning, and, since he got
whipped for it, do not call that a grim and Augustinian
self-condemnation. Along with the vague but constant
instinct of God's presence went the impression of an other-
worldly life, and, with the human punishments, the idea of
eternal ones and everlasting joys. Monica must have driven
very deep into his imagination that Eternity and the relation
to it of baptism. When he fell into some brief but violent
childish indisposition, and in their agitation they fancied he
might die, he cried wildly to be baptized. He recovered, and
they postponed it, with results he deemed disastrous. But
he insists, almost more than on anything, that with his
mother's very milk he had drunk in a tender love for the
Name of Jesus ; this affection went so deep that ever afterwards, in his most cultured hours, he felt that something was
lacking from a literature that did not contain it. Hence, a
true though indistinct feeling for God, for an eternal life,
and for the Name of Jesus, were so inwoven in his soul that
his destiny was bound to be affected by it.

[1] Technically her name should be spelt Monnica and is quite probably a
native one. But it would seem pedantic so to spell it here.

There is nothing unlikely, let alone impossible, about this. Experience proves again and again how hard it is for even the would-be atheist and materialist to rid himself wholly of the belief in the Unseen which as a boy he absorbed ; and when the incomparable music of the Bible – not alone the New, but the Old Testament – has been an integral part of an education, all other literature may for ever seem to lack an essential grace.

Even in his little school at Tagaste, and still more when he went to Madaura, Augustine showed the passionate and perhaps unstable temper of the African. He hated pain and liked pleasures, but so far kept, says he, his senses uncorrupted. His world was still that of the imagination – he told lies in plenty, as children do who hardly can distinguish the dull and unshapely truth from the vividness and rhythm of imagination – for elsewhere he says that really he hated lying ; he was as fiercely keen on his games as afterwards – very soon – he became thrilled by literature. The sensitivity of the boy reacted to the sonorous rhythm and agitating melancholy of Virgil, so much so that even when deploring in adult years this susceptibility he cannot help passing without a break from prose into hexameters and back again. He remained puzzled about his permanent distaste for Greek – it is exaggerated to say, and for him to say, that he never really knew it. Here indeed is, I think, a piece of Augustinian uncalled-for self-condemnation – he thinks he took kindly to Latin just because he wanted to say this or that and Latin was the language in which to say it. He gave Greek the go-by because there was no need for talking in it. I think that from a distance we detect another reason. It was not for nothing that he went to school at Madaura. I do not mean that he consciously imitated Apuleius of Madaura, but I think that each wrote a Latin so akin as to argue they were temperamentally akin. And that kinship was the kinship of Latinized Africans. We can, not unduly, think also of Tertullian. Possibly, of Cyprian. Greek is not gorgeous – after Æschylus, volcanic with black rocks and molten lava of speech, the Greeks became as strong and exquisite as steel inset with mother o' pearl. Afterwards they weakened into silver, then debased themselves to tin – but always it is these faint elusive tints that make lovely their discourse. Part of the enchantment of Apuleius, it is true, consists in his delicious diminutives and fantasticalities of speech : Augustine may not have been too " respectable," when he began to teach and to write, to risk such trickeries ; but afterwards he was too much absorbed in topics whose dignity forbade them ; later still, he would have had a horror of that worldliness. But never could he rid himself of his African ferocity dominated by his Latin, Roman splendidness : elaborate as may be his phrases, superb, rhythmic, rhyming his style, it was and remained as un-Greek as possible : not through naughtiness but because of a radical South-ness and West-ness in his make-up, he never could find an affinity with Greek.

Not without cause was it his destiny to transfer the centre of theological gravity from East to West, nor that, after him, the Catholic Church talked Latin and still predominantly does so.

Patritius was anxious for his son to go to Carthage for, as we might say, his university career. For that, money was lacking. It had to be collected, and the ambitious man was ready to ask for it and did so – successfully ; but it took a year to obtain it. During that year Augustine lived at home, and it was the fatal year, he reckons, the year during which he initiated himself into every immorality. I know that it is the custom now to say that Augustine, obsessed later on with the doctrine of human depravity, painted a picture of himself absurdly black. After all, he was but in his sixteenth year ! But even though when he wrote the *Confessions* he had not begun to be thoroughly preoccupied with

Pelagianism, you cannot deny that something must have happened to him to make him think very ill of his adolescent years. What had happened was, quite simply, that they were very bad. People insist on alluding to the girl with whom after a while he co-habited and to whom he consecrated " fidelity in sin," and suggest that this after all was practically marriage, and that apart from this there could but have been, at that age, mere trivial sensual slips. Authors write thus because they are not Africans or even Latins. I doubt if they know very well even their own world. But you must start by realizing that a youth like Augustine was, at twelve, what we are at sixteen ; at sixteen, what we are at twenty-two – rather, what we never are at all. After speaking with much friendliness to certain young Southerners whom I esteem, I have been amazed by the precocity, frequency, and versatility of their sexual experiments. I esteem them, because of their realism, because of the victorious survival of the spiritual thing in them that the senses never slew ; for their ultimate self-rectification. In the South you do not find the miasma of romance ; the suffocation of excuses ; the entanglement in cobwebs so delicate and so dense as to mask self from self. Patritius did not mind much. The realism of Augustine's view of the situation is far too direct to be called naïve. He says just what his father thought about him. As for himself, at first he was frightened, and prayed : " Give me chastity ! " yet added, with that interior honesty which a Northerner will never understand – he will call it hypocrisy ! – " but not yet." The Southerner, realizing that the Northerner has not the slightest intention of seriously aiming at chastity " just yet," while keeping up who knows what façade of good behaviour, accuses him of the hypocrisy. But Augustine rapidly outgrew the awkward phase. After a year, in 370, helped by the Mæcenas-like Rominianus of Tagaste, he actually went to Carthage. In that tumultuous city – city of study and of favourite jockeys, of ecstatic yet obscene religion and of dance-girls, captured gorillas whom they took for savage women, sea-monsters exhibited as mermaids, and philosophy – Augustine held himself " ridiculous if innocent ; despicable if pure – the greatest shame of all was to feel ashamed." He belonged to a gang – the *Eversores* – " Upset the lot of 'em ! " – till in the midst of this an infatuation captured him which became a true devotion, and for fifteen years he remained loyal to the girl who was the mother of his son – to him, so naturally ; to us, so unexpectedly – named Adeodatus – God-given.

(ii)

Yet, paradoxically, it is clear that this alliance was the first step, so to say, in Augustine's " stabilization." What began as a vague desire passed into true affection, and thence into a *love* for *one*, which is always a humanizing and civilizing factor, and may become a spiritualizing force. At first, naturally, the tempestuous Augustine was racked by every attendant emotion of jealousy, suspicion, panic, and rage : such love made him loathe his life. Help reached him in 373, when he chanced on a treatise by that Cicero whom till now he had ardently studied for rhetoric's sake. This book was the *Hortensius*.[1] In it, Cicero sings the praises of philosophy – the serenity of a Wisdom that at one stroke severs a man finally from the mad enchantment of a thousand things. But, poor Augustine ! It was *incredibili cordis aestu* – " with passion unbelievably vehement " – that he rushed to

[1] *Habent sua fata libelli.* Cicero wrote that small treatise, which, save for fragments, has disappeared. Perhaps he meant what he wrote in it, as much as he meant anything. Anyhow, after four hundred years, it effected a revolution in the man who was to shape the Western world ; six hundred years later, it was the joy of one of the sweetest figures in our " Dark Age " period. Herman the Cripple, the little monk of Reichenau, who could neither sit nor stand nor lie without pain, but who, " always cheery, always happy," occupied his soul with music, astronomy, history, poetry, and read and re-read *Hortensius*. And so, after another near-one-thousand years, its name returns upon our lips.

the pursuit of the Serene, the capture of the Immutable. Just when he perceived that the beauty of the True existed outside of sects, and that the " As Such " brooked no departmentalism, he became involved with the sect of Manichæans.

He returned to Tagaste already a fervid young convert, and received a real shock when Monica, suddenly obdurate, refused to accept him under her roof. She had deplored the sins of the flesh : wantonness of mind appalled her. Augustine, however, was just then less susceptible than usual. His head had emerged into a crystal air where reason and not dogma dominated. Manes " proved " his doctrines and did not impose them like the Catholics. Moreover, though a spiritual jejuneness in Cicero had sent Augustine back to the once-loved Scriptures, the young man found them clumsy, so that it was a relief when the Manichæans said he need not trouble about much of them. But, above all, more even than the fact that the Manichæan god was in some sort material – another relief to Augustine since he could not at that time entertain the notion of sheer " spirit " – the Manichæan doctrine of evil took a great load off him. One can clearly see that Augustine, during the whole of this period, had been feeling obscurely, and at times violently, that his life was " all wrong " – that *he* was wrong. Now he was taught that the evil principle existed, and resided *in* a man without precisely being *of* him, let alone *he*. " Something sins within me ; it is not I who sin." Therefore, while a mysterious instinct kept him sure that God in no case could be Author of Evil, he found a reason for the existence of evil which hardly involved his self. All the same, he wanted to be " better," and early grew distressed not only because he did not improve, but because the Manichæans seemed so much better at attacking Catholic dogmas than at proving, after all, their own. He fought down this anxiety for a while ; returned to Carthage and opened a " school " ; began to collect disciples to whom he feverishly taught the lore he was already disbelieving in. And for a while the excitement of this period, for which Romanianus once more had furnished the needed money, rescued him from the black melancholy into which the death of a friend – the first death that mattered to Augustine – had plunged him. For a while the school of eloquence went brilliantly. He found he could influence minds and wills more than he had suspected. He delivered a sarcastic speech on the iniquities of the Circus and the folly of being enslaved to its exhibitions. His friend Alypius, who had been unable to keep himself away from it, now suddenly, totally, and for ever, renounced it. Never had Augustine foreseen or intended that. Then Monica had a dream – she saw (in the semi-nonsense that a dream supplies) that she was on a " wooden Rule " and that Augustine, gay and debonair, came and stood beside her. He said : " Where you are, I am." When she woke and told him this, he argued that this meant she would turn Manichæan.

No, she insisted ; it was he who would one day stand where she was always standing. He awaited with eagerness the arrival of a Manichæan bishop of high repute, Faustinus. The old man came, was charming, polite, and modest ; but confessed candidly that he could not answer Augustine's difficulties. The young man was definitely chilled. And he suddenly woke up to the vulgarity of the average Carthaginian student. Their " rags " and senseless horseplay infuriated him. He decided to go to Rome, where he heard that youth was earnest. At the cost of telling Monica a lie, he sailed in fact from Carthage, arrived in Rome, fell very sick, nearly died, but still did not think of baptism. On his recovery, he opened his school of eloquence.

But Rome was always a mixture of extravagance and parsimony ; Augustine could not get his fees paid : when he learned that Milan was demanding from the city-prefect, Symmachus, a professor of eloquence for its own schools,

Augustine applied for the post, and, despite his African accent, won it. He now embarked on the career of teaching lads how to make speeches, and of making them himself on occasions that asked for panegyrics. No wonder that after no long time his soul loathed such emptiness.

You might have thought that by now (383-4) Augustine would have been a thoroughly disillusioned and embittered man. He knew he could not manage his body ; and was exasperated to find that often he ceased to want to, though the knowledge that he *could* not remained to gall him. He found that what he expected to help him – Manichæism – was as unable to do so as to help its own no less immoral " elect " : also, the sect cheated – it falsified the scriptural evidence to which it appealed ; also it could not construct, but only tried to destroy. So his mind too was out of his control. Even his curiosity had been tricked by an excursion into that astronomy which turned almost at once into astrology ; and as for panegyrics and " agonistic crowns," they began to nauseate him with their insipidity.

(iii)

But an austere and patient Providence attended him. The Roman rhetorician Victorinus had translated some works of Plato and Plotinus, and these rescued him from the brief period of " academic doubt " into which indeed he had fallen in his despondency. It is here that the dispute, alluded to at the beginning of this chapter, really arises. It is maintained that Augustine simply handed himself over to neo-Platonism and that his imminent conversion to Christianity was but technical – he remained essentially neo-Platonist. The truth is, that he already knew quite well the philosophy of Christianity, and read Plotinus with Christian eyes – discerning in him, therefore, grave omissions. We can safely

allow that " Plato " revealed to him the " True God " –
God, that is, quite different from the semi-material god of the
Manichæans ; Plotinus shed dazzling light upon the notion
of God's Word : but that the Word was " made flesh," that
the Word " redeemed " – this was not there ! At the same
time, he was frequenting the sermons of the great St.
Ambrose. That senatorial personage had not much time to
offer to Augustine, though he accorded him a gracious yet
embarrassing interview or two. Ambrose, however, assisted
him, by means of the precarious method of allegorization, to
think better of the Scriptures ; though, even so, Augustine
was grateful that he had met Plato before Paul.

Tempting as it is to indicate Augustine's approximations
during this period to Plato or Plotinus, and his withdrawals
from their spell, these have nothing to do with his character
as such, but with his mental progress towards Christianity.
I think that all his life through Augustine had felt that he
must be a Christian or " something else " – I mean, that
Christianity stood all alone upon the one side, and plenty of
options on the other. Christianity was never for him one of
many, as the rest of the warring philosophies had been. In but
a short time, the conflict revealed itself as entirely moral. " I
had found the goodly pearl ; and, at the price of all I had, I
should have bought it, and I hesitated. " His two wills,
" one old, one new, one of the spirit, one of the flesh, fought
angrily together, and my soul was on the rack." Monica had
arrived at Milan ; tenderly she had persuaded her son's companion to go away (I like to think that the suffering of this
girl, who surely loved Augustine as much as he did her, and
maybe more, merited for him help in his difficult hour) ; but
another woman had replaced her. The man was sure he
never could live chaste. Someone read the life of St. Antonius
to him. This created a crisis.

" Thou, Lord, in his words wast twisting me back to myself . . . wast setting me before my face, that I might see how

foul I was, how distorted and filthy, how soiled and ulcered. And I saw, and shuddered, and could flee myself nowhither. And if I tried to turn my gaze from myself, the reader went on reading, and Thou placedst me once more before my own face, and thrustedst me before my own eyes, that I might find my iniquity and loathe it. . . . The day had come when I lay naked to myself. . . . With what scourge of argument lashed I not my soul, that she should follow me who sought to follow Thee ! But she struggled and refused, and made no excuse. For all her reasonings had been consumed and de-feated : only a dumb shrinking still remained."

Augustine, on reaching home, sought the garden, with his friend, Alypius, terrified, at his side. The " merciful severity " of the Lord was there, scourging him to the snap-ping of the last meshes of sin.

" And I kept saying in my heart, ' Let it be now ! Let it be now ! ' And as I spoke, I made towards the resolve. I was all but doing it, and I did it not : yet I stepped not wholly back, but I would stand still hard by, and draw breath. And again I would try : and by a little less I was there, and again by a little less ; all but – all but – I reached and I held ; and lo, I was not there, and reached not, and held not, hesitating to die to death. . . . The empty trifles, and the vanities of vanities, my loves of yore, still held me back, plucking softly at my robe of flesh, and softly whispering, ' Wilt thou dis-miss us ? And from this moment shall not this and that be allowed to thee any more for ever ? From this moment shall we be with thee never any more for ever ? . . . Thinkest thou to do without these things ? ' . . . But from the other side be-hold a vision of the chaste dignity of Continence, serene in cheer . . . smiling and calling me."

It was the army of the pure, boys and girls, men and women, virgin equally. " What they could do, cannot you ? " The words came back and back. Bursting into a storm of tears, Augustine tore himself from Alypius, ran to the farthest part of the garden, flung himself on his face beneath a fig-tree, and sobbed and prayed. A child's voice reached him, singing from the neighbouring house some trifling rhyme : " *Take it, read it ! Take it, read it !* " Half dazed, Augustine rose, returned to Alypius, opened his scroll and read :

" Not in riotings and drunkenness, not in chamberings and impurities, not in contention and envy. But put ye on the Lord Jesus Christ, and make not provision for the flesh in its lusts."

In calm and silence, the miracle was worked. His will was healed ; he went direct to Monica, and the old life dropped from him like a garment.

Of this appalling struggle, the *Confessions* leave us what none shall persuade me is not the truthful document. During the Lent of 387, Augustine prepared for baptism, which, along with Adeodatus and Alypius, he received, doubtless on Holy Saturday.

(iv)

Thereupon, nothing would serve him but a hermit's life. He started for Africa, but at Ostia Monica fell ill. Her work was manifestly done. She died, untroubled – now that the son of her tears had been baptized – that her old prayer, to be buried near Patritius, could not be granted. "Nothing is far from God." One of the sweetest things in Christianity is that it prevents entirely all hardening of the heart. Augustine, become man-of-affairs, bishop, controversialist, theologian, proves by his transcendently beautiful pages on this death that his love for his mother had been intense, and became, as the years sped by, but deeper. From 388 to 391 he lived as a recluse at Rome, and later in Africa, though already his literary output became prodigious : probably in

396 the inevitable bishopric was thrust upon him. From this time onwards, it can hardly be suggested that his character changed in any substantial way or even developed. Certain episodes, however, did, I think, produce their effect on him.

I think that the duty of combating Manichæism, which soon befell him, established his intellectual conviction about the falsity of its view of evil, in a way which stood him in good stead when the Pelagian heresy came his way. I think it steadied him, and will say how in a moment. Perhaps also his experiences with the Donatists developed his statesman-like qualities. It is exasperating to hear of Augustine " using force to interfere with freedom of thought." The extreme savagery of the Donatists, their arson, pillage, and flinging of corrosives into the eyes, and in general their creation of chaos in a land where the maximum of unity was for every reason needed and would be needed even more when the invasions began in earnest, made it perfectly necessary for Augustine to admit and even apply for coercion. This did not in the least affect his disposition, which was, never to use force, let alone torture, upon his fellow-men. But so much of his early life had been spent in theorizing and in talking, that he needed at any rate a very great deal of actual experience of men and of what might be expected of them, and of what one who seeks to govern justly may find he has to do in order, precisely, to be just. The Pelagian controversy – Pelagius, like a good Northerner, was ready to believe that human nature could do more than it really can, and was tempera-mentally averse to the full doctrine of the supernatural – might quite possibly have driven Augustine into a pessimist extreme had not this double lessoning given him equilibrium. Even as it was, I cannot but think that Augustine despaired increasingly of human nature, and leant nearer to a belief in its radical corruption, towards the end of his life and under the Pelagian pressure, than he did in his middle years. After

GA

all, this was the easier because he had spent so long despairing of himself ! And the state of the world was becoming
more and more desperate. The days were approaching when
he would have to pray to die before his city should be sacked,
his flock scattered, if the barbarian disaster might not be
prevented. He did indeed die before the siege of Hippo ended
fatally, on August 28th, 430, having his eyes fixed on the
Penitential Psalms, of which he had caused a huge copy to
be hung on the wall before him.

But what we ought really to study, in Augustine's Letters
and Sermons, is that character which he displayed in his
adult years, though he had formed, long before, that which
only responsibility was needed in order to co-ordinate, harmonize, and establish. Only by the piling up of a thousand
little phrases could this final product be expressed and conveyed to a reader. You would have to be shown Augustine
the financier, and the lover of poverty : the ready manipu-
lator of those old tricks of rhetoric, when a popular audience
could not do without them, and the speaker quite conscious
that they were but tricks, and disdaining them, and only
using them with a sort of kindliness which in him replaced
humour – I am alternatively tempted to think that Augustine had a true and very active sense of humour and that he
had none at all – you would have to see him dealing with the
great civil and military officials of the empire, and with the
average congregation – he had his crack-of-a-whip phrases :
" Attend better " ; and his charming, half-mocking, quite
realist courtesies : " I mustn't keep you too long – you,
standing up to listen ; I, sitting down to talk." I will only
say that, once a Christian, Augustine harmonized himself
with extraordinary rapidity ; everything fell into its place,
and at last you saw how much there was, so to speak, to fall
there.

There might have been more originality, and perhaps
more charm, in dwelling on this complete and harmonious

Augustine than in rehearsing the hundred-times told tale of his youth. After all, there is something almost morbid, and, some might say, quite frivolous, in emphasizing the erratic career of a young and passionate man. Still, I do not believe that you could guess the aged Augustine without remembering his youth. I do not believe that anything of that youth was lost in his old age, though it had become invisible, as details do, when the whole demands your total admiration. Let it be said that Augustine contained within himself every human ingredient in rich measure and each of them intensely. For you can have many qualities, and all of them palely. I would be almost content if I had done no more than insist that Augustine never was an Englishman – not even an Italian. Africa is not Italy. Skies of hard staring blue ; sunlight on white walls to make your eyes ache ; nowhere a reticence – the purest woman saw daily the most loud-laughing vice ; creeds cursed one another ; affectation itself was crude. A world of blaring horns and clashing cymbals, hardening the Roman dignity (such as by then it was – but at least the tradition was intangible) into harshness ; coarsening Greek beauty (which long ago had weakened into " good taste ") into fleshiness, and volatilizing Greek intellectuality (already thinned down into cleverness) into phantasmagoriæ. Augustine, nervously impressionable, a boy of quicksilver like Arab boys even now, was still able, unlike the Arab boy, to " last out " into adolescence – not that he could become (behave as he would) the Tunisian youth of to-day, dreaming down the street with the thick-scented jasmine-tuft hanging over his ear, able to wake up only when lust flares suddenly. To the end his body would remain wiry, short, vibrant. And to the end his mind leapt and pounced and ricocheted from notion to analogy, from phrase to assonant word, from tiniest grain of thought to remote association of idea. It must always have been his difficulty to *resist* the hurricane-swift alliance of ideas, and keep to what he was really talking of. His sentences that begin so suddenly with *et*. " I was asleep. And You were waking and You were arousing me. And there was the sleep in Truth and You, O Wakefulness, were arousing me and lulling me and I did not know it, but You ceased not."

Sometimes thus he talks ; and for him an idea almost instantly suggests its opposite – he tosses it away only to recatch it before it has escaped him ; he inverts it, he inserts it – who knows how : the result is not only true but limpid. Perhaps, had St. Paul been a rhetorician, he would have written like that ; but there is all the difference between Paul and Augustine that exists between Jew and African, quite apart from that between two different educations. Perhaps Augustine makes us think also of Chrysostom ; but the Asiatic had not ever had the deep Romanization of Augustine : Chrysostom (whom none can fail to revere) sometimes almost shrieks at his delinquent empresses ; his recrimination becomes shrill. Augustine never shrieks. He makes us, too, turn our thoughts to Jerome, with whom he had hard wrestles. But though Augustine from time to time becomes severe and even sarcastic, he retains always his respect for the fierce old scholar ; and, though he can argue hotly, he is not what I would call ferocious. Let us just say " intense," with an intensity proper to no English author who has ever written.

But it was not an affair of authorship. All in Augustine was intense. His tenacious memory showed him distant events – even interior ones – under a vivid illumination. As in a Southern landscape, there was no distance ; there were no smudged edges. Of the rapidity and devouring advances of his intelligence, I spoke a moment ago. Lucretius spoke with pain of his " wavering will " – *incerta voluntas* ; this hurt him more than almost anything in man's composition : Augustine shows his intensity in the horror he has of anything in himself that is *not* intense – of his will, when it seemed to waver. Possibly his will wavered when his sympathy itself rose to intensity ; Augustine could hold no mere frozen idea before his mind – the thing palpitated forthwith and came to life and he hated it or loved it. If there was intellect in his mysticism, there was passion in his philosophy. And with it all, was that strange, enduring tenderness of heart, such that unconsciously he swerved, lest he should weaken, towards taking the harder course, sometimes with others, always with himself.

E. I. WATKIN

THE MYSTICISM
OF ST. AUGUSTINE

THE MYSTICISM OF ST. AUGUSTINE

Perhaps no other figure embodies in such massive simplicity the essence of religion as does St. Augustine. A vertical movement of the soul to her depths, seeking the Absolute Good – God – that alone can satisfy her, has found in St. Augustine's life and writings its classical expression. The prophets of the Old Testament, the apostles of the New are concerned primarily with the Kingdom of God – the society of souls in union with Him. They are first and foremost messengers of Divine Truth to mankind. Nor was it otherwise with our Lord Himself; His earliest message is the proclamation of the Kingdom, His latest the proclamation of Himself as its Messianic King. Even the most intimate moments of His communion with the Father bear a social reference ; if He prays all night on the mountain it is to appoint His apostles the following day, His baptism and transfiguration are solemn declarations of His divine mission, and when He prays in the garden of agony the subject of His prayer is the redemption of mankind. Indeed, the biblical writings take for granted the fundamental fact of religion – God and the soul's relationship to God. St. Augustine, who must learn it by years of painful search, sets it before us in its stark simplicity. " Thou hast made us for Thyself, and our heart is restless until it rest in Thee." These classic words, quoted until they sound almost a commonplace, express perfectly the foundation of religion and the approaches to it.

From the outset St. Augustine was dominated by a passion for lasting happiness. " Nothing very unusual," you might say ; " we all desire lasting happiness." No doubt, and no one is more insistent than Augustine in pointing it out. In

every sphere the genius is the man who realizes with exceptional strength and expresses with exceptional felicity fundamental needs and intuitions of the human spirit. He is the
voice of humanity. The saint, the religious genius, is the
voice of religious humanity. But whereas most of us are content with a compromise – with brief spells of joy, like splashes
of vivid colour in a life mainly a grey monotony of half-awake
humdrum content or discontent, as the balance inclines –
St. Augustine had the artist's demand for intense living,
for a complete satisfaction of hungry capacities – an ecstasy,
and a permanent ecstasy, of life, love and joy. " I was in
love with love " – love in which the individual passes out of
himself to live the fuller richer life of union with that which
is beyond himself.

As we might have expected from a man who did not
begin life with a strong personal religion, Augustine began
with the short-lived succession of amours which offered
themselves so easily to a young man of great personality
and brilliant gifts. Many artists get no further, and pass
their lives tossed from rapture to disillusionment. But St.
Augustine was harassed by that longing for permanence which
dominated his life and thought to the end. So he exchanged
his light loves for one deep and faithful attachment. But
his soul was still hungry – there were empty depths that no
human love could fill, and the shadow "of change and mutability " darkened the pleasures of corruptible flesh. Cicero
first, then the neo-Platonist mysticism of Plotinus and his
school, invited him to the love and possession of an absolute
and immutable Good. He was in love with Love. He drew
closer to God, Whose call he heard ever more clearly. He
shrunk back. For him there could be no half-measures ; it
must be all or nothing. Already he felt from time to time a
divine touch, enjoyed moments of union with God probably
unknown to the majority even of good Christians. " I entered
into my inward self, Thou being my Guide . . . and beheld

with the eye of my soul above my mind " – above the level
of discursive thought, with the obscure intuition or touch of
the centre of his soul, the apex or *fine pointe* of later
mystical theology – " the Light Unchangeable. Thee [my
God] when I first knew, Thou liftedst me up that I might
see there was what I might see, and that I was not yet such
as to see. And Thou didst beat back the weakness of my
sight, streaming forth Thy beams of light upon me most
strongly, and I trembled with love and awe ; and I perceived
myself to be far off from Thee in the region of unlikeness.
Thou criedst to me from afar : ' Yea, verily, I am that I
am.' And I heard, as the heart heareth, nor had I room to
doubt, and I should sooner doubt that I live, than that truth
is not. . . . And yet I did not press on to enjoy my God : but
was borne up to Thee by Thy Beauty, and soon borne down
from Thee by mine own weight, sinking with sorrow into
those inferior things. This weight was carnal custom. . . .
By degrees I passed from bodies to the soul, which through
the bodily senses perceives ; and thence to the inward faculty
[the imagination] to which the bodily senses represent things
external . . . and thence again to the reasoning faculty, to
which what is received from the senses of the body, is referred
to be judged. Which finding itself also to be in me a thing
variable, raised itself up to its own understanding . . . with-
drawing itself from those troops of contradictory phantasms,
that so it might find what that light was, whereby it was
bedewed, when, without all doubting, it cried out ' That
the unchangeable was to be preferred to the changeable,'
whence also it knew that Unchangeable, which, unless it
had in some way known, it had had no sure ground to prefer
it to the changeable. *And thus with the flash of one trembling
glance it arrived at* THAT WHICH IS. And then I saw Thy invisible things understood by the things which are made.
But I could not fix my gaze thereon ; and my infirmity being struck back, I was thrown again on my wonted habits

[my normal experience], carrying along with me only a loving memory thereof, and a longing for what I had, as it were, perceived the odour of, but was not yet able to feed on."[1]

The passage from which this extract is taken contains all the leading principles of Augustinian philosophy and mysticism. For the present we need only remark the ascent of the dissatisfied soul to the unchanging Good for which it thirsts, and the fact that already before his definitive conversion Augustine enjoyed a genuinely mystical experience of God in which, " with the flash of one trembling glance," his spirit " arrived at THAT WHICH IS." How, it may be asked, could a soul not yet wholly and definitely devoted to God be united to Him even for a moment? The objection, I think, reads back unwarrantably the present of the convert Augustine into the past of the Augustine who is feeling his way or more truly being led on to the Light. Already he possessed sufficient knowledge and love of God to desire a life incompatible with that which he was actually leading, and to find the latter therefore a barrier preventing the permanence of the union reached in a momentary flash. But that is not to say that he had then attained that conviction of the sinfulness of his life which would make it a barrier to even a temporary union with God. In the spiritual life everything depends on love, and already Augustine loved God far more fervently than the vast majority of Christians. Newman radically misconceived the relationship between religion and ethics when he made the moral conscience the organ of religious intuition and the sense of sin the foundation of belief in God. On the contrary, sin – as distinct from merely ethical faultiness – is the shadow cast by the light of God intercepted by any attachment of the will which prevents it from illuminating the soul. Thus knowledge of God gives rise to the sense of sin, not vice versa. Surely, then, we

[1] *Confessions*, VII, xvi, 23 (Pusey).

need find no difficulty in admitting the plain meaning of the *Confessions* and in granting that Augustine even before his final conversion received the grace of mystical prayer? What is regrettable is that the saint, who in his earlier writings recognizes ungrudgingly the genuinely mystical character of the neo-Platonist ecstasies, should later have narrowed his outlook and denied that philosophers like Plotinus or Proclus, who were wholly given to the service of God as they understood it, simply because they did not accept Christianity, and therefore gave to their experience an inadequate intellectual formulation, could not have received a grace bestowed on himself while yet outside the Church and living in a state which he had already begun to believe definitely sinful.[1]

On the other hand, his belief that if he had been a Christian, and living according to the highest Christian standards, his experience would have been permanent must surely be pronounced an illusion, and, moreover, strangely persistent after years of Christian life during which his conscious contacts with God (as is plain from his own words, *Comm. in Psalm. xli*) continued to be short-lived and transitory. If anything is certain, it is that not the holiest saints have enjoyed in this life a permanent consciousness of the Divine Presence. Always the positive mystical experience is followed by a dark night in which the Divine Union is hidden from consciousness. Indeed, in this very book, speaking of a post-conversion experience, he says that his mother and himself " barely touched it [the life of union with God] with the whole effort of the heart " and " in swift thought touched the Eternal Wisdom so that the experience was but one moment of contemplation."[2] Here no lack of faith or sinful

---

[1] That he felt this from the outset seems doubtful, for two reasons : (i) he called his child Adeodatus – the gift of God ; (ii) he was then a Manichee, and for the Manichees all forms of sexual union were indeed equally evil, but for the majority inevitable.

[2] *Confessions*, IX, xxiv, 25. Quoted by Butler, *Western Mysticism*, second edition, p. 66.

attachment drew him back. Yet the rapture is but for a moment. And elsewhere in the *Confessions* the saint complains that the law of alternate pain and joy, desire and possession, holds good even of the love of God (VIII, iii). There seems, therefore, a certain confusion in this passage between permanence of the experience of God and permanence of His actual union with the soul, His possession of the will by charity. The latter St. Augustine received at his conversion – the former was reserved for the " blessed life " of heaven, the only life rightly so called which in the first rapture of conversion he too rashly – so he afterwards thought – expected from contemplation on earth.

We need not retell here the story of this conversion – of the decisive moment when he gave his will wholly and irrevocably to God. If already on the way he had received the favour of infused contemplation, we should expect that he would now receive it at profounder levels, in richer abundance, in greater frequency, and for a longer duration. Sufficient evidence confirms our expectation. There is the famous conversation at Ostia during which he and his mother were both rapt to a foretaste of the joy of heaven. There is his famous commentary on Psalm xli, with which Abbot Butler fittingly introduces his study of St. Augustine's mysticism,[1] a study so exhaustive of the evidence, and so careful in its interpretation, as strictly to render superfluous this chapter or any further treatment of this aspect of St. Augustine's life and teaching. There is the account in *De Genesi ad Litteram* (ch. xii) of the highest form of Divine knowledge accessible in this life. A transient intuition of God – he calls it, misleadingly we think, a vision – accompanied by delight and spiritual sweetness, this certainly was Augustine's. There can be no doubt that his God-hungry soul was fed with the infused contemplation of God. But when we would inquire more exactly into the nature and degree of his

---

[1] *Western Mysticism*, second edition, pp. 26-34.

mystical elevations, and compare them with the detailed descriptions of later mystics – for example, Ruysbrock, St. Teresa, St. John of the Cross – we are disappointed. There is so little evidence.

" Sometimes thou admittest me to an affection, very unusual, in my inmost soul, rising to a strange sweetness, in which, if it were perfected in me, I know not what would not belong to the life to come "[1] Is this indescribable sweetness – which apparently describes the climax of St. Augustine's spiritual experience more than the Prayer of Full Union – the perfected Prayer of Quiet ? There is certainly no hint of the psycho-physical ligature of ecstasy.[2] In the window at Ostia he certainly did not enter into a state of trance. On the other hand, when he is discussing the ecstasies of St. Paul, he insists on his alienation from normal consciousness. And as we shall see, he assimilates all mystical experience – all *direct* intuition of God – to these Pauline raptures.

" We glow inwardly with Thy fire."[3] The words are applicable to anything from sensible devotion to the consuming fire of the transforming union as described by St. John of the Cross in *The Living Flame of Love.* " The leadings of a certain delight, an inward mysterious and hidden pleasure . . . a certain inward sound, the Perception of something Unchangeable."[4] The mystical intuition on some level, no doubt. But which, precisely? There is nothing to tell us. *A priori*, indeed, we should expect this mighty lover of God to have attained the supreme degree of mystical union possible in this life – the transforming union or mystical marriage. A favour granted to St. Teresa, and St. John of the

---

[1] *Confessions*, X, xl.

[2] Butler quotes from *De Genesi ad Litteram* (xii, 26, 54) a passage which he regards as the autobiographical echo of ecstasies enjoyed by Augustine (*Western Mysticism*, second edition, pp. 74, 99). But so far as the passage refers to this life it witnesses only to infused contemplation generally, as opposed to sensible and imaginary visions. There is nothing specific to the ecstatic degree of such prayer. Dom Butler in this entire section appears to use *ecstasy* widely, to cover every degree of infused and direct contemplation of God.

[3] *Confessions*, XIII, ix.   [4] *Comm. in Ps. xli*, trs. Butler.

Cross, and a host of other mystics, including the pseudonymous wife and widow whose journal has been published under the name of Lucie Christine, was surely not denied to Augustine? Again, we do not know. If Augustine contrasts the Christian's union with God with the ecstasy of the neo-Platonists,[1] it is not because the former enjoys a fuller and richer experience of God ; it is because in Augustine's view, which we may well think too short a measure of God's love for men, the Christian, even if he does not, like the Platonist, " touch to a certain extent the light of immutable truth " is by his faith on the sure road to the beatific possession of God after death – they are presumably doomed to everlasting separation from the Good of which they have caught a passing glimpse. That even experimentally Augustine had himself out-distanced the Platonists – who never seem to have got beyond ecstasy and to have attained that but rarely, Plotinus only four times during the long period in which Porphyry was his disciple, Porphyry himself but once, at the age of sixty-eight[2] – is probably to be inferred from his dissatisfaction with the pre-conversion experience recorded in the seventh book of the *Confessions*. But it is not for any superiority in his *experience* of God that the Christian is preferred to the Platonist – admittedly Plotinus did experience God where the majority of Christians must be satisfied with simple faith – but for the solid possession of God – experienced or otherwise – which Augustine too narrowly confined to Christians. To be sure, the *De Quantitate Animæ* formally enumerates the steps by which the soul ascends to God. But of these only the last, *contemplatio* – contemplation – can be a state of mystical prayer. Moreover, *contemplatio* covers a wider field, and includes any kind of thought directed to God – especially the contemplation of God in His creatures. That is to say,

---

[1] *De Trinitate*, IV, xv ; quoted by Père Maréchal, *La Vision de Dieu au Sommet de la Contemplation, d'après S. Augustin*, p. 12.
[2] Cf. Hastings, *Encyclopedia of Religion and Ethics*, " Ecstasy."

Augustine's ladder ends where those of the mystical theologians begin.

The fact of the matter is that mystical theology, understood as the scientific study of infused prayer, was as yet nonexistent. Neither St. Augustine nor any other primitive saint thought of answering questions which it had occurred to nobody to ask. Enough that in some very real sense a direct intuition of God was possible in this life, and that he, Augustine, had enjoyed it.

The obscurity is increased by the fact that not only was St. Augustine's account of his religious experience – as indeed his theology in general – inextricably involved in his Platonist philosophy – so that for him philosophy and theology are not two but one discipline[1] – but his mystical experience, like those of the neo-Platonists, was given on occasion and at the conclusion of a process of *intellectual* introversion and abstraction from the manifold of sense through the ideas they embody to God the Absolute. To be sure, whereas the Platonists concluded that their ecstasy was the direct and necessary result of this intellectual process, for St. Augustine it is a free supernatural gift of Divine Grace. Indeed, he falls into a mistake the reverse of that made by the Platonist. He is inclined to ascribe to the intellectual process the supernatural character belonging in fact only to its actual but not necessary goal, the free gift of infused contemplation, because in him, as indeed in the case also of the neo-Platonists (though he later ceased to perceive this), it was inspired by love of God. This is because he held that every true judgement, being as such a perception of unchanging being (for a truth is *qua* truth always and everywhere true) owes its truth *directly* to an illumination of the Divine Truth above the human mind – the Word of God which enlightens every man coming into the world[2] – the

[1] Gilson, *Introduction à l'Étude de S. Augustin*, pp. 41–43.
[2] *Ibid*, ch. v, especially pp. 97, 102–6, 112, 118–20.
HA

interior, indeed strictly speaking the sole, teacher : *illuminatio nostra participatio Verbi*. This illumination must, of course, be admitted in all knowledge – even secular – and in the knowledge of pagans. When, however, the Divine Source of truth is explicitly recognized, and becomes the direct object of thought, we have wisdom (*sapientia*) as opposed to mere knowledge (*scientia*), and the highest form of wisdom is the mystical experience of God. The gradual transition, however, from the order of natural knowledge, itself an enlightenment by the Divine Teacher, to the intellectual study of the truths of faith in the supernatural order, as exemplified by the appeal to God in the closing books of the *Confessions*, to guide Augustine to a true understanding of the first chapter of *Genesis*, and so on to the direct intuition of the Teacher Himself, makes it difficult to demarcate exactly the boundaries between these different levels of Divine Teaching. For the Christian, every level and mode of knowledge is, or should be, subordinated to the love and knowledge of God ; they thus constitute a whole in which every form of knowledge, even the study of the secular sciences, is motived, inspired, elevated, by the search for God of which the mystical intuition is the earthly crown. Indeed, in his opposition to a barren intellectualism which cannot give life, and which treats the discursive reason and its apprehensions as an end instead of a means – that is to say, which substitutes the abstract for the concrete, a mirror for direct vision of the object – St. Augustine underrated the value of science. He would admit only whatever studies are *directly* serviceable to the knowledge of God. But by this very contraction of the intellectual sphere the mental, the spiritual but non-mystical, and the mystical lives and activities are united still closer. This union, rather fusion – indeed confusion – had been effected by Plato (or, if you prefer, by Socrates), completed by the neo-Platonists ; and Augustine never succeeded in extricating himself entirely. " Mysticism or Platonism ? "

Dom Butler asks himself. He answers, " Not Platonism, but mysticism." No doubt, but a mysticism to the end sufficiently Platonic to assume, as its body, the intellectual life with its hierarchy of increasing abstraction. Augustinianism is thus, like man, a *compositum* – of which the soul is mystical prayer, the body theological-philosophical thought.

The object of the mystic's intuition is the immutable and timeless but obscure Absolute, God. The object of scientific contemplation is also immutable, timeless, and derivately absolute (but clear) abstract laws : for the ancients pre-eminently the laws of mathematics, the properties of numbers and geometrical figures. From Plato onwards the contemplation of the latter clear but abstract absolutes had been employed as a pathway to the contemplation of the former, the obscure concrete Absolute. This was at once a consequence and a cause of the distinctively Platonic fusion of the intellectual and spiritual lives. It had, however, two unfortunate results. One, to which Baron von Hügel has called our attention, was the abstract formulation of the concrete Absolute, that which was experienced as the Whole being described as bare abstract unity, the Good which is the supereminent possession of all concrete goods formulated as the abstract quality of goodness common to them all. The other was the hope to attain in this life as the climax of an abstractive process a clear perception of the supreme Principle and Good on which the abstract secondary principles or ideas depend as the source of their intelligibility. Because God is more, not less, intelligible than the mathematical laws which to some extent rationalize the world of matter, and His finality more rational than man's most reasonable purposes, the philosopher, given the necessary moral dispositions, should be able, the Platonists thought, to attain clear knowledge of this ultimate Rationality and, in that vision, a science of final causes. In reality, mystical experience yields only the certainty of an Absolute unintelligible in His infinite excess of our understanding. The Platonist, however, is loath to admit that this supreme experience is, and for man must always remain, contact, not vision – the more so, when, as by St. Augustine, clear knowledge of any kind is ascribed to direct illumination by the light now attained in its Source. If the sight of objects in the light of the Luminary be vision, much more must direct contact with that Luminary be vision. Further confusions follow. St. Augustine speaks of vision when the experience is no more than an obscure intuition. Moreover, under the influence of his Platonic longing for a vision of God in this life, he interprets Moses's peculiar sight of God and St. Paul's rapture to the third heaven as foretastes of the beatific vision granted, indeed, to others besides Moses and St. Paul, including, it would seem, himself.[1] True, his own experiences, as he describes them, are obviously not visions but unintelligible intuitions – flashes of spiritual light too bright for clear gazing, a sweetness indescribable. But they would seem to have been accompanied by vivid realizations of philosophic or theological truths not themselves due to mystical intuition but evoked under its stimulus from the subconscious memory. Is not the luminary then apprehended more directly than the objects it illuminates? Directly, immediately, yes, but with the immediacy of touch, not sight. But the Platonist theory, as opposed to practice, knew only of intellectual sight[2] : the touch too dim for vision had no place in their system, nor even in the christianized Platonism of Augustine.

We thus find the mystical teaching of Augustine obscured at every turn by the lack of any tradition of mystical theology and by a confusion due to Platonism. Such confusion

---

[1] See Butler: *Western Mysticism*, pp. 77–88 ; also Maréchal: *La Vision de Dieu*, etc., pp. 29–37.

[2] Cf. Plato : *Symposium*, 211 ; *Republic*, VII, 516, 540 ; Plotinus : *Enneads*, V, iii, 17 ; VI, vii, 34–5, ix, 11. There is a hint, certainly, in this last passage that the mystic's experience is touch, not sight ; but the language of vision is immediately resumed.

is indeed inevitable in the infancy of every branch of learning as it is in the mental life of the individual. The baby's experience, his knowledge, that is to say, is at first *in globo*. Only as he develops is it analysed and the various elements, sensible, mental, volitional, etc., sorted out. In Augustine, philosophy, speculative or dogmatic theology, devotion and mystical intuition are still mainly *in globo*, and we cannot hope to sift out completely any one of these factors – least of all the most obscure – the scientific study of which is therefore the latest formed of all the theological disciplines.

Scientific mystical theology, understood as a detailed account of mystical experience and its stages, has therefore, it must be confessed, little to learn from St. Augustine. But as regards the foundations of mystical theology – its psychological and theological presuppositions and principles – the case is quite otherwise. " Life as it flows is so much time wasted, and nothing can ever be recovered or truly possessed save under the form of eternity." As Professor Santayana intended these words, they are but a half-truth, for his eternity is an eternity of abstract thought or artistic embodiment, not a concrete life. Rightly understood, they are the key to Augustine's religion, of which his mysticism is but the flower. For him life is indeed wasted because it flows – and the sense of this is, as Baron von Hügel has pointed out so emphatically, itself due to the presence and operation of something which does not pass. But that for Augustine was no lifeless abstraction, but a concrete Fullness of Life – ever the same because it contains in itself all the values produced at each passing moment of time.

The intuition of eternity as a comprehensive whole is specially emphasized by Augustine. In his subtle study of memory he shows that the human mind already in its normal operations in some measure transcends time, for example when we apprehend as a whole a metre or a melody, though the individual sounds and notes are

successive, not simultaneous.[1] But it is more than an
argument *a fortiori*, it is actual experience which enables
him to speak with such conviction of " the glory of that
ever fixed Eternity " in which " nothing passeth, but the
whole is present," and to cry for God " to hold the heart
of man [evidently in this life] that it may stand still to see
how Eternity, ever still standing, neither past nor to come,
uttereth the times past and to come," contains them, and
expresses their value. [2]

This apprehension of eternity, the absolute Givenness of
God[2] – this no doubt the source of the Augustinian
emphasis on the factor of grace in the economy of salvation
– the rapture of the mystic's experience yet its necessary
impermanence on earth, the intuition of God as the
ground, guarantee and goal of all knowledge whatsoever –
such are the experiences directly mystical or tending
towards infused contemplation which moulded the religion
of Augustine. Even his limitations – his contempt for any
knowledge not *directly* serviceable to religion, his lack of
belief in any essential amelioration of the conditions of
human life (he treats the absurd cruelty of school punishment, on which he comments, as an inevitable penalty of
human sin[4]), his underestimate of the power of free
will and the value of natural goodness – are insufficiently
criticized concomitants of the mystic's radical experience
that God is man's all, and creatures, by comparison, worth-
less nothings.

Sed non omnes possumus omnia, and it was well that the
absolute character and claim of religion – of God, as revealed by the mystic's direct contact with Him – should
be thus massively embodied in the life and system of

[1] *Confessions*, XI, xxxiii, *sqq.*   [2] *Confessions*, XI, xiii.
[3] "Unless it [the soul] had in some way known the Unchangeable, it had no
sure ground to prefer it to the changeable." *Confessions*, VII, xvi.
[4] *Confessions*, I, xiv–xvi, xix, xxiii.

Augustine. If he has not left us a mystical theology
in the later sense, the soul of his theology and philosophy,
or more truly his theological philosophy, is mystical. We
shall go to Augustine, not for a detailed description of
mystical experiences, their characteristics, conditions and
order, but to observe in a supreme instance the essential
nature of that experience in every degree, and how it reacts
upon the entire system of a thinker of genius, a rich complex
of non-mystical and in part non-religious interests and knowledge. If St. Augustine is a churchman, it is because he has
learned by experience the need for an objective institution
to explain, fructify and render permanent in substance,
though not in consciousness, his intuitions of Divine Union.
If the doctor of Grace, it is because mystical experience reveals, as nothing else, the sheer gratuitousness of the Divine
self-gift and self-manifestation. If a subtle psychologist especially in his analyses of memory and will, it is because it
is in and through these obscure depths of the soul that the
Divine Presence and Working come to consciousness. If a
student of time, it is because the analysis of time reveals the
need and reality of the Eternal – of the laws of number,
because their absolute and immutable character reflects and
points to the Divine Absolute. Only here and there can
we find a passage descriptive of an indubitably mystical
experience, but everything he writes is inspired by such experiences, and looks backward or forward to them. A clergy-
man once said to the writer that Augustine put his entire
experience into his prayer. It is true, and that prayer at its
height was mystical or infused contemplation. It is in his
mysticism, therefore, that he baptized everything he experienced or learned. *Cor Augustini, cor igitur Augustinismi,
sedes Dei, Dei vivi et Dei tactu intimo animæ cogniti.*

FR. JOHN-BAPTIST REEVES, O.P.

ST. AUGUSTINE AND HUMANISM

ST. AUGUSTINE AND HUMANISM

" European civilization," " Western ideas " – what do these phrases mean ? Usually something definite though not easily definable. We hear, for instance, that Japan is adopting Western ideas, or that India is resisting European civilization. This may mean no more than that certain fashions of dress, concoctions of alcohol, industrial mechanism, or commercial methods, which first appeared in Europe in fairly recent times, are being favoured or discountenanced elsewhere. But as a rule it means much more. It implies something spiritual, ethical, cultural. It implies a reference to history – the history of Greece, and Rome, and Christianity. Above all, it implies a tradition of books, and learning, and schools – especially schools. The religion of Europe has manifestly influenced the culture of Europe ; but not exclusively or immediately. It is not directly due to Catholicism or Protestantism or to ancient paganism as a religion that Homer, for instance, holds his present place in the cultured minds of Europe. If culture were immediately dependent on religion alone, every change in European religion would have been accompanied by a corresponding cultural change ; thus the great change in the essentials and externals of religion at the Reformation should have produced both a fundamental and a superficial change in culture. This did not happen. Between Dante and Milton, for instance, the religious difference is in every way greater than the cultural difference. It is only by schools that culture is directly determined. Even religion must use them as a medium to influence it. Christian culture is the immediate result of the scholastic system which Christianity has used throughout many centuries. Apart from the spirit which Christianity infused into it, and the Christian purposes to which it was applied, that system is a human institution independent of Christianity. It is older than Christianity ; it was derived from Greek and Latin sources distinct and very different from those Jewish sources from which alone the Christian religion has drawn anything ; and it has long outlived Christianity here and there.

Modern civilization, unwilling to acknowledge its debt to Christian schools, has narrowed the meaning of Christian scholasticism to include no more than the purely philosophical and theological elements which reached their full development in the educational system of Catholic Europe in the thirteenth century and have dominated it ever since. But from the fourth to the thirteenth century and for long afterwards the term " scholastic " connoted, not a special kind of philosophy or theology, but the discipline in arts which must precede any and every philosophy, and all theology that pretends to be a rational science. A *scholasticus* originally meant a schoolmaster, or master of arts. By the eleventh and twelfth centuries the meaning of the word had been extended to include pupils who were being trained to be schoolmasters, and therefore graduating in arts. If a special kind of philosophy or theology is still called " scholastic," this is not, and cannot be, as many vainly try to show, a description of the nature of that philosophy and theology. It is an extrinsic description, dictated by an almost unconscious memory of the past, and justified not so much by any analysis of the things described as by attention to their historical associations. Scholastic philosophy and theology are so described because they were first produced, and are still supported, by the scholastic tradition of arts, and especially by the first three, or *trivium*, upon which the entire culture of the Western world is based in so far as it is consistent with itself and has a continuous history behind it.

The history of European schools and education reveals scholasticism as a complete culture. St. Thomas Aquinas is not more entitled to be called a scholastic than are Dante and Shakespeare. He was a scholastic because he was educated in the liberal arts ; in the *trivium* by a certain Martin, Master of Arts, and in the *quadrivium* by Peter the Irishman, another Master of Arts. As well as being a scholastic, he specialized later in theology ; we therefore call him a scholastic theologian. Dante and Shakespeare received the same education in the liberal arts ; to be consistent we should call the first a scholastic poet and the second a scholastic dramatist.

The discipline of the liberal arts, or scholasticism, was eminently a tradition ; after the Christian religion itself it is the best example in European history of a really living tradition. The ambition of the *scholasticus* of the Middle Ages was to master, and to hand on to others the discipline that had been established by the schoolmasters who had preceded him. From the sixth to the thirteenth century no scholastic ever dreamed of improving what had been done for this tradition by his predecessors. Frequently he was able to master a little more than he had received from his own immediate master. This, however, he did, not by going outside the tradition, or by developing it on his own initiative, but by going back as nearly as he could to the first and most perfect master of all, from whom the whole line of scholastics was descended, and to whose complete culture it was the consistent aim of Scholasticism to approximate. This first of all the scholastics was St. Augustine.

With St. Augustine, scholasticism entered the Catholic Church. He was not the first Christian to be also a scholastic. St. Jerome, for instance, was a master of the liberal arts. But St. Jerome was never quite clear in his mind whether as a Christian he ought to be proud of this or ashamed of it. He was not a lifelong scholastic in the sense that he continued all his life to educate others to be scholastics. St. Augustine was a professor of the liberal arts before his baptism, and continued to practise his profession to the end of his life, and for generations afterwards. Immediately after his conversion he maintained that nobody could be a Christian who was not educated in the liberal arts. Later he modified this view, observing that many saints had never had this education, and many others who had were not saints.[1] But he always maintained that the scholastic training which he himself had received in his youth was an advantage to good Christians, and willingly offered himself to them as their schoolmaster.[2]

The influence of St. Augustine on Christianity is sometimes exaggerated. It will be well if we distinguish here his influence on Christianity from the influence of Christianity upon him. He was obviously not the founder of the Christian religion. At his baptism he submitted himself to it just as it was. And it was, and had long been, a solidly established and highly developed religious society. Its beliefs were well defined ; its liturgy had already asserted all its characteristic elements ; its primary documents were generally acknowledged and attentively studied everywhere ; its laws and system of government were settled and in working order. In the West even its common language was fixed. Although Greek was predominant in the theology and liturgy of the East, where these important elements were most advanced, it did not hold the same promise of permanent vitality and development as the Latin of the West. Western converts to Christianity have always been converts to Latin too, unless they possessed it already. Though St. Augustine did much to strengthen this tendency, it existed before his day.

[1] *Retractationes*, I, iii, 2.
[2] He writes to the deacon Deogratias : " As for myself, I am not at all unwilling, nay, charity and duty towards you and the whole church compelling me, I am ready and eager to do anything God wills to help my brethren by the example (of skilful teaching) which I by his bounty am able to give " (*De Catechizandis Rudibus*, I, 2).

Amongst the African Christians Latin had already replaced the native Punic which they spoke and wrote with some culture when Christianity was first preached to them. Greek, which was showing more vitality than Latin before the advent of Christianity, afterwards showed less ; as a liturgical or theological language it tended rather to submit to translation into other tongues than to replace them. Most particularly is this noticeable in Western districts like southern Italy and southern Spain, where there was once a prospect of its being a successful rival of Latin. Before St. Augustine's conversion the Latin world was very deliberately adapting to its own habits of speech, thought, and action all the elements of Christianity which had hitherto been more highly developed in the East. His elder contemporaries, St. Ambrose and St. Jerome, were both keen students of the example of the East ; but the Roman genius was too strong in both of them to allow them to be slavish imitators of any foreign example. In the liturgical work of St. Ambrose only the inspiration came from the East. In character his hymns are a more natural product of the West, and less influenced by Grecian forms than the works of Virgil or Horace. And St. Jerome was not prevented even by the exigencies of accurate scholarship from infusing a characteristic Latin spirit into translations which from the necessity of the case had to be as close as possible to their Greek and Hebrew originals.

To these religious elements of Christianity, as they had been unanimously developed in the West, St. Augustine simply submitted himself. Their influence on his life and character was absolute. He can only be said to have influenced them in so far as he strengthened them by the example of his whole-hearted acceptance. Every saint and teacher may be said to have influenced Christianity in this way. But it is one thing for a saint to strengthen the influence of Christianity as the result of being himself influenced by it ; it is quite another thing for a convert to influence the character of Christianity in consequence of what he was before he became a Christian. When St. Augustine became a Christian he repudiated his former sins and nothing else. In all other respects his character remained what it was before. Christianity enriched it and enlarged its scope, but did not change it. When he was baptized, at the age of thirty-two, his character as a man of the world was very mature and very strongly marked. The schooling, the reading, the employments, and all the experiences which had moulded it continued to be operative all his life. Not one of them was ever forgotten or disowned. He was the first of the great converts to Christianity who have always remained thankful for the early education they received outside it. That education had brought him to Christianity, and made him a better Christian than he would have been without it.[1] As a Christian teacher he took his disciples through the whole schooling in which he himself had been educated, making the pagan arts the introduction to Christian doctrine. His contribution to doctrinal development was no addition to the substance of the Church's teaching ; it was merely a new presentation by a master of all the arts. In the best sense of the word he was an artist who could touch nothing without adorning it. He was a master in the sense in which we still call every great artist a master. He had a masterly grasp of the Christian religion, and gave a masterly presentation of it to others.

The results of his early training appear most conspicuously to us in the use he himself makes of secular learning and pagan authors in his Christian writings, and in the zeal with which all succeeding generations of Christians strove to follow this example. But that is only a sign, not the full measure, of his influence. He was much more than a literary humanist and the father of literary humanism. For his own and all succeeding ages he solved, both in theory and practice, the attitude

[1] In the *Confessions*, VII, xx, 26, he attributes his having read Plato before the Scriptures to the benevolent Providence of God.

to be adopted by Christians towards those things which in their origin are human and not peculiarly Christian. Before his day, in the West at any rate, there was no such example of a Christian humanism so complete as this. As for theory, no Latin Christian had achieved anything worthy of the name. There had been much speculation on the matter, but the crude solutions reached left even those who offered them in great confusion of mind, and liable to very distressing scruples.

Loyalty to supernatural religion needs to be very clear-minded if its attitude to all the good things that God has made is to be above all suspicion of sectarian prejudice, and to bear the mark of catholicity in the eyes of those who are dependent on reason alone for the formation of their judgements. Simple faith in any authority requires that authority to be very explicit. Whatever it approves must bear the seal of its approval. Whatever carries the hall mark of any rival authority will be at least suspect. The more it appeals by its natural goodness the more it will be resisted as a diabolical seduction from the true faith. This is seen in our own day, as when, for instance, a simple Irish Catholic woman, very sensitive to beauty, is induced to step inside an old English cathedral now in Anglican use, and at once rushes out as from an inferno, faint with holy horror of a seductive loveliness that it would be sinful to contemplate for a moment. This unreasoning delicacy of faith is always strong when the faithful are an oppressed minority in a society abounding in the good things of this world. It was very strong indeed in the first Christian centuries. Whatever was not marked with the Cross of Christ was of the world, worldly, and therefore not of God. Unless it was Christian, or at least Jewish, in its origins and associations, it was pagan, and therefore a thing sacrificed to idols.[1] Faith naturally precedes thought and

---

[1] See the correspondence between St. Augustine and the rich African landowner Publicola, *Ep.* xlvi, xlvii.

IA

makes it modestly afraid of itself even when authority en-
courages it. Christian thought advanced very timidly to the
conclusion that human nature is not wholly corrupt ; that
both the natural and the supernatural law proceed har-
moniously from the same divine Lawgiver ; that even
paganism is good in so far as it springs from principles of
natural religion, and only bad when it becomes a perver-
sion of them, or asserts itself to be equal or superior to
Christianity, thus leading men away from Christ instead of
towards Him, as it easily may and often does.

As long as Christians remained for the most part simple
people, none of these doctrines caused them any perplexity.
Their faith was simple, practical, and unreflecting. The
trouble began with the conversion of the more educated
classes, who brought with them into the Church talents and
accomplishments cultivated under pagan influences, memories of the good things of their pagan days that had led
them to Christianity, and the educated habit of reflection,
analysis, synthesis, and inference.

There was much food for reflection in their new faith ;
and much more when they attempted to harmonize it with
what they already knew by reason to be both good and true.
To such minds the strongest recommendation of the Church
was its claim to be Catholic. This was a philosophical notion
already familiar to them, but there was some difficulty in
adjusting the notion to the fact. In fact, Christian society
was only a section of humanity. Its claim to be Catholic was
a claim to a universal mission. In so far as this meant an
ambition to embrace all mankind, it must remain a hope as
long as any considerable number of men resisted it. But
Catholicity must also mean that the Church had accepted
for its province the entire range of human affairs and interests. The victory promised to its faith was a conquest of the
whole world : " Behold," it said confidently, " I make all
things new." But with regard to the old things that were to

be made new a difficulty arose. The birth of the new man, it was agreed, must be preceded by the death of the old man. At the same time, not one jot or tittle of the good old things was to be taken away. As far as the Jews and their law were concerned, these apparently conflicting maxims could raise no doubt or difficulty. At a very early stage the attitude of Christianity to Judaism had been very clearly defined. But its attitude to mankind in general, and to such things as are human, was not yet explained by any clear definition that could easily be applied to the complicated problems arising daily now that Christians moved with equal liberty in two worlds, the one religious and purely Christian in origin and association, the other secular and so intimately associated with the worship of pagan gods that it seemed to be, and often claimed to be, originally sprung from them.

In practice a pagan schoolmaster or a pagan classic could be treated as potentially Christian. The paganism of both could be overlooked for the sake of the good things in each that favoured Christianity. But on reflection, was it not clear that these good things favoured paganism even more, or at least as much ? Would they have been now available for Christian use if they had not long ago been begotten of a zeal for false gods whose hall-mark could not now be effaced from them ? These questions were especially pertinent in the case of the arts, the poetry, and the philosophy which had grown up under the inspiration of the religious ideals of paganism and were inalienably dedicated to pagan muses and deities. Four centuries of prosperous Protestantism have not yet purged English speech, laws, or education of the signs of their Catholic origin. Four centuries of struggling Christianity had done very much less to empty Latin civilization of the influence of the immortal gods. Not unlike the atheist who surprises himself in the act of swearing by God that there is no God, the Christian often found himself virtually invoking the pagan gods in the very act of denouncing them. The discovery was embarrassing, emotionally and intellectually. Some teachers, like St. Jerome, fell into scruples of conscience and into inconsistencies and eccentricities of conduct. Others, like Tertullian, condemned the use of pagan culture in language that was a more accomplished exhibition of it than the instances they were condemning. Others, again, naïvely reproved pagans for using pagan inventions which they encouraged Christians to imitate. Whatever is good, they argued, is out of place in paganism and in its rightful place in Christianity. All pagan virtues being vices, it follows easily that pagans are all thieves, and all their good things stolen goods. " Whatever good they taught," says Justin, " belongs to us."

The practical genius of Rome had accustomed the West to obedience, and thus disposed it to live more by faith than by reason. Speculation advanced more rapidly amongst the Greeks in the East, and Christian faith, far from impeding it there, stimulated it. And eventually, in early Christian as in pagan times, the philosophical habits of Greek civilization influenced the Latin West, without, however, diminishing its native practical character. Good philosophers are formal and emphatic in their theories, but temper their practice of them by playing one against another. Good practical men are cautious in theorizing, and so emphatic in practice that theories are easily forgotten and contradicted by the practice they were meant to justify. That is what happened in this matter of the Christian attitude to good things of natural origin.

In the fourth century the Greeks had reached a clearly defined solution of the problem, and were applying it consistently yet temperately. " We consider this human life of ours," says St. Basil, " to be of no value whatsoever ; nor do we think or call anything absolutely good which is profitable to us while we are here . . . ; but we run forward in hope and act in everything with a view to another life. Whatever, therefore, is helpful to that life ought, we say, to be loved and pursued with might and main. . . . We are led to it by the sacred writings, teaching us through mysteries ; but as long as it is not possible for us, because of our youth, to take in their deep meaning, our mental faculties are given a preparatory training by means of other books not altogether different from these – their shadows, as it were. . . . We must use poets, historians, rhetoricians, and all men from whom help may be expected for the cultivation of our mind. . . . Having first become perfect in this foreign learning, then, and then only, shall we be able to follow the sacred and revealed doctrines ; being accustomed to look at the sun in the water, so to speak, we shall thus turn our eyes to the light itself. Then, if there is anything in common between the secular and sacred books, the knowledge of them will be helpful to us ; if not, at any rate our knowing the difference by having compared them will be a strong argument in favour of whichever sort comes out better. Great Moses, whose name is the most celebrated amongst all men for wisdom, is said to have been educated in the learning of the Egyptians and so to have gone on to the contemplation of God's essence. In like manner we are told that in later days Daniel the wise, having in Babylon learned the wisdom of the Chaldeans, then attained to divine learning. But enough has been said to show that this learning from outside the Church is not without its use for souls."[1] He goes on to show that while much in pagan literature must be disapproved and avoided in practice many noble examples of virtue are to be found there. " It is worth our while to love and to imitate these, and to try with all our might to be such men ourselves."[2] He accepts the opinion that " the whole of Homer's poetry is praise of virtue."[3] He remarks that Plato, speaking of purity, "says things rather like St. Paul."[4] "But

---

[1] *Ad Adolescentes de legendis Libris Gentilium*, P.G. 31, col. 565, 568.
[2] *Ibid.*, col. 568 D.   [3] *Ibid.*, col. 572 B.   [4] *Ibid.*, col. 584 B.

such things," he concludes, " we shall learn more perfectly
in our books ; nevertheless, in the doctrines of those outside
let us trace, at least during the time we are studying their
works, the outline of virtue's shadow."[1]

St. Basil's theoretic approval of the good things in paganism is quite consistent with his practice, though at first sight
it may not seem so. On the whole, he rarely names a pagan
author or openly displays his knowledge of pagan writings.
But neither the names nor the writings are ever far from his
mind. They are exactly where his theory says they should be :
underneath his Christian learning and culture as a shadow
moving on the earth in advance of the substance, and larger
than it though less important and scarcely noticed. Both in
theory and in practice the two Gregories, Nazianzen and
of Nyssa, agree with him. There is little actual sound, though
many an echo, of classical learning in their more mature
work. The actual sound is very distinctly heard, however, in
such a youthful work as Gregory Nazianzen's philippic
against Julian the Apostate : " O who will give me the
leisure and the tongue of an Herodotus and a Thucydides,
that I may hand down to future ages this man's villainy, and
leave the history of these days graven as in stone for pos-
terity ! "[2]

The West, in its practical way, adopted the theories of the
East only to outrun them in practice and so involve itself in
contradictions both theoretic and practical. St. Ambrose
was directly influenced by Basil and the Gregories, and applied their theories with such characteristic Roman thor-
oughness as to exaggerate them in practice and contradict
them verbally when he himself fell into theorizing. He quotes
freely from almost all the poets and philosophers of pagan
Greece and Rome, Homer and Euripides, Virgil and Horace,
Plato and Aristotle and Cicero – especially Cicero, who

---

[1] *Ad Adolescentes de legendis Libris Gentilium*, P.G. 31, col. 588 B.
[2] *Contra Julianum*, I, xcii, P. G. 35, col. 624 B.

supplies the inspiration and the model for his *De Officiis Ministrorum*. But though he makes more open use of pagan writings than any of the Cappadocians, he apologizes a little uneasily for doing so, and is more concerned to show by how much than by how little they fail of perfect truth and goodness. " Although certain students of philosophy have written works *de officiis*, I have not thought it inconsistent with my ministry to do the same myself."[1] " Natural science, left to itself, has failed to hold its own. The extravagant debates of philosophy have left it empty. Its teaching is only half perfect. Let us, then, observe how clear and perfect is the teaching of Sacred Scripture about a subject on which we see philosophy to be so complicated, so involved, so confused."[2] He still clings to the view that the good things in pagan books are derived from the Old Testament, and that the Christians who use them are therefore only taking back what is their own. Before the pagans defined the moral virtues these had been defined, and, what is more, practised too, by Abraham, David, and Solomon.[3] David wrote before Aristotle, before Socrates, before Pythagoras even ; the last named followed his doctrine, but so absurdly as to outrage nature, which David safeguarded.[4] " The pagans teach that truth must be zealously sought after, must not be confused with falsehood, must not be wrapped up in obscurities. But what is more obscure than to treat of astronomy and geometry, as they do ; to measure the space of heaven and apply mathematics to sea, and sky ? Great Moses, educated in all the wisdom of the Egyptians, made trial of these things, but he judged it a foolish waste, and left it to seek God with his inmost heart. Who was ever wiser than he ? He was taught by God Himself, and he made void by the power of his works all the wisdom of the Egyptians and all that the liberal arts can avail."[5]

Contemporary with Basil and Ambrose, St. Jerome vividly

---

[1] *De Officiis Ministrorum*, I, vii, P.L. 16, col. 34 A.
[2] *Ibid.*, II, iii, col. 112 B. [3] *Ibid.*, I, xxv, col. 63 A. [4] *Ibid.*, I, x, col. 36 B.
[5] *Ibid.*, I, xxvi, col. 64 A.

exemplifies the painful uncertainty of mind which could still harass a Christian who reflected on the use he made in practice of the human elements in paganism. He varies both his theory and his practice ; when his practice is challenged by others, he suits his theory to it ; when the challenge comes from his own conscience, then he inverts the process. At one time he is tortured with scruples, and sees himself damned for being an enthusiastic Ciceronian, and therefore no Christian.[1] At another time he struggles for years to reduce the number of classical quotations he is wont to use in his writings. The habit of a lifetime is too strong for him. When nearly seventy, having abandoned the struggle he replies to a critic[2] : "You ask why in my writings I propose examples from secular literature. You would never ask that if you were not wholly obsessed by Cicero, or if you read the Scriptures and those who interpret them." He goes on to explain that in the Books of Moses and in the Prophetical Books there are things taken from pagan works. Solomon exchanged questions and answers with the philosophers of Tyre. St. Paul quotes Aratus and Menander and misquotes Epimenides ; he had learnt from David to take Goliath's sword and cut off his head with it. It is in this context that St. Jerome gives his celebrated account of the classical accomplishments of the Greeks, Romans, and Jews who wrote in defence of the Scriptures ; he includes his contemporaries, "Hilary who imitated, in style and number, the twelve books of Quintilian," and "the Cappadocians, Basil, Gregory, and Amphilochius, who (amongst others) so packed their books with the doctrines and opinions of the philosophers that you cannot decide which you ought more to admire in them, their secular learning or their knowledge of the Scriptures." It is as he says with himself ; he cannot decide. "There is, you see, a wealth of matter for debate ; but it is time that what is only a letter should be brought to a close."

---

[1] *Ep.* xxii, P.L. 22, col. 416.   [2] *Ep.* lxx, col. 665.

The debate which St. Jerome could only close by leaving it open was closed for ever by St. Augustine, whom Jerome more than once rebuked for being a younger man and not considerate enough towards his elders. He was able to do so because he remained a young man all his life, and was one of the most considerate of men. He had a memory which kept his childhood and youth always vividly present to him, an understanding that saw the good in everything, and a will that loved it.

Augustine was an African, born and bred on the shores of the Mediterranean facing Europe. From his childhood all the influences that have gone to the making of our civilization were focused upon him : Semitic influences transmitted through the society, perhaps through the blood, of the Phœnicians whose language and traditions were still alive and familiar to him ; Persian influences, brought to bear on him by the Manichæism in which he became involved ; Latin and Greek influences, infused into him by way of education by his father, his nurses, and his schoolmasters ; Christian influences, urged upon him gently but persistently by his mother from his infancy, and at last by the overwhelming force with which it recommended itself to his great heart and his great mind.

St. Augustine anticipated our modern civilization even so far as to provide us with his own psycho-analysis, upon which he built a whole philosophy. The key to his character and his influence on future ages is his catholicity : the catholicity of a tenacious memory, a mighty understanding, and an all-embracing will. He forgot nothing ; he ignored nothing ; he despised nothing. The only thing he turned away from in his life was evil. From that he only turned his will away ; even his sins were never banished from his memory or exempted from close scrutiny by his understanding. He remembered them, and constantly thought of them, not merely because he could not forget anything, or refuse to understand

anything, but because he could not resist loving anything ; the only way for him to resist loving his sins was to
remember them exactly, and so exercise his understanding
upon them as to see that they were not anything, but only
vanity and privation of good.

In his analysis of himself and of all mankind, memory is
the primary spiritual faculty in man, and the foundation of all
rational life. He would not, could not, did not, forget anything. It never occurred to him that memory need ever seek
to purify itself by trying to forget. In his theory and practice,
it is naturally purified by the understanding, which is the
next in order of the human faculties. The memory retains
everything indiscriminately, good and evil, truth and falsehood, realities, phantasms, sensations. The understanding
faces them all, recognizing only goodness and truth as realities, and showing evil to be naught, phantasms and sensations next to naught. Hence the fascinating play of optimism and pessimism which has been frequently noted in
Augustine and in the Christian culture dating from him, but
which is absent from all pagan culture preceding and following. The delight of pagans in fancies and sensations is never
turned to wistful tears by the discovery that they are naught.

St. Augustine's supposition that he was a common man
died with him. But his psychological theory of common man-
hood went unquestioned for eight hundred years until St.
Thomas Aquinas, his greatest and most devoted disciple,
equal to him in memory, superior in understanding, more
fortunate in a will that never loved naught, quietly and
reverently rejected it. But his example has stood unassailed,
and will stand unassailable as long as Christian memory
shall last. For the memory of Christendom is the memory of
St. Augustine : it remembers whatever he did not scruple to
remember. He was troubled with no scruples, like St.
Jerome, about having a memory full of pagan poets, play-
wrights, and philosophers whom he never could forget. Nor

has Christendom ever since scrupled about such memories. Though it has not, like him, found it impossible to forget them, it has laboured to preserve his memory of the good natural human things of pagan antiquity ; to recover it when lost, to increase it even. Christian schools are still the " schools " of good pagan " Grammar," " Poetry," " Rhetoric," and " Philosophy " in which he was first a pupil, then all his life a master.[1] All the great schoolmasters of Christian Europe, Boethius, Cassiodorus, Isidore, Alcuin, Lanfranc, Bernard of Chartres, Hugh of St. Victor, and the rest, have striven, first to preserve the memory of the Greek and Latin classics, the liberal arts, and all the secular beginnings of our civilization as he remembered them ; either compendiously, like Isidore and Alcuin in difficult days, or with amplifications, like Boethius and Bernard in happier days. All the leaders of Christian thought – Anselm, Abelard, Bonaventure, Aquinas – have followed his understanding with theirs. All the poets – Theodulf, Hildebert, St. Bernard, Dante, Petrarch – have learned from him to sing out their hearts joyously in praise of beauty ever old and ever new, and to weep when things that seem fair are found to be naught.

This is a view of literary history little likely to win favour in a generation which maintains that it owes nothing to its ancestry except examples of the primitive simplicity out of which men must escape in order to become men at all. To justify it in our day we should need to set forth in detail all St. Augustine's rich store of ancient learning, his whole philosophy, his theory and practice as an artist ; and, besides this, to write a full history of the ways in which learning

[1] In England, Ushaw alone, I believe, still uses the word " schools " in the vernacular in its traditional sense ; though the phrase " in the schools " survives everywhere, and such language as " scholæ vacant " is part of the Latin vocabulary of all scholastics. Classes or forms are still called " Grammar," " Poetry," and " Rhetoric " in places where tradition lingers longest, like Ushaw, Upholland, and Stonyhurst ; but even in such places the full traditional significance of these names is obscured by modifications in educational practice dating from the Renaissance.

survived through the Dark Ages, and in which philosophy
and art were developed from the eleventh century to the
thirteenth. This is a task requiring more time and space than
any man or group of men has yet found for it, though some
beginnings have been made.[1]

It will suffice here to sketch the outline of an argument
that may provoke the sceptical to reflection and research.

．　　．　　．　　．　　．　　．　　．　　．

St. Augustine learned Latin in the nursery, and his education was almost exclusively in that language. He never knew
Hebrew, but was familiar with Punic, though it is doubtful
whether he spoke it. He was taught Greek as a boy, but it was
a foreign language to him, and through disinclination for
the aridities of text-books he made little progress. He regretted this afterwards, and for the better understanding of
the Scriptures made the most of what he knew. He seems
thus to have acquired a useful reading knowledge, though he
shows no sign of having read any classical Greek author in
the original.

His education followed the plan described in the *Institutio
Oratoria* of Quintilian. In the elementary stage he was taught
to speak correctly, to recite, to read, to write, to count. From
these " first schools " at Tagaste he went away to Madaura
to a " school of Grammar." Here he was introduced to selected passages from the Latin poets, his masters commenting
on their meaning at great length. These readings gave him
much pleasure, and, eager for more, he went beyond his
text-books and steeped himself in Virgil and other authors.

[1] For an excellent account of St. Augustine's classical learning, his theories
of literature and art, and his fusion of classical and Christian culture, see
Gustave Combes, *Saint Augustin et la Culture Classique*, Paris, 1927.

A fairly full bibliography will be found in *Bibliotheca* " *Commentarii pro Reli-
giosis*," *Sectio Bibliographica*, Vol. I ; *Bibliographia Augustiniana*, by Eulogius
Nebrada, C.M.F.

To this list should be added : E. K. Rand, *Founders of the Middle Ages* (containing a valuable chapter on *St. Augustine and Dante*), and C. H. Haskins,
The Renaissance of the Twelfth Century. Much that is illuminating is to be found
throughout the *Obras Completas* of Menendez y Palayo.

The text-books published in Carthage at this time contained extracts from Terence, Horace, Catullus, Ovid,
Juvenal, Persius, and Martial. His intimacy with all these
poets appears to date from this early period of his life.

His success in these studies fired his own enthusiasm and
excited the ambitions of his parents for his future. They destined him for the Bar, because of the honours and emolu-
ments to which it led, and he readily responded to their designs. At fifteen he finished his schooling at Madaura, and
after a year of idleness, disastrous to his morals, spent at
home till his father could afford to send him to Carthage, he
went to a " school of Rhetoric " there. Here he read again,
more widely and deeply than before, all the great models of
Latin prose and verse, attending to their style now more even
than to their matter. His chief text-book was the *De Oratore*
of Cicero, and, following the course of study it prescribes, he
became interested in philosophy. The *Hortensius* of the same
author greatly excited him ; it elicited from him the first unmistakable signs of a powerful understanding and an intense
intellectual hunger for abstract truth. He began to indulge
this with his wonted intensity. Though he later condemns
as pride the part played in this by his will, it had the effect
of sobering down his morals a little. But he still frequented
the theatre and other public shows, including pagan sac-
rifices, attracted by their lasciviousness. In competition with
others he wrote poems for public recitation, and the public
taste of the time awarded him the first prize.

On the completion of his studies for the Bar, his enthusiasm for reading and philosophy caused him to renounce
his former intention of practising in the courts. Instead, he
returned to Tagaste as a teacher of Rhetoric. This was his
regular employment until his conversion, and his success in it
took him in turn to Carthage, Rome, and Milan. He continued his own education in the arts and philosophy. His
master in the first was Varro, whose writings, prolific and

prodigiously learned, included treatises, based on Greek
originals, of nine liberal arts : Grammar, Dialectic, Rhetoric,
Arithmetic, Music, Geometry, Astronomy, Medicine, and
Architecture. Augustine's education so far, according to the
custom that had grown up during the general narrowing
and hardening of all cultural traditions under the Empire,
had been restricted to two only of these : Grammar and
Rhetoric. Now, at the age of twenty, he studied Dialectic,
reading the *Categories* of Aristotle in translation. " With restless impatience," he confesses, " I craved to understand it as
a thing sublime and divine. I read and understood it without
help. Others, I found, who had studied it with great difficulty, and under masters with diagrams, understood it no
better than I did." He read all he could find on the other
arts also, and began to write treatises on them. Only the
four books *De Musica* have survived. Their subject-matter is
elementary, as the tradition of the arts has always intended
it should be ; but in the treatment there is much profound
philosophy and psychology, and the first fine outline of the
theory of esthetics by which the culture of Europe has lived
and prospered through the centuries. In the early letters from
Cassiciacum to Nebridius there is some discussion of Arithmetic and Geometry. It is in the form of philosophical speculation, again on very elementary points. To us it sounds
crude, like all the speculations that follow it for centuries.
Nevertheless, it marks the sure beginnings of a Latin appetite
and aptitude for such studies. We have since gone to school to
Greece for Geometry and to the Arabs for Arithmetic ; but
it was principally and primarily Augustine who disposed our
forefathers to go there so eagerly. Astronomy for him meant
astrology, by which he was at first captivated, but which he
subsequently abandoned, moved at last by arguments drawn
from Scripture, but at first by arguments drawn from
Medicine,[1] which art has a very conspicuous and honoured

[1] *Confessions*, IV, iii.

place in all his writings, though there is no trace of any formal treatise on it. Of any study or doctrine of architecture there is no vestige either ; which of itself is enough to explain why Latin countries have been more independent of classical traditions in this than in any other art.

In philosophy he was led by Cicero and driven by the Manichæans to the Greeks, and especially to Plato and the Platonists, of whom very much was accessible to him in Latin. Their doctrine of eternal memory suited well his experience of the workings of his own mind. As a Christian teacher he preserved as much of it in his psychological theory as his faith allowed, and so – the one instance of his tremendous influence leading to disorder – delayed the advent of Aristotle for eight hundred years, involving in much danger of heresy, and many an involuntary step towards it, every Catholic philosopher of that period, and every Christian Platonist to the present day. Aristotle he considered " a man of outstanding ability and eloquence but not equal to Plato." The *Perihermenias* and *Topica* existed in translations by Victorinus, whom Augustine learned to admire at his conversion, and all of whose work he most probably studied ; his knowledge of Aristotle was clearly limited to this acquaintance with them.

With his discovery of the Platonists and his own treatise *De Pulchro et Apto*, his purely secular education and his career as a purely secular schoolmaster come to an end. But their influence has been endless. He forgot nothing and disowned nothing that he had read or thought out for himself. He thanked God all his life for everything he had learned from his infancy, both because it had led him into Christianity and because it made him more faithful[1] and more serviceable[2] there than he would have been had he never gone to

---

[1] *Confessions*, VII, xx, 26, mentioned above.

[2] *Ibid.*, XV, 24 : " May whatever useful things I learned as a boy be of service to Thee. May it be of service to Thee that I can speak and write and read and count."

school with pagan masters. In their school, he insists, much is empty and vain, but from their vanities he has learned much that is useful, " many useful words." These same things could be learned in matters that are not vain – that is, in the sacred history and poetry and philosophy of Scripture, the greatest of all literature. This is a safe school in which children might be taught to walk. When he said this he was already laying the foundation of such a school in which the Scriptures were to be the great text-book. But in the careful grammar with which he says it there is a clear implication that such a school is still a thing to be desired. [1]

When grace came to him at Milan its first effect was to produce a type of Christian literature which was rare, if not quite unknown before, but which began a long line of masterpieces very dear to Christendom, the first to follow being the *De Consolatione Philosophiæ* of Boethius, one of the first and greatest of all Augustinians. In this type there is no mention of anything specifically Christian or supernatural ; no such authority or example openly appealed to, no such doctrine openly concluded. The appeal throughout is to reason and humanity, preferably pagan humanity, which is turned against itself if it needs correction. The language and examples are of this world of nature, not of the world of grace. In the interests of good literature scriptural language may creep in, for it is always the best way of saying the best thing ; but it is never acknowledged, and this against the tradition which purely Christian writing has always preserved in scriptural quotations even when (on the grounds that all men are spiritually equal, without rights of private property in natural truth or human language) plagiarism amongst men has been held no sin. The conclusions stay at the threshold of the Church, worshipping the Creator and renouncing evil there, but not yet venturing in.

These firstfruits of grace form a series of dialogues and

---

[1] *Confessions*, I, xv. : " . . . *tuta via . . . in qua pueri ambularent."*

soliloquies begun and for the most part completed while Augustine was still a catechumen at Cassiciacum. Though he had abandoned his secular ambitions, he says, he was still puffed up with the mannerisms of secular literature. But he does not by any means on that score discount them as Christian literature. As a bishop finally revising his published works, he includes them with his other writings, giving them the first place according to chronological order, and insisting that this order is important for the study of his works as a whole, since the earlier must explain the later, and the later the earlier. Christians may read the earliest with profit provided they are indulgent, or at least indifferent, to a few faults in them, and do not make these faults a precedent.[1] They must not, for instance, speak of Fortune and the Muses as he has done, as though they were gods. They must not, like him, exaggerate the importance of secular education as though it were impossible to be a saint without it, or to fail to be a saint with it.[2] In spite of these warnings, however, he is setting a precedent he does not exactly intend. His followers will often be writing, not for themselves, but for their readers. They will eliminate the name of Christ and His teaching, not because they are too weak or too modest to utter it, but because their readers are only being disposed to hear it. Augustine is writing, not for others weaker than himself, but for his own and his friends' sake, to dispose himself and them humanly for the reception of revealed truth. Hence his reticence continues after his baptism, as in the *De Magistro*, written in Africa to his son,[3] in *De Quantitate Animæ*,[4] *De Libero Arbitrio*,[5] and the numerous letters to Nebridius.[6] As late as 391, when he is already a priest, he begs his bishop to leave him to study undisturbed by pastoral work, since, having everything to learn from Scripture, he is quite unqualified as yet to come forward as a Christian teacher.[7]

[1] *Retractationes*, Prol. 3.   [2] *Ibid.*, I, iii, 2.   [3] A.D. 389.
[4] A.D. 387-8.   [5] A.D. 388-9.   [6] *Ep.* vii–xiii, A.D. 389-90.
[7] *Ep.* xxi, Ad Valerium Episcopum.

KA

He was allowed at most two short years of study before he preached his first published sermon.[1] How much he profited by this study is evident from the sermon and the flood of authoritative Christian writings that follow it. With what aim and according to what method he studied he himself explains in great detail in the *De Doctrina Christiana*.

This book instructed Christian scholasticism what its method and aim in education was to be, and was most faithfully followed. No book on education has ever been studied more attentively or profitably than this was in the twelfth century by the great men, humanists and philosophers, who laid the first complete foundation of European universities.[2] It is not a long book, but takes longer to read than we who have more books than can be read in a lifetime are prepared to give to so few pages. The best way to read it is to see what had been made of it after 700 years of unremitting study by the first, and therefore the greatest, educationalists in Europe. Let our reviewers be St. Anselm, Abelard, Hugh of St. Victor, John of Salisbury, and Robert Kilwardby.

There are two kinds of things : things to be enjoyed as an end in themselves, and things to be used as a means to an end. God is the only perfect example of the first kind of thing. There are two kinds of things to be used. First there are those that serve simply in virtue of what they are in themselves. Then there are those which, apart from what they are in themselves, serve by making known some other thing quite distinct from themselves ; and these we call signs. There are two kinds of signs : those which have some natural relation with the thing they signify (and these we call natural signs, as smoke, which is a natural sign of fire, being its effect) ; and those which signify other things simply because

---

[1] *De Fide et Symbolo*, preached at the Council of Hippo, 393.

[2] See G. Robert : *Les Ecoles et L'Enseignement de la Théologie pendant la première moitié du XIIe Siècle*.

it has been agreed by the free will of man that they shall do so (and these we call artificial or conventional signs). Among such conventional signs which men must use as a means to the end they were made to enjoy are words, writing, and books. The most important of these are the sacred words written in the Books of Scripture. These books, being signs only, do not interpret themselves ; they must be interpreted, and can only be interpreted by those whose free will decided what they were to signify. In all other books it is the free will of men alone that has decided what written signs, or letters, shall be used to signify a spoken sound or word ; what word shall signify each thing ; and whether one thing, itself signified by its appointed word and letters, shall itself be also a sign of some other thing, as, for instance, whether a serpent shall be a sign of wisdom or of venom, and a dove a sign of simplicity or love. Therefore to use, or, as we say, read, such books, we must learn what is signified by each letter and word and other sign. This we can only do by applying for instruction to those whose free will decided what each should mean ; or to those to whom the knowledge of this has come down as a tradition. The body of such tradition is known as the liberal arts. Therefore whoever would use human books as a means to the end he is made to enjoy must be instructed in the liberal arts. The Sacred Books of Divine Scripture are signs fixed partly by the free will of God, partly by the free will of man ; for in the writing of them God has not fixed everything arbitrarily, as He fixed the two trees in Paradise, but has used men, and with them the words and letters in which they were instructed according to the tradition of the liberal arts. Hence to read the Scriptures we must be instructed in two traditions : the tradition of the Apostles, who received from Christ the meaning of the signs that God Himself has fixed ; and the liberal arts, or the traditions of men who have received from other men the meaning of the signs that yet other men have fixed in times long past. The arts

are Grammar, which teaches the use of words as signs ;
Dialectic, which teaches how the meaning of these signs
may be conjectured when there is no master at hand ;
Rhetoric, which teaches how signs may be made anew by
the head and heart of each generation. The other arts study
the use of the elements of nature as signs. The waves of the
sea, the raindrops, and all the element of water are signs of
multiplicity, intermission, and repetition ; they give us the
art of number, or Arithmetic. The sounds of the air are signs
of flowing movement, of rise and cadence, and give us the
art of Music, which treats of the numbers in which poets
sing. The solid earth is a sign of all things that are constant,
having figure and proportion, and gives us the art of Geometry. The element of fire is a sign of things that are constant,
with their parts ever in movement, and gives us the art of
Astronomy. Each of these liberal arts has a long line of
masters coming down from their first human author. A
scholasticus represents all these masters in his own person. He
is a Donatus in Grammar, an Aristotle in Dialectics, in
Rhetoric a Cicero, in all other arts a Plato. He is in the tradition of all these secular teachers. But the proper business
of the Christian scholastic is to teach the signs of God, for
which human signs only prepare the way. Therefore he must
be in the tradition of the Apostles. That is to say, he must be
a Bishop. The first Bishop to stand firmly and faithfully in
both traditions was the Bishop of Hippo, who founded the
Cathedral schools like Chartres, Lyons, Orleans, Canterbury,
and the rest.[1] As not every Bishop could be a complete
schoolmaster like Augustine, most have had to employ a
scholasticus, called also a Chancellor, who, being in the
secular tradition, is able to read, write, and count, and teach
others to do the same. The Bishop is in the Apostolic tradition ; the Chancellor is his man of letters, and as his

---

[1] It was St. Jerome who founded monastic schools like Bec and the rest,
which still in the twelfth century were scrupulous about secular learning.

representative has authority over all clerks in matters of secular learning.[1]

The twelfth century was more conscious of its traditions than any succeeding age has been, and understood them better. But the best minds of every generation have always understood their debt to St. Augustine, and the obligations it placed them under of being masters in his schools and artists after his example. Outside his theological tractates Boethius mentions no Christian name except Augustine's. Cassiodorus, in his enthusiasm for books and all learning, sacred and secular, is forever turning to Augustine for support. Quotations from Augustine and summaries of his doctrine appear on every page of Isidore's *Etymologies*. Alcuin wrote little original work; he was so busy schoolmastering, with Augustine as the treasury from which he compiled his primers. The schoolmasters he trained all launched out into theology, exegetics, poetry, all closely modelled on Augustine even in their choice of subject-matter. Scotus Erigena learned to speculate like another Plato when there was none to show him how save only Augustine. In St. Anselm's thought and manner of speaking St. Augustine lives again. Abelard's vanity is never greater than when his successes remind him of St. Augustine's *perspicax ingenium*. In his disgrace he recovers his self-esteem and public credit by a dramatic gesture which shows him another Augustine; the talents he had once used to gain money he now uses to gain souls.[2] The humanism of the school of Chartres was Christian Platonism inspired directly by Augustine. Everything characteristic of the school

---

[1] The troubles in Paris in the thirteenth century were due to this last part of the tradition being called into question. The clerks studying arts desired a Rector of their own who should not be the Bishop's deputy. And this Rector desired authority, not only over the secular arts, but over theology also, in which only a Bishop had been able to make a master before theology became an art. Reference to the inclusion of theology amongst the arts by the new scholastics appears in the question at the beginning of all the thirteenth century *Summæ* : Whether theology is an art? Art and science were still used synonymously by writers like Alexander of Hales.

[2] P.L. 168, col. 979 C.

of St. Victor was a studied reproduction of his example :
Hugh went to him for his theory of education, for his distinction between faith and reason, between natural and supernatural, *opus conditionis* and *opus reparationis* ; Richard studied
his psychological doctrine more closely than anyone before ;
the Mystics, Walter and the rest, in their loyalty to Augustine's mysticism exaggerated it.

When specialization began in the thirteenth century, each
specialist appealed to St. Augustine to prove the importance
of his own branch and the exaggerated importance of every
other. The deadliest blow the reactionaries could aim
against the progressives was a simple assertion of the Augustinian tradition. At the beginning of his *Summa Theologica*,
St. Thomas has to invoke the authority of St. Augustine to
show that he is not obliged to accept with blind faith every
word Augustine says. Dante refers Can Grande to the *De
Quantitate Animæ* in justification of the mysticism in Canto I
of the *Paradiso*. In the lyric sadness of vernacular poetry, so
noticeable in Petrarch, the tears of Augustine on the futility
of human love are wept over again.[1] The troubadours sighed
wistfully as they tried to withdraw their hearts from created
beauty to eternal beauty. The pagans of the Renaissance
moved the other way ; undoing the work of Augustine, they
lost the gift of tears. In England, Spenser led the fashion
which has tried to make the best of both worlds ; he separated
his Hymn of Heavenly Beauty from his Hymns of Earthly
Beauty, attempting to sing without sobbing in either. It was
Shelley who, rebelling against English religion and thinking
himself an atheist, began the reaction of English poetry from
the pagan naturalism of Wordsworth, who could not weep,
to the religious poetry of Faber, Keble, and Newman, who,
in their impetuous return to the traditions of Augustine, wept
a little too much.

Evidence of vital Augustinian influence in our culture can

[1] Rand, *op. cit.*, p. 271.

be found in all directions. Even those who can only measure spiritual things by statistics can test it. They have only to examine the existing catalogues of European libraries from the earliest to the latest times. In the earliest they will find the works of Augustine heading the list and forming its largest section. Then they will find the list increased by works recommended by Augustine. The last addition consists of the books written or recommended by those who have authority because they follow Augustine.

M. C. D'ARCY, S.J.

THE PHILOSOPHY OF ST. AUGUSTINE

THE PHILOSOPHY OF ST. AUGUSTINE

St. Augustine had so many diverse interests, and in his writings he passes so swiftly from one subject to another, that his philosophy has not received the attention it deserves. He is too big to be classified as a philosopher, but, nevertheless, he made a distinct contribution to philosophy. A school was formed under his name, and recent historical investigation has confirmed the tradition of the paramount influence of that school in the West from his death to the thirteenth century. Even after the coming of St. Thomas, St. Bonaventure, and in a lesser degree Duns Scotus, suffice to show that Augustinianism did not die ; and there can be little doubt that Descartes and Malebranche are of his ancestry. St. Augustine is indeed one of the most striking embodiments of a type which recurs again and again in the history of thought, a type which can be recognized by one chief characteristic. It refuses to allow natural reason the whole field in philosophy. Sometimes this tendency reaches an extreme and substitutes another activity, feeling or desire or faith or, more vaguely, experience, in place of reason. In the Augustinian system reason is not ousted, but abetted, if not led, by love. More definitely, St. Augustine does not admit the division of labour, the forced neutrality between philosophy and faith, desire and reason, which was adopted, for instance, by St. Thomas, and has become since so widely accepted. He does not cease to be a Christian when he is writing philosophy, and he wants answers to questions, not for their own sake, but for peace of soul. *Nulla est homini causa philosophandi nisi ut beatus sit.*

Such an attitude may seem to some fatally unphilosophical.

But there is ground for questioning their opinion. The humanity of Augustine does not cause him to abate the severity of his reasoning, and the picture he paints for us has a distinction which few others possess. He has the same power as Pascal and, at times, Newman of making what is intensely personal pass into the universal, so that the reader seems to be following his own story. To use the language of his system, his own experience evokes in the memory of others an echo which is recognized to be true. Hence his mark on philosophy has been described by a modern writer as that of *interiorizing* it. He is the first explorer of the hinterland of the self. " And being thence admonished to return to myself, I entered even into my inward self, Thou being my Guide : and able I was, for Thou wert become my Helper. And I entered and beheld with the eye of my soul, (such as it was) above the same eye of my soul, above my mind, the Light Unchangeable."[1]

Now if this be the unfailing attitude of St. Augustine, his philosophy and the story of his life should be read together. From youth onwards he suffered from a divine discontent and sought eagerly for happiness in wisdom. But after many years his only reward was the discovery that the flesh could degrade the spirit and blind it. After nine years spent in the school of Manichæanism he owned that his mind had become so clogged by material images that he habitually thought of mind and of God in terms of matter. The memory of these dark days was, no doubt, in part responsible for his love of the immaterial and reaction against matter in his later philosophy. When finally disabused of the pretensions of the Manichæans he found that the scepticism of the New Academy answered the despair of his soul.

Of the events preceding his conversion there is no need to give a history, as they are recorded elsewhere. One fact, however, is relevant and may be recalled, namely, the close connection in time between the reading of the neo-Platonists

[1] *Confessions*, VII, x, 16, Pusey's translation.

and his conversion. It has been argued that the narrative of the *Confessions* is inaccurate, that he antedates his conversion and that his writings at Cassiciacum prove that he was then, not a Christian, but a pagan neo-Platonist. An interpretation which is consistent with his own words becomes obvious, if we reflect on his previous history and character. He had clearly a deep natural interest in philosophy, so deep that to him wisdom and happiness were synonymous. On his conversion he found peace and happiness, and he had been reading the neo-Platonists with intense intellectual satisfaction. What more natural than that in the first flush of his faith he should conduct an argumentative campaign against his old opponents, using neo-Platonism as a weapon? Furthermore, faith had brought insight. He knew now that his old doubts had lost their cogency, but it was imperative that he should dispose of them effectively by reason and slay the monster which had for so long blocked the gateway to truth and peace. As he says in his *Retractations* in reference to the Academy : " I wrote against them first that I might put away from my mind with the strongest possible reasons their arguments, because they used to have an influence also on me."[1]

When as a Christian he took up philosophy with the motto, *fides quærens intellectum*, he found neo-Platonism to be a most suitable instrument. It had taught him the distinction between sense and intellect and opened out for him a new world, the world of " yonder," where dwelt the numbers and the ideas and Truth and the One, like fixed and imperishable stars in a firmament. His opinion of its function is clearly expressed in the *Contra Academicos*[2] : " After many centuries and many disputes at length a system of philosophy was discovered, which, in my opinion, is most true. It is not, what our sacred religion so rightly abhors, a philosophy of the material world, but reveals another and intelligible

[1] *Retractationes*, I, i, 1.   [2] III, xix, 42.

world." He adds, however, that not the cleverest reasoning of itself could avail to reveal this intelligible world to the sense-darkened mind of man, were it not for the mercy of God; and, as he grew older, he came to feel more and more the defects, not so much of the system, as of its exponents. He therefore confidently adopts its language and arguments, and nevertheless his thought remains unmistakably his own. He cannot cease to be himself, and, as the object of all his study was God and his own soul, he has bequeathed to us truths " ever ancient and ever fresh " on these two greatest of subjects.

Before examining them in detail it will be well to state some of St. Augustine's characteristic views in his own words. Philosophy has for its object truth and happiness; the two are inseparable and together sum up the meaning of life. " Think you that wisdom is other than truth, in which the supreme good is beheld and possessed ? "[1] Of truth he says : " Here then is Truth ; embrace it if you can, and enjoy it and rejoice in God and He will give you the desires of your heart ; . . . and shall we deny that we are happy when we are watered by and feed on Truth ? "[2] And if Truth means happiness, " the happy life consists of joy in Truth : for this is a joying in Thee, Who art the Truth, O God, health of my countenance, my God."[3] In this last outburst it is remarkable how philosophy and faith join hands. No sooner does St. Augustine think of truth than he passes to God, or, as in other places, to the Word. " Truth is immortal ; Truth is unchanging ; Truth is that Word of Whom it is said : In the beginning was the Word."[4] Before his conversion he had had no such *gaudium in veritate* ; life was to him an exile in dark and lonely places. *Et factus sum mihi regio egestatis.* His conversion meant a metamorphosis not only of his morals, but of his mind. He could now see and delight in liberty and

---

[1] *De Libero Arbitrio*, II, viii, 26.   [2] *Ibid*, II, xiii, 35.
[3] *Confessions*, X, xxiii, 33.   [4] *Enarr. in Psalm.*, CXXIII, ii.

truth. " Fairer to me, I own, is philosophy than Thisbe, than Pyramus, than their Venus and Cupid and all such loves " ; and with a sigh he gave thanks to Christ.[1] Sensible joys were, as the Platonists rightly maintained, only the far-off reflections of a spiritual Beauty, of the One God Who was nearer than hands and feet. Creatures and the world of sense, the troops of contradicting phantasms, fell away, and within the chambers of the mind Augustine found Him whom he had sought. " And thus by degrees I passed from bodies to the soul, which through the bodily senses perceives ; and thence to its inward faculty, to which the bodily senses represent things external . . . and thence again to the reasoning faculty, to which what is received from the senses of the body, is referred to be judged. Which finding itself also to be in me a thing variable, raised itself up to its own understanding . . . that so it might find what that light was, whereby it was bedewed, when, without all doubting, it cried out, ' that the unchangeable was to be preferred to the changeable ' ; . . . and thus with the flash of one trembling glance it arrived at That Which Is."[2]

The sentences just quoted contain in an epitome all the thought of St. Augustine. His own wisdom, he felt sure, if it was to be worth anything, must be a scintilla of the Wisdom of God. This explains why he begins philosophy with a somewhat surprising postulate. The object of philosophy being truth, it is usually assumed by students that one must begin with reason and reason unaided. No, says St. Augustine, with a glance at his past, one should begin with faith. " If you cannot understand, believe in order that you may understand."[3] " Whence then shall I begin ? With authority or with reason ? The natural order is that authority should precede reason when we wish to learn anything."[4] These are not stray texts chosen from sermons to the faithful ; it is

---

[1] *De Ordine*, I, viii, 21.   [2] *Confessions*, XVII, xvii, 23.
[3] *Sermo* cxviii.   [4] *De Moribus Ecclesiæ*, I, ii, 3.

his deliberate conviction that neither the truth of the
Christian religion nor a true philosophy of life can be seen
until faith enlightens the mind. The high things of God are
visible only to the disciplined soul and by a spiritualized
insight.

To prevent misunderstanding two cautions are needed.
St. Augustine is not discussing the powers and limits of the
natural reason of man. Man with nothing but his natural
endowments is an abstraction ; he has never existed. Augustine is thinking of men as he knew them and of himself,
creatures fallen from grace, and in fact, if not by nature,
blind to their own best good. Again he is not denying the
native capacity of the intellect to know what is truth. On the
contrary, he tells Consentius to cherish his reason dearly,
Intellectum valde ama. " Far from us the thought that God de-
tests that whereby he has made us superior to other animals ;
far from us an assent of pure faith which should dispense us
from accepting or demanding reason."[1] Faith, he insists,
does not exclude reason, nor does wisdom exclude faith. In
every branch of learning we begin with authority ; the child
learns from his parents and the schoolboy from his master.
As time goes on, no doubt, reason justifies or rejects belief,
but even in mundane beliefs it is of the first importance to
try to accept provisionally another's point of view. Reason
without interest or sympathy takes us such a little way. And
if docility be requisite in all branches of knowledge, will it
not be essential in what concerns Wisdom itself and Happiness ? Here all is at stake, and for our own part we are not
immutably wise, but only feeble participants in what is far
greater than ourselves. Besides, as he says with magnificent
rhetoric, " What soul hungering for Eternity and shocked
by the shortness of this present life would resist the splendour
and the majesty of the authority of God ? "[2]

St. Augustine does not, therefore, appeal to faith as a

[1] *Epist.* cxx.   [2] *Epist.* cxxxvii.

counsel of despair, but as the beginning of wisdom. Wisdom is made up both of intelligence and desire. It betrays a lack of intelligence to make the human mind the measure of reality, and there is no successful discipleship without good dispositions. " Talent enough is yours," he writes to Consentius, " to think out your thought ; but, what is more, you are upright and humble enough to deserve to know what is true."[1] The thought occurs again in the *De Moribus Ecclesiæ*.[2] " For the present, my aim in dealing with you must be not to make you understand [the Catholic faith] for that you cannot do – but to excite in you some desire to understand." Desire, therefore, and learning go hand in hand in knowledge.[3] The judgement which discerns is led or cozened by the soul's desire, for where the heart is, there also is our treasure. Hence the imperative need of singleness and purity of purpose. Truth " unveils itself to him who lives well, prays well, studies well."[4] It is then that the soul " begins to take the shape of truth (*incipit configurari veritati*),[5] and it is in accordance with reason for faith to precede reason. Thereby the soul is washed clean and made fit to see and bear the shining of what is mighty in reason." " Unless we walk by faith, we shall not be able to reach that vision which passes not but abides, that vision which comes from our being fastened to truth by a purified mind."[6]

These quotations show that it is false to think that Augustine means to impoverish philosophy at the expense of faith. The Christian philosopher does not use revelation as a premiss in an argument, but he is better off because faith enlightens his mind to seize the true meaning of what baffled him before ; he becomes familiar with the context of

---

[1] *Epist.* cxx.   [2] I, xvii, 31.
[3] Cf. *In Epist. Joan. ad Parth.*, II, ii, 14 : " *Talis est quisque, qualis eius dilectio est. Terram diligis ? Terra eris. Deum diligis ? Quid dicam, Deus eris.*"
[4] *De Ordine*, II, xix.
[5] *De Doctrina Christiana*, I, xx, 19.   [6] *Ibid.*, II, 12, 17.

the text of nature and his soul. There is only one philosophy, one wisdom. The neo-Platonists indeed glimpsed the truth, but from afar. "They saw indeed the fixed, lasting, and indefectible truth, where abide all the forms of all creaturely things ; but they saw it from afar (*de longinquo*) ; they saw, but their camping-ground lay in error ; and so to that mighty, ineffable, and blissful possession they found not the way."[1] How then could their error be set right ? Not by a further extension of knowledge of external objects, but by the recognition of the true Master within. St. Augustine is apt to baffle the modern reader by his insistence on some mysterious and apparently esoteric doctrine of illumination. We shall have to show later in detail what this illumination means. For the moment, a simple explanation may suffice. What he means to say is, that to know the changeless and the true, to apprehend or judge, for instance, the laws and numbers or forms of the intelligible world, one must possess some absolute standard in oneself. It is necessary to be in truth to see truth. "What is seized within is within the mind ; nor is the possession of it anything other than the beholding of it. But now the fool has no wisdom within him ; therefore he knows not wisdom."

In the confidence of his faith, St. Augustine straightway set himself to solve the difficulties which had harassed him for years, and at Cassiciacum he composed various dialogues, which form the most purely philosophic of his writings. The first had for object to establish certainty and truth against the New Academy. He felt it vitally important " to get past that boulder which stood in the way of those entering on philosophy."[2] Philosophy for him meant knowledge of God and his own soul. These were the two realities for knowledge of which he had always hungered. " *Deum et animam scire cupio. Nihilne plus ? Nihil omnino* "[3] ;

---

[1] *Sermo* cxli.

[2] *Contra Academicos*, III, xiv, 30.   [3] *Solil.* I, ii, 7.

but that they should shine out in their due splendour, he had first to establish the possibility of truth.

The arguments he uses to lay these ghosts of his former doubts are many. They are pursued with a tireless and almost fanatical fervour. First he attempts to show that the position of the sceptic is inconsistent. In denying absolute truth the sceptic by his very assertion affirms it. Moreover, how can the philosopher of the New Academy make any profession of wisdom if he has no particle of knowledge of what it is ? He has indeed no right to set his pupils' steps in the direction of so-called happiness, seeing that he knows not in what direction it lies. All human action depends on knowledge ; therefore high probability is, like scepticism, a paralysing blindness. But scepticism of all sorts is not merely inconsistent ; it can be shown to be wrong by positive proofs. The fundamental error lies in the confusion of the intelligible with the sensible world. Sense may deceive us ; we may dream or walk in our sleep ; but the neo-Platonists were on the right track when they turned the mind to its proper object, the region of the intelligible and unchanging. There are truths which cannot be doubted. A man may dream, but it is certain that he is either dreaming or not dreaming, or again that he is either knowing or not knowing, acting or not acting. Numbers are not counterfeit coins ; addition is not subtraction nor multiplication division. Every argument has its rules, and these cannot shift and change ; every step in conduct must have one direction or another. There can be no justice if there be no stable truth – no preference that has worth – no virtue distinguishable from mediocrity or vice.

Like Plato, St. Augustine takes his opponent from the field of the sensible and bids him contemplate the objects before the mind. " It is sufficient for my purpose that Plato felt that there were two worlds ; the one intelligible, where Truth itself dwelt ; the other sensible, which, as is clear, we feel by sight and touch."[1] In the former the soul moves in a familiar atmosphere ; it encounters itself and God, and truth is unveiled. The argument is really finished so soon as St. Augustine has shown that the data of sense are not the only objects of apprehension. His intention, however, is to penetrate still further into the realm of Truth. We are not material bodies influenced by and in contact with other material compounds. Behind the appearances there is the noumenon, subject to law and number and order, and within us is the soul, not visible to the eye of sense, but most evident to us by its own radiance.

Having established the existence of a supra-sensible world, he is free to concentrate on the two objects of his predilection, God and the soul. The soul comes first in order of demonstration, and the method he follows has a striking likeness to that of Descartes. But whereas Descartes began with doubt and tried to deduce all else from one sole indubitable truth, namely, the existence of a thinking self, St. Augustine regards the self as a *primus inter pares*, a leader or companion among other truths equally undeniable. The line of argument he follows and the connection of this truth with others, such as the existence of the intelligible world, of Truth and of God, is excellently expressed in the following passage. " Everyone who knows himself to be in doubt, knows truth, and is certain about what actually he knows ; therefore he is certain about truth. Everyone therefore who doubts whether there be truth, has within himself truth whereby he should not doubt ; nor is there anything true which is not true by truth. He therefore that can doubt in any wise should not doubt of truth. Where this is seen, there there is light, pure of all space be it of places or times, pure too of all representation of such a space."[2]

The same argument is repeated in various treatises with slight variations. In the *Contra Academicos* it is not developed;

---

[1] *Contra Academicos*, III, xvii, 37.   [2] *De Vera Religione*, XXXIX, lxxiii.

in the *De Beata Vita* it can be found in its simplest form ; in the *De Libero Arbitrio* it forms part of a proof of the existence of God. The *Soliloquies*[1] gives it in dialogue form as follows : " *R.* You who wish to understand yourself, do you know that you exist ? – *A.* I know it. – *R.* How do you know it ? – *A.* I know not. – *R.* Do you know that you are thinking ? – *A.* I do. – *R.* Therefore it is true that you think. – *A.* True." Still more Cartesian is the style of the argument in the *De Trinitate.*[2] "Truths of this kind have nothing to fear from the arguments of the Academicians. They say : yes, but you may be deceiving yourself ! If I deceive myself, I am. For he, who is not, cannot, clearly, deceive himself, and so I exist if I deceive myself. Since then I exist if I deceive myself, how could I deceive myself about my existence, seeing that it is certain that if I deceive myself, I exist ? It follows, therefore, that even if I deceive myself, I needs must exist in order to deceive myself, and it is beyond all doubt that I do not deceive myself when I know that I exist." *Intima scientia est qua nos vivere scimus.* There is nothing more certain for Augustine. Instead of that deceptive phantasmagoric world in which he had lived a slave to sense, he trusted now to what was indubitable, and he saw himself, a pinpoint of light in an intelligible world, a soul with intimations of truth and therefore of God.

The natural order would be to proceed now with the soul and set down what St. Augustine thought about it. But, as the thought of God influences all his teaching, it will be well at this point to anticipate and sketch his proof of God's existence. The gist of it is that truth exists, the soul exists, therefore God exists. Between each of these truths there is scarcely any interval ; strike one chord, and the others immediately respond. It is not surprising then that various schools of philosophy, the Cartesian and the Ontologist, can support their views by quotations from his writings. They fail,

[1] II, i, 1.   [2] XII, xxi.

however, we think, to extract all that is contained in the
argument. Just as conscience meant so much to Newman
that alone with it he felt alone with the Alone, so in the intimacy of his soul St. Augustine felt that Truth and God
made one sound. He did not disdain the argument from external creatures, but he made it living for himself by carrying it within. That argument, as sometimes stated, suggests
that we have to start with a pagan segment of reality and
derive from it the existence of a hitherto unknown God. On
the contrary, so Augustine thought, the creatures are coins
which already bear His inscription, and our interest and
thought are also already His. The mind and the will are
carried by the very *pondus* of the soul to beatitude and God,
so that God must be called the chief Huntsman to the pack
of thoughts, as well as the quarry.

In keeping with this view, he thought that faith should
precede proof. " Nor does anyone become fit to discover God
unless he shall have first believed what he is later to come to
know."[1] On the other hand, the *Confessions* make it clear
that there are innumerable ways along which the soul can
fly to God. Creatures call out his name and summon the soul
to recognize within itself laws of truth and goodness which
it did not make. " Wherever you turn you encounter the footprints of God made upon His work. It is by them that God
speaks to you, and if you lean to the exterior, God uses the
very forms of these exterior things to bring you back within.
So it is that the approval or disapproval you show of objects
perceived by your senses, supposes already in you the laws
of beauty, to which you refer whatever beauty is seen in the
external world by you."[2]

In one place in the *De Libero Arbitrio* he draws out the argument to a considerable length. The dialectic is neo-Platonic,
and the cogency of it depends on the proper understanding
of terms like truth, numbers, wisdom and law. That there is

[1] *De Libero Arbitrio*, II, ii, 6.   [2] *Ibid.*, XVI, xli.

truth he has shown, and also that there is a soul which thinks. He begins with a division into three classes : things, living beings, and thinking beings. He then grades them. Thinking beings are the highest, because, if they exist, the other two must exist, whereas neither of the other two implies the existence of the third. Next he turns to analyse this latter, and he elicits from that examination the fact that reason is higher than the senses because it measures them and judges them. Even amongst the senses themselves there must exist an interior sense to correlate each particular sense and serve as a dépôt or exchange. The reason, however, does far more ; it regulates and judges sensation and certifies its truth. If then there be nothing higher than reason to judge it in turn, then the human reason must be the final arbiter and divine.

St. Augustine has now cleared the decks for his main argument. Truth exists and human reason exists. If he can show that truth is higher than our reason he will have reached his goal. " If," he says to Evodius, " we can find something indubitably superior to our reason, would you hesitate to call that, whatever it be, God ? " The answer of Evodius brings out the apparent weakness in the suggestion. " I would not straightway . . . call that God. For it is not one to whom my reason is inferior whom I would call God, but one who has no superior." Augustine agrees, and continues ; if you find nothing above your reason save what is everlasting and immutable, as contrasted with bodies which change and our reason which advances and falls back, succeeds and fails, must not this unchanging reality be God, or point to One even higher than it ? What he wishes to persuade Evodius to admit is that the human mind is subject to something higher, and that this higher reality is Truth which changes not. For the argument to hold it is clear that the idea of Truth must bear an enormous weight. That it could do so was Augustine's firmest conviction, and he had behind him the Platonic

and neo-Platonic tradition. He enjoyed, moreover, the certitude, which came with his conversion, that absolute Truth
and Beatitude were words of life and no abstractions. " For
if he ask whence he is, God created him ; whence his wisdom,
God enlightened him ; whence his happiness, God has given
him to enjoy God ; as existent he is fashioned, as spectator
he is enlightened, as participant he is gladdened ; he is, he
sees, he loves ; in God's eternity he thrives, in God's truth he
shines ; in God's goodness does he take delight."[1]

The steps in the argument are, therefore, the following :
What measures and judges is higher than what is measured.
Now the mind of man finds itself in touch with an intelligible
world and knows truth. But this intelligible world is not a
product of the senses or of the soul of man. It is unchanging,
whereas the world is passing ; it is steady, whereas the soul's
glance is unsteady. Truth is found and not made, and the
human mind is subject to it. If then there is truth and it be
immutable and eternal, this is God or something belonging
to a being who must be God. The premiss which St. Augustine is most anxious to establish is that there are truths, and
that these truths are immutable and absolute norms. In the
De Vera Religione he shows that beauty and goodness and
unity are not borrowed from sensible things. On the contrary, sensible things have received from above these per-
fections, and it is because we know them dimly within ourselves that we are able to know and measure the sensible
beauty and order of things. Then from those interior experiences we are able to rise to absolute beauty and unity, which
is God.

In the De Libero Arbitrio he makes a greater use of the doctrine of numbers and Ideas, though it is not necessary to
know the exact relation of the Ideas with God's essence to
prove God's existence. He considers with evident delight the
mysterious character of numbers, and illustrates at length

[1] De Civitate Dei, XI, xxiv, 41.

their importance in music, in architecture, and in all the arts and sciences. Unity, symmetry and proportion are the conditions and factors of beauty, and prevail everywhere. Now whether we take a simple arithmetical truth, such as *seven and three make ten*, or the form and proportions of any sensible object, we are in the presence of the intelligible. Sense is not aware of unity and cannot give us order. The mind then it is which apprehends something intelligible and unchanging, and does so in a way like to that of the artist, who expresses in sensible design a still invisible ideal and perfects the image in accordance with an internal law of numbers and beauty dimly present in his soul. " I have seen the lines of architects, the very finest, like a spider's web ; but those (the intelligible) are still different, they are not the images of those lines which the eye of flesh showed me : he knows them who without any conception whatsoever of a body, recognizes them within himself. I have perceived also the numbers of the things with which we number all the senses of my body ; but those numbers wherewith we number are different, nor are they the images of these, and therefore they indeed are."[1]

Two affirmations stand out in this account ; first that numbers are not sensible, and second, that they exist apart, a kind of galaxy in the mind's firmament. St. Augustine had a natural love of numbers, and the studies of the period, neo-Platonism, and Scripture all contributed to make him emphasize their importance, and at times, it must be confessed, in his sermons and sacred commentaries, to indulge in fanciful and wearisome speculation. They are not for him abstractions derived from the sensible, as the Aristotelians held. The sensible cannot give birth to the intelligible, and numbers are clearly objects of the mind. " What can be more intolerable and irrational than to admit that we surpass animals by reason, and then to admit that what is seen by

[1] *Confessions*, X, xii. Cf. *De Libero Arbitrio*, II, xvi, quoted above.

our bodily sight is real – though certain animals see it better than we do ; and nevertheless to maintain that what is seen by our reason is nothing?"[1] The contrary is true ; numbers exist everlastingly and immutably, and the sensible is real only by participation in those numbers.

What is true of numbers holds with still more force of wisdom and beatitude. " Before we are happy we bear imprinted in our hearts the idea of happiness. . . . Likewise before we are wise we bear imprinted in our hearts the idea of wisdom."[2] Men may differ about the content of happiness, but the very variety witnesses to the reality of the idea, and all our judgements in conduct are measured by goodness as they are also in other matters by truth. Once more we perceive that we are in the presence of an unchanging norm and of a Truth which surpasses us and subdues us.

Such is the argument St. Augustine proposes. It is, as can be seen, based on the neo-Platonic doctrine of degrees, but genius has given it an original form. The visible is the starting-point, but, in contrast with the well-known cosmological argument, the next step mounts to truth as seen within the mind. Mind is higher than matter, and has its own world clear to those whose soul has not been darkened by the Circean enchantments of sense. Within itself the soul can contemplate the order of truth. " Gaze upon the sky, the sea," the works of art, the soul of the artist ; " pass beyond the soul, that you may behold number everlasting ; then it is that the splendour of wisdom will shine out from the inner dwelling-place and very sanctuary of truth."[3] But here the human mind is no longer master ; it must take the second place and confess to the existence of a truth which in its everlasting serenity and perfection directs it into paths of happiness whither it is already tending.

It is now time to return to the soul, the existence of which

---

[1] *De Vera Religione*, XXXII, lix.
[2] *De Libero Arbitrio*, II, ix.   [3] *Ibid.*, XVI, xlii.

was quoted as an example of certitude against the New Academy. St. Augustine does not use a consistent technical language in his description of the soul and the mind. *Anima* means generally the vital principle or man as stirred by desire and love, and *animus* the highest grade of *anima*, that is, the soul as the principle of thinking. Of the *intellectus* he says : " And so in our soul there is something called the intellect. This part of the soul which is called *intellectus et mens* is enlightened by a higher light. Now that higher light whereby the human mind is enlightened is God."[1] The *ratio*, on the other hand, is " the movement of the mind (*mens*) capable of distinguishing and interrelating what is learnt."[2] The *mens*, in turn, is distinguished into a higher and lower activity according as it is engaged on contemplation or action.

These distinctions do not conflict with the unity and substantiality of the soul. As a spiritual being the soul is indivisible, and its spirituality and subsistence are given directly in self-knowledge. This certainty disposes of pantheism and of the opinion of Tertullian that the soul was material. " The soul is conscious that it lives, that it remembers, that it knows, and that it desires. It recognizes all this within itself. . . ."[3] Not that the soul need or can possess all this knowledge at all times with full awareness – in fact, one condition of a right knowledge is that it should keep near and try to come closer to the centre of that spiritual kingdom to which it belongs. Nor, again, are we to suppose that the soul comprehends its nature fully. In a sense it must do so, as it cannot know itself in part; and yet, since it is still searching for this knowledge, it is unable to enjoy it completely.

St. Augustine insists so strongly on the spirituality and substantiality of the soul that he is faced with a difficulty

---

[1] *In Johann. Tract.* XV, iv, 9.   [2] *De Ordine*, II, ii, 30.
[3] *De Trinitate*, X, x.

when he has to explain its relation with the body. His language is indefinite, and he is frankly puzzled. " The manner in which spirits are united to bodies ... is marvellous, and it exceeds the understanding of man."[1] Fortunately he does not leave the mystery altogether unprobed. " The soul is a rational substance fitted to rule the body."[2] The separatist tendency apparent in this definition is counterbalanced by others. " Man is a rational, mortal animal," and, " man is a rational soul using a mortal and earthly body." This "use" of a body does not imply a conception of the body as an alien substance. Man is one being, and the soul vitalizes the body and is present in every part by what he calls an *attentio vitalis*. The body is a " sleeping partner " or like the wife in a Roman household ; the soul gives it its rights, its share in life and intelligibility, even as the soul in turn receives its light from the Source of all light and unity. All that we know of body which makes it worthy of attention consists of order, form and beauty – and this grace of order descends upon it from the soul, which is in contact with the world of ideas in the divine mind. The soul, in other words, is an intermediary between matter and supreme spirit. " Nor is there to be found anything between the highest life, which is unchanging wisdom and truth, and the lowest to receive life, that is, the body, save the soul which quickens it."[3]

The neo-Platonism inherent in this half-worked-out theory created fresh difficulties when he tried to square it with the Bible. He had to retract in later life language which suggested a soul of the world, and he never succeeded in hitting upon an explanation of the origin of the soul that did justice to the doctrine of Original Sin. He inclined to a form of traducianism, but in the *De Libero Arbitrio* he offers four hypotheses : either every soul issues by God's act from

[1] *De Civitate Dei*, XXI, x.

[2] This definition of the soul is not peculiar to St. Augustine. It is to be found in the neo-Platonist writings.

[3] *De Civitate Dei*, XI, xxiii.

the first soul created by God, or God creates a special soul for each individual, or all souls pre-exist in God (*in Dei aliquo secreto*) and are sent at the appointed time to govern a body, or lastly they descend into a body of their own accord. In case of the two latter alternatives the soul can have no memory of its pre-existent state. This uncertainty shown by St. Augustine is, however, only a *penumbra* round what is shiningly clear, to wit, that the soul is not a part of God, but created by Him and of an immortal texture. Self-knowledge reveals infirmity and subsistence, whereas God is unchanging perfection ; and as the soul cannot be dependent on matter it must be dependent by creation on God.

The argument for immortality is also governed to some extent by neo-Platonic principles. He recurs to the dependence of the mind on God, the Truth, and to his favourite conception of the soul, in the garden enclosed of spirit, speaking with itself and contemplating its object. For an object to be known it must exist free from its spatial limitations, as an idea. Things pass and perish, but their truth abides in the mind of God and in the idea of it which we possess. " The mind could not contemplate its object were it not united to it in some way." That object " is not known as external to the spirit which knows it." It is therefore an idea, and as such we could not know it were not our mind illumined by the Light of all ideas and united with Him. This union with God gives St. Augustine the premiss for his conclusion, because such union is of its nature immortal, as can easily be shown. The soul is not Truth itself, because Truth is immutable and the soul is subject to change ; nor is it a part of Truth, because it is aware of itself as alive and thinking, and therefore as a substance. There is left only one other alternative. God must sustain it and unite it with Himself in such a way that it perseveres in existence and participates in His light. Such participation is everlasting, for matter cannot molest the substance of what is higher, and there is nothing which could conflict with it. " If no essence, in so far as it is essence, has its contrary, still less can the primordial essence have one. If, moreover, it is from this essence that the soul has all that it is (and in truth it cannot have it from any other source, seeing that it does not exist of itself and must therefore exist by this substance superior to itself), if, I say, it is from this substance that the soul holds all that it is, there is nothing which can destroy it, as nothing exists which is opposed to the substance it has. Consequently the soul cannot cease to be."[1]

This metaphysical and Platonic line of reasoning is sup-ported by other arguments. What we love we become ; to love immortality is to become immortal, and it is certain that all men, willy-nilly, love to persist in some sort of being. If this be doubted, do not all men seek truth and certainty and happiness ? For certainty we require a state which is enduring, a state of contemplation in which there is a joy which cannot be taken from us ; and in this mortal life there is no such state to be found.

In this discussion some connection of the mind with supreme truth, of the soul with God, is constantly assumed. The precise nature of this connection must now be inves-tigated. Unfortunately St. Augustine has, in the abundance of his thought, left material for several and divergent answers. According to some he means by truth God, and the mind is in direct communication with God as truth. In God all else is perceived, as Malebranche thought ; or in God's ideas all else is recognized, as many Augustinians have held.[2]

[1] The point of this argument is brought out by an illustration. Cold is the opposite of heat, and dissipates it ; disease is the opposite of health, and ruins it. Now falsehood is the opposite of truth, and " it is obvious how much falsehood can harm the mind (*animus*). Can it do more than deceive? Why, no man is deceived unless he is alive : hence falsehood cannot destroy the mind." *De Immortalitate Animæ*, XI, xviii.

[2] The influence of the doctrine on early Scholasticism has been thoroughly worked out by M. Gilson in an article " *Pourquoi S. Thomas a critiqué S. Augustin* " in *Archives d'histoire doctrinale et littéraire du Moyen Age*, 1926–7.

God sheds the light of the eternal ideas on the mind. In this latter hypothesis these ideas may be the first objects known, or norms whereby experience is judged. On the other hand, many commentators maintain that the theory differs in little, if at all, from that of St. Thomas Aquinas. What St. Thomas called the " active intellect " (*intellectus agens*) is said to be described in fact, if not in word.

Leaving aside a detailed examination of the arguments for the various views, we have to answer two main questions : first, what do the senses contribute to knowledge ; and second, what does St. Augustine mean by truth of judgement and knowledge ? He appears to be in a quandary. He has vigorously denied that sense can act on or inform the mind on the ground that the lower cannot determine what is higher. Truth lies within, and the human mind reaches truth because of its participation in the highest Truth, the ideas of God Himself. But without experience the mind has no content, so that it looks as if the content must somehow come from above. It is possible that St. Augustine was not fully aware of this dilemma, and, if so, the nonchalance with which he ignores difficulties can be explained ; or it may be that M. Boyer is right, and that the difficulties rest on a misunderstanding of his doctrine.

Sensation certainly is a necessary condition for knowledge. " Whatever is known to us is known to us by the senses of the body and the experience of this life." It is equally true that knowledge is not the product of sensation. " The thought cannot be entertained that a body can cause anything in a spirit, as though the spirit, like matter, were subject to the action of a body."[1] What happens then is this : that a sensible body affects one of the physical organs of sense. There is no sensation as yet. Matter is affecting matter. But now the soul by its very nature is allied with the body in so intimate a way that it takes care of the body and is vigilant

[1] *De Genesi ad litteram* XII, xiv.

for its welfare. The impact on the human body may escape its notice. If so, the reaction will be unconscious. If, on the other hand, the soul in the exercise of its vigilance is able to attend to what is happening, we have sensation. To use a revealing phrase, the soul *exserit attentiores actiones*, and it is this act of attention or consciousnesss which is sensation. The explanation is obviously based on Augustine's theory of the interrelation of body and soul. The soul ensconced within its own spirituality lives in conjunction with a body of its own. When something happens to that body, it listens and raises to its own level the response to be given. Sensation belongs not to the body, but to the soul through the body. *Sensum puto esse non latere animam quod patitur corpus.*

To give an example : the body is in contact with other material bodies, and its functions are furthered or impeded by interaction. Where, then, the welfare of the body is at stake the soul exercises its vigilance and attends to the wound or increased activity of an organ. This act of attention constitutes the sensation of pain or pleasure. " When, then, [the body] resists what is adverse . . . [the soul] becomes more attentive because of the difficulty in the way of action. This difficulty . . . is called feeling and goes by the name of suffering or effort."[1] The body, then, does not feel, but the soul through the body, and St. Augustine describes the action of the body rather as an appeal, like the sending of a message, than as a cause. " For it is not the body that has sensation, but the soul through the body, and it uses the latter as, so to speak, a messenger in order to form within itself what is announced from without."[2] We may think, as an image, of a telephone, or remind the reader of the view of Bergson which bears a remarkable likeness to the analysis just given. As St. Augustine pointed out in discussing sound and lines of verse, the impact of the notes on the ear does not make us hear *Deus Creator Omnium*, much less understand

---

[1] *De Musica*, VI, v, 9.   [2] *De Genesi ad litteram*, XII, xvii, 33.

its meaning. One impact succeeds another, but it is the soul which " gives something of its substance to the formation " of the sensible image. Out of the succession the soul by memory – that word so full of meaning in Augustine's philosophy – preserves a unity, and in the production of an image within itself is aware of its operation and has sensation. The soul speaks to itself, and all is carried on within its own theatre.

How then guarantee the objectivity of sensible knowledge ? The question so framed belongs to another age, but Augustine has an answer, I think, and it depends on numbers. He dismisses the question of the fallibility of the senses. " The eyes do not deceive, for they can only tell the soul (*animus*) how they are affected. Now, if not only they but all the other bodily senses relate their condition, I know not what more can be expected of them. . . . If a man think that an oar is broken in the water and set straight when it is taken out, his witness is not wrong, but he is a bad judge." Nevertheless, we can go farther because the unity and the proportion and the numbers of sensible objects can be appreciated by the *mind*. The soul in sensation is assimilated in its harmony of number to the excitations of the body by sensible objects. Moreover, wherever there are objects there is order and some kind of unity showing itself in equality, symmetry, beauty. Such beauty is a participation of Beauty itself, and belongs to truth. The mind recapitulates that order and within itself is aware of an absolute standard or norm, which guarantees its judgements to be true. It must not be forgotten that St. Augustine does not claim for the human mind a knowledge of the essence of tables and chairs and other material things. His world is that of the intelligible, and he is content to find the trace of God in the order and unity of the world outside us, in the proportion and harmony of numbers which relate to us something of its nature. In answer, then, to the question of the source of our knowledge

MA

St. Augustine bids us look up, and not down to the material world which so faintly participates in truth.

The doctrine of illumination completes the theory. Unfortunately, as has already been pointed out, the passage from sensation to knowledge is not at all clear, and this obscurity has been the source of many explanations. The Platonic leanings of St. Augustine are in part responsible. Convinced that knowledge is not wholly due to the experience of sense, he found a clue in the example of the slave in Plato's *Meno*. The slave who knew no geometry could nevertheless reply intelligently and show that in some way he possessed the requisite knowledge already. Knowledge, then, is not a lesson learned from without. Our minds do not contain furniture brought in from outside and stacked within. St. Augustine is at great pains to establish this. He points out that language and gestures are signs, and often enough do not convey the thought within ; disputes are over words and the ideas are understood despite the words. Words, then, cannot cause ideas, though they are the vehicles of communication. If the subject-matter be sensible, explanation is useless without some personal experience ; if the subject-matter be ideas, then the teacher suggests something to the pupil's mind. The former's task, however little he know it, is to direct the pupil to foregather with himself and, in the chambers of his mind, find the truth which is there. " In my heart, then, they were, even before I learned them, but in my memory they were not. Where, then, or wherefore, when they were spoken did I acknowledge them, and say, ' So is it, it is true,' unless they were already in the memory, but so thrown back and buried as it were in deeper recesses that, had not the suggestion of another drawn them forth, I had been unable to conceive of them ? "[1]

Lest this argument sound fantastic, it must be remembered that for St. Augustine sensible experience is necessary for

[1] *Confessions*, X, xvii.

knowledge. He is here thinking of truths which the pupil learns, and he is arguing that such truths come to light within us ; they are not merely the private singular views of a professor. Is he then committed to some form of innate ideas or Platonic reminiscence or to Ontologism ? In his first years as a Platonist he was in all probability affected by the doctrine of reminiscence, but its influence declined as he pursued his meditations. As for innate ideas, the truth seems to be that St. Augustine steers a middle course between them and a direct vision of God. The nearest approach to them is found in passages devoted to memory. This word has a suggestion of the Platonic *reminiscence*, but in St. Augustine it covers a multitude of meanings. It refers to the present as much as to the past ; it emphasizes his belief that within the soul resided knowledge and truth, and I think it served a useful purpose as suggesting that that truth was derivative, whether from past experience or from God. " The memory, then, is as it were the belly of the mind," or in other phrases a place " of spacious chambers furnished with innumerable stores." Now, in listening to the words of others, it was not the words nor the private opinions to which he assented, but something common to all minds, something universal, something within, which goes by the name of truth. Whosoever can perceive this universal " is within, the disciple of truth ; and without, the judge of him who speaks, or rather of the discourse itself."[1] " Truth is near to all, is eternal for all ; it prompts from without, it teaches from within."[2]

To the soul itself then we must turn. But memory here reveals to us that it cannot be the human soul which begets truth. The soul must listen and be taught. As God is the Author of our existence, so must He be the Doctor. The soul, which changes, cannot have produced the unchanging. " And I entered into the very seat of my mind (which it hath in my memory, inasmuch as the mind remembers itself also),

---

[1] *De Magistro*, XIII, xli.   [2] *De Libero Arbitrio*, II, xiv.

neither wert Thou there . . . because Thou art the Lord God
of the mind and all these affections are changed, but Thou
remainest unchangeable over all and yet hast vouchsafed
to dwell in my memory since I learnt Thee." And again in
the next chapter he writes : " Everywhere, O Truth, dost
Thou give audience to all who ask counsel of Thee, and at
once answerest all, though on manifold matters they ask Thy
counsel ; clearly dost Thou answer though all do not clearly
hear."[1]

Truth then, which is God, is the Teacher and Master
within, enlightening the mind. There are innumerable
passages in which St. Augustine struggles to explain and develop the thought, but the correct interpretation remains
uncertain. Many critics think that St. Augustine has in mind
the formation of concepts. The problem then would be, how
and whence has our knowledge any intelligible content ?
Sensation cannot provide the content, because sensible experience cannot be the cause of knowledge. As is well known,
St. Thomas Aquinas followed Aristotle in positing an active
intellect which abstracted the intelligible from the *datum* of
sense, and this active intellect was a power belonging to man.
At the time when Scholasticism ripened, the influence of
Arabian Aristotelianism led to the interpretation of the
doctrine of illumination in terms of the active intellect. Hence
William of Auvergne taught that God was as it were the book
from which the human mind reads all the principles of knowledge, and Roger Bacon definitely calls God the active intellect of man. M. Portalié[2] inclines to think that when all
the texts are considered, this view is the nearest to St.
Augustine's meaning. M. Boyer, on the other hand, follows
Kleutgen, Zigliara and Lepidi in so assimilating St. Augustine to St. Thomas Aquinas that their views become indistinguishable save by accent. " God enlightens us by the very
fact that our own intelligence enlightens us. Our intellect is,

---

[1] *Confessions*, X, xi.   [2] *Dictionnaire de Théologie.*

in fact, nothing else than the divine Light tempered to the infirmity of our nature. The truths we perceive are partial, limited, made clumsy by the multiplicity of the terms. Nevertheless, they are the expression, suited to our nature, of the total and simple truth, which is God. No one of our ideas, whatever we do, reveals to us the pure Idea which is in God, but each of our ideas, in its positive content, expresses something which belongs to God, although under a form which the idea does not reveal. This is the sense in which God is our Light and the manner in which we see truths in God."[1]

This view is satisfactory, at least in so far as it makes the necessary distinctions between God's Light and our intellect, and God's ideas and what we know. St. Augustine holds fast to the existence and separate functioning of the human mind, and he is too sure of the infirmity of human nature and the human mind to give the latter a vision of the ideas as they are in God's mind. Again, the analysis which St. Augustine offers makes it certain that God does not introduce into our intellects the subjects of knowledge. His theory of sensible perception is given as a faint replica of what happens in a higher order. God is like to the sun in the visible world in that the objects seen are lit up by its light and the eye is enabled to see by means of the sunlight. [2] But does this comparison of God's illumination with the light of the sun indicate a theory of abstraction, as some contend ? [3] A serious objection is that

[1] Boyer, *L'Idée de la Verité*, p. 206.

[2] This is the sense of the famous passage in the *De Trinitate*, IX, xv, 24 : " The nature of the soul is so made that by the disposition of its Creator it is naturally united to intelligible things ; hence it is that it sees them in a kind of incorporeal light of a special sort—*in quadam luce sui generis incorporea* – just as the fleshly eye sees what lies round it in this corporeal light, for which it has been made and disposed." St. Thomas takes *luce sui generis* to mean " of the same nature as " that of the soul, and many commentators follow him. It is then suggested that the passage proves that the light must be a created light. On the other hand the expression may mean only that the light is of the same genus as the soul – incorporeal.

[3] M. Boyer remarks pertinently that in the Thomist theory of abstraction the phantasm does not strictly cause conception, but only presents a content from which the active intellect abstracts the potentially intelligible element.

this theory of abstraction is at variance with the Platonic outlook of St. Augustine, and therefore an anachronism.[1] It is much more likely that Augustine is thinking not of the formation of concepts, but of the truth of judgements. In his philosophy there is no sensible image to be spiritualized, because the image is a product or expression of the soul acting through the body. If this be so, the office of the active intellect would be a sinecure. The sensible has no drawbridge to cross, because sensation is a sentinel of the mind. St. Augustine was exercised by a problem, but it is not that of sensation and abstraction. The mind recognizes in its activity a feature, the feature of truth, which does not fall within its own scope. Whence comes this universal and adamantine quality ? He answers that it must come from God, and that the soul perceives in the light of God's truth the truth of its judgements. Therefore, as M. Gilson says, whereas the Aristotelian active intellect produces the concept, the Augustinian illumination produces truth. " Illumination of the thought by God in Augustinianism, illumination of the object by a thought which God illumines in Aristotelianism : that is the difference "[2] between the two systems.

This interpretation is perhaps more in accord with the neo-Platonist school from which St. Augustine took his premisses, but it leaves, nevertheless, a gap in the system, of which he may not have been aware. He has not shown what is the content of the judgement, nor divulged whence and how it has been obtained. In the Aristotelian philosophy the object specifies the concept and the concept is the result of an abstraction from a sensible *datum*. St. Augustine has

---

[1] To this M. Gilson replies that the very idea of a sensible phantasm, as understood by St. Thomas, is foreign to St. Augustine. It should also be noted that the word *abstraction* does not cover the whole operation of the Thomist active intellect. There is an Augustinian ring in such expressions as " *Lumen intellectus agentis est nobis immediate impressum a Deo, secundum quod discernimus verum a falso et bonum a malo* " (*Spir. Cre.* a. 10), and " *Sicut virtute judicativa . . . per intellectum agentem judicamus de veritate* " (*ibid.*, a. 8).

[2] Gilson, *Introduction à la Philosophie de S. Augustin.*

shown, for his part, how in experience the soul attends to the report of the body, and in this active attention has sensation. This may suffice as an analysis of feeling or pure sensation, but it appears to neglect consideration of the object felt or perceived. In knowledge, again, of objects which do not fall within sensible experience, illumination may suffice to explain judgement, that is, the mind's power to acclaim their truth ; but what of the objects themselves ?

This criticism, formidable as it may appear, may possibly rest on a prejudice in favour of a sharp distinction between concept and knowledge, simple apprehension and judgement, which St. Augustine would not have accepted. In his view there are degrees of reality, and what is not God is graded according to its likeness to Him. But this likeness or participation is not something supplementary to a being's constitution ; the likeness is its constitution. Objects have meaning in so far as they reflect the unity and immutable perfection of God, and this meaning is identical with their order, unity, and beauty ; they are, in fact, like sentences or musical themes whose meaning can be read or heard. When, therefore, critics assert that the image or concept in this philosophy has no content, they are assuming the psychology of Aristotle or their own, and they forget that for Augustine the soul has no difficulty in conversing with the intelligible by means of the numbers. They start from the lowest, the world of things, while Augustine starts with the highest, the centre and measure of every order ; and since things and living bodies and souls live only by their participation in abiding truth, the concept of them and the judgement of them tend naturally to run together.

This same consideration throws light on the doctrine of illumination and the relation of the soul to God. St. Augustine has argued that no object can be beautiful and true save by the diminished presence in it of absolute beauty and truth, and as in his own soul he finds only borrowed gleams, he urges that man must submit to the unchanging truth. But now man's soul is active and intelligent as well as intelligible; it commands a view of nature and judges what is true. Here divine Truth must be active, and God must be its Teacher, revealing His presence in the absolute standards wherewith the soul judges. The most significant texts in this connection are those in which the cry of Pascal is anticipated : " Thou wouldst not be searching for Me, hadst thou not already found Me." We cannot desire what we do not already know ; we judge of truth because the Truth already abides in us ; our very love lets fall the secret of His love, for " He is in our memory though we suspect it not." This fact of psychology and metaphysics is the burden of his language about God as the Light and Truth within us. *Et ecce intus eras et ego foris et ibi Te quaerebam ; mecum eras et tecum non eram.*

The idea which the soul has of God is therefore not God, for it knows Him not, and nevertheless God is the Truth and interior Master which that idea intimates. In art and morality the ideal can remain indistinct and control withal execution and conduct and apportion merit. It must then be present as it presides as a norm. God presides in a similar way in knowledge, and just as conscience can without contradiction be recognized as a dictate of reason and at the same time the will of a living God, so for Augustine a true judgement is both the natural expression of our minds and the word of God which enlightens every man. With such an Accomplice it is no wonder that our minds possess an immutable certainty in their judgements and are able to behold the veritable nature of the objects contemplated. Their nature is their truth, and there is no adequate distinction to be made between the form or content of the object and its participation in Him, whom St. Augustine invokes as the God of Truth " in whom and by whom all the things that are are true."

Deus qui scitur melius nesciendo ![1] We know God better by
our inability to know Him. Nevertheless, He is not, like the
One of Plotinus, beyond all knowledge. " He exceeds all
understanding save without doubt His own."[2] All perfection is His, and " what He has, He is " (*id quod habet, est*).
St. Augustine has favourite terms of address. " God is the
supreme good, above all good, and for that reason He is
unchanging." Change implies imperfection, and so it is that
the immutability of God comes to mind in the consideration of the passing show of things and the soul's inquietude.
And with changelessness truth is connected. " He truly is
because He cannot change." Also as change denotes time,
so changelessness denotes eternity. " But Thou precedest all
things past by the sublimity of an ever-present eternity ; and
surpassest all future because they are future, and when they
come, they shall be past, but Thou art the same and Thy
years fail not."[3] And as He overflows time, so He fills all
space and is not contained. " God is not contained by any
place, but is everywhere in Himself."[4]

In all that God does He is free, and we cannot rightly ask
the question, why God chose to create other beings than
Himself. We have to start from the contingent as a fact, learn
what God does, and not inquire into what He ought to do.
The proof of God's existence moved, as we have seen, by
steps from the changing to the forms which endure, and
thence to their immutable source. The panorama of creation
is looked at in the same perspective, but from above. God is
immutable. He is goodness and truth and all perfection.
These pure forms exist as ideas in God's mind, as the pat-
terns by which the creative activity is directed. Like the
sun's luminous envelope or photosphere, layers of being are
formed from the central point where God is. In this radiance –
the Plotinian *Kathodos* – unity breaks up into multiplicity, and

[1] *De Ordine*, II, xxiv.   [2] *De Civitate Dei*, II, xxix.
    [3] *Confessions*, XI, xiii.   [4] *Epist.* clxxxvii.

what is multiple is real in so far as it participates in the unity
and beauty of the One. The forms are dispersed in time and
space, but however far off from Truth and Unity, however
lowly and materialized, they have meaning and reality, because the music of the divine theme can still be heard in their
numbers. " Behold the sky, the earth, the sea, what shines
above, creeps in the lowest regions, flies and swims ; all these
things have forms because they have numbers ; take away
their numbers and they are no longer anything. Whence
come they, then, if it be not from the source of numbers, seeing that it is the same thing for them to be and to be a melody
of number ? "[1] Such is the scheme of creation and participation by means of the ideas. St. Augustine adds that, since all
that is creaturely resembles its prototype, Resemblance or
Likeness must itself be an idea, and this he identifies with
the Word, Who is the perfect image of the Father.[2] Image
and word are therefore closely connected. Indeed, as M.
Gilson has pointed out, the Augustinian theory of knowledge is constructed on an analogy with the generation
of the Word by the Father. The expression of our feeling
or our thought is a *dictio*, and the thought expresses a
verbum, an interior *verbum*, which is not lost after it is
begotten.

In his account of creation St. Augustine has constantly in
mind his own former Manichæan errors, and his reply to
them is couched in Platonic language. He is, it must be
owned, at times somewhat embarrassed, as the tenets of
Plotinus do not always easily square with the story of creation as given in Genesis. God ceaselessly upholds all creatures
in existence, but is this by a mode of participation or by

[1] *De Libero Arbitrio*, II, xvi.

[2] An image is a likeness expressed. The Word is the Only-begotten of the
Father and His perfect image and likeness. This thought of St. Augustine has
its influence in his application of *image* to objects of sense and knowledge. He
also introduces a likeness of the Trinity in every department of the universe.
For a full treatment of this, cf. Gardeil, *La Structure de l'Ame et l'Expérience
Mystique*, Paris.

causality ? The two modes are joined together, and not always too smoothly. The world as intelligible has form and exists by participation in the ideas of God. Like a work of art, it proceeds from the divine mind according to an eternal plan. Forms, therefore, have at least two modes of existence, the one eternal, the other in time ; and the latter ought by right to constitute the reality of changing objects, because they are nothing else than tones re-echoing truthfully the hymn of God's nature. " True things are true in so far as they exist ; but they exist only in so far as they are like to the sovereign One."[1] Now we have seen in what that likeness consists. Nevertheless, St. Augustine lays it down that all things, even, probably, the human soul and angels, have a matter as well as a form, and that this matter had a relative, though not temporal, precedence in order of creation.[2] It is possible, too, that Père Gardeil is right in thinking that the term " creation " should be reserved for this matter alone. More probably form, too, belongs to the creative act, but, be that as it may, matter is separate from form and real. It would even appear from certain texts as if it were possible for matter to exist without form, though in matter of fact God " created matter impregnated with form." It is described as *quædam informitas sine specie* and like to sound, which is the material of song, but this does not help us to understand what this strange visitant, " which no intellect can seize owing to its lack of form," is doing in Augustine's world of numbers and participation.

In this world of matter and forms " everything that comes to be and passes away is said to take form " from the forms which do not change. These latter are the primary ideas or " the fixed and unchanging reasons of things, which are

---

[1] *De Vera Religione*, XXXVI, lxvi.

[2] This " matter " is not of course the Aristotelian *materia prima*. Professor A. E. Taylor, in his commentary on Plato's *Timaeus*, has explained carefully its place in the Platonist system, and offers a useful comparison of it with the description of matter in Professor Whitehead's recent works.

themselves not formed, and persist therefore eternally and always in the same way, being contained in the divine intellect." In this manner, what is lowest shares in what is highest and manifests its unity. But, as all that is below God has life only by participation, and as God created all at the beginning, as Genesis declares, creatures must fall into two classes, the actual and the potential. All is created at once, but not all comes to completion at once. The second class consists of seminal reasons or ideas or causes, as they are variously called. All that will ever be on this earth is already there in them " invisibly, potentially, causally, *quomodo fiunt futura non facta.*" Both the account in Genesis, so Augustine thinks, and neo-Platonist principles reserve to God the power to produce something new. Participation is nearer to final than to efficient causality, and formation is close in meaning to illumination. Now, objects and the human soul are illumined by the ideas existent in God. Hence development depends on what is already a created *ratio seminalis*, and secondary causes do no more than plant and water what can only receive its increase from the First Cause. The origin of this view is to be found in the Enneads, but whereas Plotinus conceived the seminal reason as a kind of development of the content of an idea or of an intuition by deduction, St. Augustine transfers the seminal reasons to the physical world. They are assigned to the wet element of the earth and become the germs of physical forms, and, being permeated by numbers, they develop by means of these " most active numbers " to their pre-ordained perfection. Some would see in this theory an anticipation of modern evolution ; but the points of view are so different that it is difficult to establish any profitable comparison.

In his reflections on creation St. Augustine grew more and more fascinated by that mysterious creature of God, time. The world is not eternal because eternity is a divine prerogative. "Time, because its passage involves change, cannot be

coeval with unchanging eternity."[1] Thus on the ground of
change he settles one vexing question, but as to the nature of
time, " if no one asks me I know ; if I wish to explain it to
one that asketh, I know not."[2] It cannot be identical with
movement. A poem is measured by its feet and syllables, but
such measurement is spatial, not temporal, and if we recite
it we can draw it out or shorten it independently of its
arranged *tempo*. Does it not seem to be some kind of pro-
traction ? " But of what, I know not ; and I marvel if it be
not of the mind itself ? " Such a solution is characteristic of
St. Augustine. In every question he finds the trail within,
and here it is in memory that he catches sight of his quarry.
Already he has defined the soul in terms of an *attentio*, and
as the human mind is but a dispersed image of the One, it is
natural that it should have to stretch itself out in recollec-
tion of the past, and strain to the future. Lacking the simul-
taneity of God, it nevertheless captures in its memory the
succession of changing objects and its changing self. " Who
shall hold the heart of man that it may stand still and see
how eternity, ever still-standing, neither past nor to come,
uttereth the times past and to come ? " Almost impossible it
might be thought, but St. Augustine has an inkling of an
answer, because his mind shares in the divine light, and his
soul has heard the utterance of that word.

The neo-Platonist universe is easily adapted to the Christian notion of Providence, and St. Augustine, long tormented
by Manichæan difficulties, saw in the doctrine of " ideas " a
saving solution. God creates and disposes of all things
sweetly. He is truth and goodness, and all that exists participates by reason of its being in the ideas ; therefore creation
and providence are one. " If it is true that no being would
subsist if robbed of its form, the immutable form, which
makes changing things to be and penetrates with harmony

[1] *De Civitate Dei*, XII, xiii.   [2] *Confessions*, XI, xiv.

their being and their action, this form is their providence."[1]

It must be true, therefore, that " whosoever looking on and considering the universe of creatures maketh his way to wisdom, feels wisdom show its merry countenance in the journey and greet him in every act of providence."[2] And yet what means it that " whereas Thou art everlastingly joy to Thyself, and some things around Thee evermore rejoice in Thee . . . this portion of things (the life of man) thus ebbs and flows, alternately displeased and reconciled " ?[3] Evil should have no place in a universe coming from God and built to the music of the Ideas ; and yet there is no gainsaying its presence. All his life St. Augustine pondered this grievous fact. His answer has its repercussions in theology, in all that he writes on liberty and grace, on Original Sin and Redemption and Hell and Heaven. Reason, schooled in neo-Platonism and enlightened by faith, gave him an answer which the succeeding ages found acceptable. Creatures which are subject to change have the seeds of death in them ; they come and go ; but in their passing they linger, as in a piece of music or a poem, and so contribute to the beauty of the whole. Evil is relative and not substantial ; it is a falling short of goodness or being. The single good thing can fail, but it is good so long as it is alive, and in its extinction may be relatively good in a larger whole than itself or to an oncoming generation.

The problem of human misery and sin is, however, hardly touched by this general answer. " Behold these things pass away, that others may replace them, and so this lower universe be completed by all its parts. But do I depart anywhere ? saith the Word of God. There fix thy dwelling, trust there whatsoever thou hast thence, O my soul, at least now thou art tired out with vanities. Entrust to Truth whatsoever thou hast from the Truth, and thou shalt lose nothing ; and

---

[1] *De Libero Arbitrio*, II, xvii.   [2] *Ibid.*
[3] *Confessions*, VIII, iii, 8.

thy decay shall bloom again . . . and all thy diseases be healed."[1] Man must entrust Truth ; that is to say, he has his liberty, and it is in his power to move into the Unchanging or suffer degradation, to bloom again even from decay or wear away in vanity. The responsibility of evil lies with him since the home of his soul is the Unchanging Goodness. Free will, therefore, is the key to the problem of evil. It may not be in our power to love God as He should be loved, but the evil that we do is certainly our fault. In this conviction St. Augustine never wavered. Free will, he says, is so evident that if we are so foolish as to deny it we have to use our freedom to do so. But though he recurs to the subject again and again, he was too much preoccupied with contemporary problems to tidy up his view. His *De Libero Arbitrio*, for instance, is directed against Manichæan errors, and in his later works the problem of grace is foremost before his mind. Consequently we do not find the necessary distinctions drawn between liberty, power, will and choice.

It is possible, however, to gather from the mass of his writings certain definite doctrines. The will is defined as " the power of the soul to hold on to or to attain an object without constraint." The evidence for freedom is of the same order as that for existence. " I know that I live ; grant me that ; I know that I wish to live ; grant me that also ; now if the whole human race is unanimous on this point, then our will is as evident to us as our existence."[2] Choice depends on motives, and consists in a judgement on the motives. " The reasoning soul yields or refuses assent to interior images by choice of will."[3] Choice, however, is not the same thing as full liberty. We may choose to do what does not, as a matter of fact, lie in our power, whereas liberty means the power to do what is good. " The choice of our will is fully free when it does not serve our vices and our

---

[1] *Confessions*, IV, xi, 16.   [2] *De Duab. Anim.*, X, xiii.
[3] *De Genesi ad litteram*, IX, xiv.

sins."[1] Our will is God's, but our freedom is not destroyed by the will of God. " God foresees also the power of the will. Therefore this power is not taken away from me by God's foreknowledge ; on the contrary, it belongs to me more surely."[2] Lastly, free as we are, " our dominant passion determines necessarily our action."[3]

This last declaration is to be understood in the light of what was said in the beginning about the relation between desire and knowledge. St. Augustine is but repeating a favourite thought of his, that we judge and are judged by our loves. " Give me a lover and he will understand what I am saying." Where our heart is, there is our treasure, and a secret love betrays itself in all that we do and think. This is the crowning thought of Augustinianism ; *pondus meum amor meus ;* and it is with this clue that we can trace out his theory of goodness and its relation to wisdom. There are two loves, avarice and charity ; there are two philosophies, knowledge (*scientia*) and wisdom ; and there are two cities, the city of this world and the city of God. Man is more than his body, more than his intellect ; he is a force of knowledge which is will or love. Consequently he is restless and in motion until he find peace, a peace of understanding and delectation. The aim of philosophy is not a dry inventory of the nature of being, but a consummation in an ideal life. Now this in the moral order is beatitude, and in the intellectual it is wisdom, and both are summed up in Charity.

In St. Augustine's vision of life, God dwells in his unchanging unity, but His perfection radiates out in an ever increasing multiplicity shot through by the forms of beauty and goodness and truth. His own favourite comparison is to music. Number and harmony inhabit and form the reality of the world of bodies, and man is a kind of high priest of nature. His soul is knit to a body and watches over it, and

[1] *De Civitate Dei*, XXII, xxx.   [2] *De Libero Arbitrio*, III, viii.
[3] *In Epist. ad Gal.* xlix.

by the senses he has contact with the external world. So it is that he hears within himself the concord of their numbers with truth, and is enabled, because absolute Truth sets the measure, to verify the unchanging in the passing sounds without and within. But just as the ideas and forms in things are, so to speak, drawn up into a higher order by man in his sensation and understanding, so ought man for his part to journey further within to find and take delight in the Truth hidden in the recesses of his memory. Looking in this direction, he attains peace and contemplates Truth and Beauty as they are in God. " O Thou Light, which Tobias saw, when, these eyes closed, he taught his son the way of life ; and himself went before with the feet of charity never swerving."[1]

For man, endowed as he is with liberty, there are two ways. He cannot help desiring happiness, for such is the *pondus*, the weight of his love. But he can seek personal satisfaction " avariciously " and go abroad and become distracted and dissipated in the multiplicity of sense objects ; or instead he can tend towards what is fair and complete and everlasting. By the first choice he degrades his soul, so far as that is possible, and his judgement is afflicted by his wrong desires. All St. Augustine's moral philosophy is governed by this consideration, and the *De Civitate Dei* works it out in the perspective of human society. " Of these two cities two loves go to the making ; the love of God it is which maketh Jerusalem, the love of the world that maketh Babylon." The one is founded on justice, and God's light and law are reflected in its peace and concord. Thereby it is most orderly and looks heavenward, as the eyes of the servant are fixed on their mistress. The other is founded on self-seeking (*cupiditas*) and looks downward. No actual state or society does more than figure these two loves. Imperial Rome is at most a type of the " world " which Christ condemned ; and

[1] *Confessions*, X, xxxiv, 52.

the Church, again, has to be expanded so as to contain all generations and all men of good will, before it can be said to do more than figure the City of God in St. Augustine's use of the phrase. In the society of living men the boundaries of the two cities overlap, even as the wheat and cockle grow together before the garnering.

The same cross-section is implied in his distinction between *scientia* and wisdom and the active and contemplative life in morals. For as " science too has its measure of good," wisdom must depend more on our attitude or apperception than on our field of study. If we love God we can do what we will, but we must be sure that our will does cleave to God in love. The thought of St. Augustine remains the same whether he is treating of morality or theory of truth. Moral principles are on the same level as the ideas which control the intellect and manifest themselves in the numbers of material objects. Justice, for example, is as universal and unchanging as a mathematical truth ; the only difference is that whereas the material world is intelligible in its harmonies for all, good or bad, for the moral norms one has to turn to the company of those who live an interior life and abide in justice. Therefore the wise are few compared to the multitudes of those who have knowledge of external nature. In both cases, however, the mind is illuminated and taught by the Master within. In morals the teaching reveals itself in conscience, and the lesson is the *lex æterna.* " This teaching is the very law of God, which remaineth fixed and unshaken in Him, and is, as it were, transcribed in the minds of the wise."[1] The Supreme Good, which is Happiness, is as the dayspring of man's moral acts, and his at first dim perception of it grows luminous in the laws which direct us unequivocally to its enjoyment.

All, therefore, that has been said of illumination applies equally to St. Augustine's moral theories. Moral laws are

[1] *De Ordine*, II, ii, 5.

the ideas, and these laws are articulated in the four cardinal virtues. The movement and unity of his thought are seen very clearly in the nineteenth Homily on St. John. " That in the soul which quickeneth the body is other than that whereby the soul itself is quickened. The soul, forsooth, is better than the body, but better far than the soul is God. Now the soul, be it foolish, unjust, and impious, remains still the life of the body. But because its own life is God, therefore just as its presence in the body yields to the body strength, beauty, swiftness and the due movements of its members, so the life of God in the soul yields wisdom, piety, justice and charity."[1] God, therefore, is the life and end of the soul, and the love of Him is the very law of our nature. For this reason love or will holds the primacy in all human activity, practical or contemplative, as can easily be shown. The intimacy of soul with body, for instance, has already been described in terms of a vital and loving attention which produces sensation. For knowledge, again, study is required, and study is an act of the will. *Partum mentis præcedit appetitus*, " desire precedes the offspring of thought." And, if this were not enough to show that knowledge as well as sensation involves the will, " what is there that the soul desires more than truth ? "[2] Now " can you believe that wisdom can be anything but the truth in which the Supreme Good is seen and possessed ? "[3] And God, Who is Truth, can He be other than the Supreme Good which all desire knowingly or unknowingly ? " The happy life is surely joy in the truth ; for this is a joying in Thee, Who art the Truth, O God, my Light, health of my countenance, my God."[4]

The claim, therefore, that " my weight is my love " is justified by every feeling and thought of man. The soul cannot but gravitate to God, drawn by the myriad imitations of the divine goodness all around it. " I sought what I might

---

[1] *In Johann. Tract.* XIX.   [2] *Ibid.*, XXVI.
[3] *De Libero Arbitrio*, II, ix.   [4] *Confessions*, X, xxii, 33.

love, in love with loving, and safety I hated, and a way without snares. For within me was a famine of that inward food, Thyself, my God."[1] And so it is that all ends as it begins in St. Augustine's philosophy. The love of God is wisdom and the journey's end is delectation. Love tends normally both to interior happiness and to the good of the beloved, and ends in equality which is the likeness of identity. In our love of God, however, there is no equality. Like the mind before unchanging truth, the will must make an entire surrender to love ; forsaking itself, the soul is possessed by God and starts afresh in charity. A new cycle begins now which belongs more to the story of grace than to philosophy. That we receive of the plenitude of Christ beyond our deserts, St. Augustine knows from the Christian teaching, but as a preparation for this good news a true philosophy had taught him the beginning of wisdom and the need of a generous will and a self-sacrificing love. As he tells us in his *Confessions*, he had suffered from a spiritual homesickness for many years, from the restlessness of a soul absent from God. Understanding came when he realized, in his own words, that God was his Truth and love his weight. " My weight is my love ; thereby am I borne, whithersoever I am borne. We are inflamed, by Thy Gift we are enkindled ; and are carried upwards ; we glow inwardly, and go forwards. We ascend *Thy ways that be in our heart* and sing a *song of degrees* ; we glow inwardly with Thy fire, with Thy good fire, and we go ; because we go upwards to the peace of Jerusalem."[2]

---

[1] *Confessions*, III, i.   [2] *Ibid.*, XIII, ix, 10.

JACQUES MARITAIN

ST. AUGUSTINE AND ST. THOMAS AQUINAS

TRANSLATED BY FR. LEONARD, C.M.

ST. AUGUSTINE AND ST. THOMAS AQUINAS

A bishop of the fourth-century, a schoolman of the thirteenth : not only are their periods, their interests, their intellectual surroundings, utterly different, but their actual vocations are quite unrelated. To compare St. Augustine with St. Thomas is not only a delicate and difficult, but a paradoxical, and, at first sight, an impossible task. The intellect is bound to abandon its most natural method of approach, which consists in juxtaposing upon one plane, contrasting in one light, and seeking coincidences and variations. It must move to another plane, and to a different light, and it is precisely in non-coincidence that it must discern unity. Concord and discord are equally valueless as criteria : each proceeds from the same optical error.

On the one hand, a comparison of Augustine's originality with that of Thomas is out of the question ; their intellectual attitudes, and, if Augustine be systematized, their systems, do not coincide. On the other hand, there is not only concord and harmony, but a fundamental unity, in their wisdom. How resolve the antinomy ? We should like, without entering into controversies on which specialists are divided, to indicate here our own principle of solution. " The heart has its order, and so has the mind, which is by way of principle and demonstration ; the heart's way is different. . . . Jesus Christ, St. Paul use the order of charity, and not of the mind, because they wish to inflame, not to instruct ; so too St. Augustine. This order chiefly consists in digressions on each point, which is referred to the end in order to show that it is still there."[1] Pascal's view needs ampler definition,

---

[1] Pascal, *Pensées*, 283.

but suggests the essential, a difference of order – from the formal point of view, a difference of *lumen*. Jesus Christ did not only wish to enkindle hearts, he meant to teach, but in the order and light of divine revelation itself; St. Paul, in the order and light of the *gift of prophecy* in its highest and holiest form ; each of them from too great a height to condescend to philosophize. St. Augustine, like them, employs the order of charity ; however copiously he may philosophize, it is in love that he instructs, and, by one and the same movement, practically directs the human being towards its last end. How so ? We shall explain in a moment.

St. Thomas employs the order of intelligence – setting it to work by means of love, and in order to exhale love, but carrying out its work in the pure atmosphere of objective demands (which seem cold only to those who do not love truth). It is in the order and light of *theological science*, and subsidiarily of *philosophy*, that he teaches : disciplines that proceed by the method of speculation, or of pure knowledge.

What, then, is the proper fount of Augustine's teaching ? We think it is on a more elevated plane – the wisdom of the Holy Ghost. We have said that he teaches in love. Why so, except that he teaches us in the order and light of the *gift of wisdom* ? This is the key for which we have been looking. That is the kind of wisdom which provides him with his special *point of view*, and from it his thought hastens forth to embrace all things and ceaselessly to lead them back to their centre.

When we say that the fountain-head of St. Augustine's teaching, which is on a lower plane than that of St. Paul's, and *a fortiori* than that of Christ's, is nevertheless situated on a higher plane than that of St. Thomas (which is imparted in human and rational fashion, and is much more perfect in that fashion), let it not be imagined for a moment that St. Thomas himself was wanting in this infused wisdom ; he abounded in it, as he did in all other mystical graces. He needed them, indeed, to carry out fittingly his work as a theologian ; but this work lay strictly within theology and philosophy as sciences, which are indeed of wisdom, yet which proceed in a human way, and hence, are techniques, inferior to infused wisdom. Offices and functions have their definite places in the Body of the Church ; the teaching function of St. Thomas, as universal as the discipline of theology, is not that of an Augustine, which is even still more universal, and above and beyond technique.

This would be the place to recall that the wisdom of the saints, which judges things divine by a sympathy or connaturality, *compassio sive connaturalitas*, and even in virtue of a union with God,[1] presupposes not only faith, but charity, that it is experimental, that it is not merely speculative but also practical, proceeding from union with God and guiding our activities towards that union, regulating human life according to divine rules ; and lastly, that it is capable of employing argument and discourse.[2]

Imagine such a wisdom, no longer ineffably concentrated on the endurance of divine things, as happens in mystical contemplation itself, but royally overflowing into a communicable knowledge : not in an attempt to express in lyrics, like St. John of the Cross, or, if I may venture to say so (without a play upon words), in oratory, like Bérulle, the

---

[1] Cf. John of St. Thomas (*Les Dons du Saint-Esprit*, tr. R. Maritain, Paris, 1930, Ch. I, II, IV) ; *Cursus Theol. in* I-II, q. lxx, disp. 18, aa. 1, 2, 4.

[2] John of St. Thomas teaches that the gifts of wisdom and knowledge, though not of themselves discursive, still " do not always proceed without discourse ; (i) because investigation and reasoning are natural to man, and the gifts of the Holy Ghost do not destroy but perfect nature ; (ii) because St. Thomas admits the possibility of discourse and comparison even in the case of Christ's infused knowledge (*Summa Theol.* III, q. 11, a. 5) ; (iii) because we do not usually experience in ourselves a light that enables us to understand truths without discourse or comparison " (*Cursus Theol., loc. cit.*, a. 5, u. 6 ; *Les Dons du Saint-Esprit*, p. 181).

Hence we are considering here, and in all our subsequent developments, not only acts (discursive in mode) produced by the gift of wisdom by itself, but also, especially, such acts produced by the gift of wisdom *making use of rational attainments and acquired knowledge.*

mystical experience itself ; spreading out over the whole
field of knowledge and completely controlling the play of
our rational energies, *employing* all the natural instruments
of knowledge, with that respect, that courtesy for nature
and reason, and also that confidence, ease, courage, and
sovereign loyalty which are the gifts of true spiritual
liberty : such is the wisdom of an Augustine, and of the
Fathers generally.

The common wisdom of the Christian, a wisdom doubly
instinctive and spontaneous – for the least instructed of the
faithful have also received the Holy Ghost and His gifts,
and in this light make use of their own natural reason
and good sense – takes on its noblest proportions, truly
paternal and episcopal, in the wisdom of those great spiritual
pastors ; the science of the theologian, not yet set apart as a
specialized discipline (that was the work of the scholastics),
is contained within it as in its source, and in an eminent
degree. (The age of technical studies had not yet begun, and
theology is the first great technique of the Christian world.)
This supreme wisdom conquers all, appropriates all, carries
all along in its universal current : the spoils of the Egyptians,
the riches of the philosophers ! Let us say, for the sake of
putting a definite line of demarcation, that the treasures here
in question are, not precisely those of theological, as distinguished from philosophical knowledge (which were not yet
made explicit in their own proper nature), but those of infused wisdom, of the wisdom of the Holy Ghost, which
dominates and envelops them, and which is linked up with
grace and charity.

Thus we may see the mission of the Fathers of the Church
in its fulness. " The Fathers and Theologians," this phrase
constantly recurring in treatises of sacred doctrine, designates two quite distinct offices. Theology is to be found in
theologians in its own specific nature of a specialized
science, the light of which is reason elevated by faith.

Theology is to be found in the Fathers implicit in a higher state, and its light is the very light of the gift of wisdom making use of reason, and proceeding, even as a doctrine, in the light of sanctifying grace. It is a *holy* doctrine. The Church will always have new Doctors. The age of the Fathers is definitely closed ; it was the age of a great pouring forth of the gifts of the Spirit, which were needed for the spiritual begetting and *education* of the Church ; what marks it above all is the purity of the waters of that impetuous flood of the Spirit, certainly far more than the finished polish of each of the stones detached from the old philosophical rock, which it bears along.

The philosophy which St. Augustine employs, one of the greatest religious philosophies of humanity, is incontestably deficient, forcibly torn away from the last defence and spiritual fructification of dying paganism : it is the philosophy of neo-Platonism. (He took what he found. And who can read Plotinus without being grateful ?) But, for Augustine, this philosophy is the instrument of the gift of wisdom ; and no one had a clearer perception than the Doctor of Grace himself of the superiority, the heavenly transcendence of that gift, and the divine mastery with which it handles the tools which it employs. What comes absolutely first, what illuminates, judges, commands, regulates, measures, what gives the right of jurisdiction over all things, *spiritualis judicat omnia*, what springs in the Christian's breast, like waters of Paradise, to fructify and renew the whole expanse of knowledge, is the gift of the Spirit in the might of love. A human instrument, certainly in no way mediocre but imperfect, blunted and risky, and, for its manipulation, a hand, the most perfect, fearful and pious, intelligent and understanding, strong, prudent, and wise, the irresistible light of the superhuman Spirit – such is the admirable paradox of the wisdom of the Christian Plato.

Should we perceive (who perceived it more clearly than

St. Thomas ?) the living *sense* of this wisdom, the goal to which such a spirit, employing such an instrument, is moving – it would be the pure universe of Christian truths, the eternal depths, there where theology takes its rise. If we consider such an instrument in any material fashion, separated from the spirit passing through it, we are at once engaged in an endless dispute, in a blind attempt to turn St. Augustine into a neo-Platonist, or in a mere literal search for discordances between him and St. Thomas.

The really remarkable feature here, and one that should be regarded as a stroke of genius, of Augustine's *holy genius*, is the certainty of instinct, the supernatural tact with which, whilst remaining a Platonist and in strict dependence on Plotinus in philosophy, he avoids (the same cannot be said of all his disciples) the most dangerous pitfalls of Platonism : at one moment magnificently setting his Greek masters right (as when he constructs the world of divine Ideas out of the Platonic exemplars), at another leaving unresolved those questions to which the Platonic method does not supply a key (as, for instance, many questions about the soul and its origin), and at yet another leaving unfinished, in a state of pathetic, because expectant, uncertainty, in a state at once of promise and of reserve, certain great doctrines (such as his doctrine of Illumination) which, with such a method, he could not bring to a higher point of precision without the risk of falling into grave error.

But what concerns us most, and what regards the central design of this short study, is not the Platonic instrument employed by Augustine, but his wisdom itself, so far as it is primarily a gift, utilizing reason and discourse. Such an approach enables us to understand how St. Augustine constantly philosophizes, and is yet in no way the inventor of a system of philosophy ; how it is that many obscurities still do not dim his light ; how he is installed above philosophy, even above theological science, in the strict sense of the word, and how he compasses the whole domain of theology, philosophy, and practical moral science. It is, we believe, in the closest harmony with the admirable doctrine on wisdom bequeathed to us by Augustine himself, which has passed in its entirety – with the requisite distinctness of statements and differentiations – into the Thomist system.

When he shows that science, as distinguished from wisdom (the supreme science), is the product of inferior reason and knowledge, in the twilight of created things, primarily directed to the labour of action, whilst wisdom is the product of higher reason and knowledge in the light of divine things, primarily directed towards the repose of contemplation, when he formulates the great law, which dominates all civilizations, of the inevitable choice between wisdom and science (for all the riches of the latter, good and necessary in themselves, are ordered to supply the needs of wisdom, so that to choose them as an end is the crime of avarice and covetousness, a deadly turning away to perishable goods) ; when he describes, in incomparable psychological analyses, the economy of science and wisdom in holy souls, it is clear that Augustine (certainly without excluding the distinction of the three wisdoms, metaphysical, moral, and infused, which St. Thomas was later to establish, though quite ignoring this distinction, because his sole idea was to oppose Christian wisdom to the false wisdom of the pagan philosophers) – it is clear that Augustine wholly centres his idea of wisdom on wisdom *par excellence* – infused wisdom. The flood of his thought, which derives from this wisdom, flows back to it and sweeps along all thought towards it. He sees sacred and profane science (so far as the aspect of science is to be found in sacred knowledge itself) participating in such wisdom, when subordinated to it, as they should be, in the Christian soul.

The essential difference between St. Augustine's teaching and St. Thomas's is a difference of perspective and point of view. With St. Thomas, it is theological wisdom in the strict sense of the word ; with St. Augustine, it is infused wisdom. With the former we explore essences ; with the latter we are drawn to an experience of Him whom we love. We have said that the wisdom of St. Augustine is the gift of wisdom utilizing the reasoning faculty. If we call to mind the special characteristics of the gift of wisdom, [1] as laid down by theologians, we shall understand St. Augustine's special point of view, and the idiosyncrasies of his teaching, without needing to refer to the marvellous attraction of his style, or the spontaneity transcending technique to which we just alluded, thanks to which the instinctive baptismal wisdom of the average Christian recognizes itself in him. We shall understand that, for him, true philosophy—we mean growth in wisdom—is the road to beatitude, and the true philosopher a friend of God, *verus philosophus amator Dei* ; [2] that, while he was perfectly well aware of the essential distinction between purely rational knowledge and conclusions drawn from principles of faith, he never dreamt of systematically distinguishing between the disciplines of philosophy and of theology : he did not draw up a plan of intellectual disciplines, but aided reason, enlightened by faith, on its way to the enjoyment of God. We shall understand how, while he had a finer sense of particular values and the dignity of speculation than any man, and rejected with his whole being (and, as a matter of fact, without even being able to conceive) what fifteen centuries later a desupernaturalized age was to know as philosophical pragmatism, this lover of the intellect was able to manipulate, with the utmost liberty, a sort of lived pragmatism – that of eternal salvation – and integrate in his wisdom the will's movement towards its last end – because infused wisdom proceeds from charity.

In Augustine's teaching faith universally precedes and prepares the intelligence. *Crede ut intelligas*. What is there to

---

[1] *Les Dons du Saint-Esprit*, IV.   [2] *De Civitate Dei*, VIII, i.

surprise us if the intelligence in question here is the knowledge of infused wisdom extended by the reasoning faculty to the whole humanly explorable field ? Such a knowledge presupposes theological faith as well as theological charity. It is absolutely essential for Augustine's wisdom to proceed from faith, because from the start it tends to experimental union with God. Furthermore, experience had taught Augustine that the sinner's wounded reason needs to be healed by *gratia sanans*, if it is actually to recover the soundness of its natural vigour, even in an order of truths accessible of themselves to the demonstrations of reason. And it is in our ordinary daily movement towards the first Truth that he wishes to guide and instruct us.

He repeats and enforces the lesson that the soul will only succeed in finding God by a return and progression *ad intus*, by a withdrawal from things and the senses in order to dispose itself for ascents in its own inmost self. For it is a question of meeting, in the depths of the heart, Him who abides there as in His temple, and in whom the heart can find rest, not indeed the God of philosophers and scholars, who may be attained without faith, nor even the God of theologians, who may be attained without charity, but the God of Saints, the life of our life offering Himself to us by grace and in love.

In this mystical experience of God, the soul also experiences, at the most hidden point of its sanctified activity, its own nature as spirit. This twofold experience, produced under the special inspiration of the Spirit of God and by means of His gifts, is, as it were, the supernatural completion of the movement of introversion proper to all spirits. That is the centre of gravity of all Augustine's doctrines concerning God and the soul. If we lose sight of this twofold experience, the full and inner meaning of his doctrines escapes us. They are under its sway from the very start, and it gives them, even when moving far from this centre, and in an atmosphere of itself natural, that indescribable note of something delightful, something experienced and lived, which is their characteristic : a far-off participation, hope, and promise of supreme joy. That is why metaphysical objects and their purely intellectual restraints, whose value Augustine takes care not to diminish or deny, whose efficacy he knows and reveres, far more than Pascal, only present themselves to him enveloped in the resonance of the soul's vibrations ; that is why the rational proof of the existence of God, without, in his case, ever ceasing to proceed *per ea quae facta sunt* and the way of causality, without ever implying that, *for us*, the evidence of God precedes that of things, still takes its point of depar‑ ture yet again from experience, and a natural one now – the inner experience of the unchangeable truths of reason which illuminate our restless minds. [1]

As for the soul's knowledge of itself, if, in the philosophical formulation of his thought on this head, and also in certain psychological theories connected with it (particularly the theory of sensation), Augustine obviously submits to Platonic forms difficult to defend, it still remains true that what he saw in the first place and infallibly, always as a more or less distant participation in, and reflection of, a divine experi‑ ence, is the nature and spiritual privileges of the human soul, whereby it is radically (but not for the state of union with the body) intelligible to itself by its substance, and is only aware of material objects by submerging them in its own special light. All St. Thomas had to do was to point out that the soul, in this life, knows itself only by acts, in order, here

[1] Hence the proof of the existence of God from the sensible world has with St. Augustine (from whom Pascal deviated widely on this point) its full value : " Behold heaven and earth have a being, and they cry out that they were made ; for they do change and vary . . . They also cry out that they did not make themselves . . . Now this voice of them that speak, is the evidence of the thing itself. Thou therefore, O Lord, who art beautiful, didst make them for they are beautiful ; who are good, for they are good ; who Art, for they also are, yet are they neither so beautiful, so good, nor are they in such wise as thou, their Creator, art ; in comparison with whom they are neither beautiful, nor good, nor are they at all." *Confessions*, XI, iv. Cf. *Sermones*, CXLI, ii, 2.

as elsewhere, to settle the matter definitely. Augustine, no doubt was forced to take too high a flight in order to make men's eyes see what lay around them : once the substance of his psychology is grasped it may easily take its place, in its entirety, as Father Gardeil has so admirably shown,[1] in the system of Aristotelian ideas, relived and, if I may so express it, *Augustinized* by the Angel of the Schools. Let us say that mystical wisdom is, in some sort, the activating agent, the catalytic element of Augustinian introspection, thanks to which the latter appears, in all the orders, as the most marvellous instrument for the discernment of spiritual things. Moreover, Augustine's psychology never abandons the concrete ; it is, perhaps, much more a moral science than a psychology, and proceeds in quite another way than the analytical psychology of St. Thomas.

In all these matters we are still in a domain quite apart from that of metaphysical knowledge : a domain which, if it were merely a psychology or practical knowledge, might be inferior to that of metaphysics, but which it would be utterly erroneous so to characterize ; a domain, in reality, transcending metaphysics, because it is, in fact, the royal domain of infused wisdom that is a prelude to vision, turning man back to the loving contemplation of the three uncreated Persons abiding in him by grace. One may say, then, with Windelband, that the doctrine of St. Augustine is a metaphysic of the inner life, or, with Gilson, that it is a metaphysic of conversion, provided one immediately adds that such a doctrine is not a metaphysic in the proper sense of the term. Windelband's phrase, and Gilson's too, are all the more illuminating inasmuch as one gets a better idea of the fundamental inappropriateness of the word " metaphysic," in such a connection.

It would then definitely seem that St. Augustine's doctrine

[1] Gardeil, *La Structure de l'Ame et L'Expérience Mystique*, Paris, 1927.

OA

is a religious doctrine in its essence, and even in its mode. He does not contemn, or diminish in the slightest degree, the scientific discovery of the nature of things (either in metaphysics or the experimental sciences) ; he is too great a friend of Plato's not to see the universe as a great family of essences, and at every moment touch on metaphysical concepts. But he touches them only obliquely and for ends of another order. If he examines the idea of *materia prima*, it is while making an act of thanksgiving. He does not even once place the object of his researches under the light peculiar to purely rational speculations. The metaphysical intuitions in which his teaching is so rich descend on us from a higher wisdom.

Finally, let us remember that such a wisdom contains within itself, inchoate and *eminenter*, the elements of separate, defined, theological and philosophical disciplines, and that, at a later period, these were disengaged by the schoolmen ; or, more precisely, and to come to closer grips, let us remember that such a wisdom contains a philosophy in a *virtually-eminent* manner, and a theology in a *formally-eminent* manner (because when the Fathers made use of a *lumen* higher than that of the simple theologian, as they were also something more than theologians, they wrought a real, true, and proper theological work) ; we see that St. Augustine's teaching differs from St. Thomas's, as we have explained, not only in its *point of view* and *habit* of knowledge ; it also differs from it in its *state*. In one there is a state of formation and specific actuation, the state of sciences and techniques constituted in their own proper orders. In the other, there is a state of transcendent fruitfulness, a state of a super-technical wisdom which envelops the sciences in question, eminently ; a state which, in relation to philosophical science and the scientific method of theology, is a state of virtuality. In any event to transfer the doctrine of St. Thomas with its peculiarly and exclusively Augustinian characteristics to the plane of philosophical systems, to make it one of their number, is *pro tanto* to deform it. Thus do we see creatures taken from great sea-depths fly into bits when they are exposed to an atmosphere and pressure in which terrestrial fauna may breathe freely.

It is just as well to point out here the ambiguity of the word *Augustinianism*, which, if taken to designate St. Augustine's thought, inevitably connotes, by its termination, the idea of a system. In this sense of the word, there is no paradox in maintaining that Augustine never professed *Augustinianism*. (And one might ask, which Augustinianism ? There have been as many different, and sometimes hostile, Augustinianisms as there have been Augustinian philosophers.)

One may see from the foregoing considerations what chiefly renders debatable the position of those philosophers to whom the history of philosophy has given the name of Augustinians. To speak plainly, such a position implies, on the part of philosophy, a remarkable ignorance of its own limitations : to ask St. Augustine for a system of philosophy is to demand for philosophy, and its peculiar light, what actually proceeds from the light of the highest Christian wisdom, of faith, and of charity. Hence philosophical Augustinianism seems to be naturally allied to an exaggerated philosophism, obvious in the Cartesian school, concealed in those of our contemporaries who despise " notional " knowledge only to overestimate the modes of apprehension that they substitute for it. Whatever veneration may be felt for St. Augustine, whatever old or new truths may be drawn from his treasure-house, whatever feeling for inner realities may be due to him, his very spirit and living thought are cruelly betrayed by such a course of action. The *Méditations touchant la Philosophie Première* resemble the *De Trinite* as much as a dark-room does the eye of a poet. Descartes's " courageous and attractive " spiritualism, the Cartesian *cogito* (which has quite another range than the *si fallor sum*), the ontological argument, the theory of idea-pictures, of thought-substance ; Malebranche's theophilosophy, onto-logism, occasionalism, the vision in God — far from being authentic forms of Augustinian spiritualism, these are merely the residues of its rational disaggregation.

An analogous process of *materialization* had already made itself felt in theology when Jansenius transmuted into the coarse texture of his own pessimism and theological hedonism the transparent, but difficult, letter of Augustine's teaching, his all too charming style, too divinely human when dealing with grace and liberty, Adam's innocence and fallen nature, the delectations of grace and the senses.[1] We are not unaware that a theological Augustinianism is possible, one that would not fall into the excesses of Jansenius or Luther, or those anti-Thomist disputants from whom Luther took his inspiration. But we do think that in such a case the rule which controls and keeps it in the path of truth is much more the Christian instinct of the theologian than the virtue of the principles of theological conceptualization taken in themselves.

As a matter of fact, medieval scholasticism vainly strove to extract from Augustine, only with weapons supplied by himself, a complete philosophical and theological systemati-zation. St. Bonaventure succeeded in recapturing Augustine's lofty inspiration, and a ray of his wisdom ; he failed to accomplish a scientific work (if he ever meant to do so.) Aristotle's weapons were needed, and so too was Thomas Aquinas. In St. Thomas's day, scholastic Augustinianism would seem to have reached and become caught in an *impasse* (and the attempts it made, after St. Thomas, to extricate itself, only rendered the state of affairs more obvious) ; it was clearly wanting in the means of establish-ing itself as a science, and consequently of making progress.

---

[1] Cf. Del Prado, *De Gratia et Libero Arbitrio* (Fribourg, 1907), I, *introductio*, pp. lxi-lxvi.

St. Thomas alone really succeeded in placing theological wisdom in its own proper and specific order, in making theology a science, whilst, at the same stroke, defining the domain of philosophy. He alone was able to extract from Augustine, but with Aristotle's and not Augustine's weapons, a science of theology and a science of Christian philosophy—for is it not by means of philosophical weapons that theology gradually establishes itself as a science? He alone was able to systematize, theologically and philosophically, the wisdom of Augustine, precisely because, while placing this wisdom in the purview of wisdoms less high but technically more perfect, and with an irreplaceable function in the economy of Christian intelligence, he had the courage to force it to submit to the conceptual re-differentiations needed to *change it within itself* on new planes of intelligibility.

It is only archaism, with its sterile zeal, that can be surprised that the natural progress of thought and culture was bound to bring about the arrival of philosophy and theology as special disciplines and, as it were, special techniques, which certainly are not separate, even if they are distinct; and the same thing was to happen at a later period to the natural sciences. Spiritual organisms grow in the same way as living bodies. It could not but happen that heterogeneous functions, vitally articulated amongst themselves, and corresponding to different objects specifying spiritual activity, should progressively be made more explicit in the course of history. The explicitation accomplished by St. Thomas Aquinas at the end of the Middle Ages was absolutely necessary.[1] Confronted with new provinces of knowledge, truths naturally accessible to

---

[1] *See* Père M.-D. Chenu's fine study, "*La Théologie comme Science au XIII*e *Siècle*," in *Archives d'histoire doctrinale et littéraire du Moyen Age*, II, pp. 37 *sq*. There is not, however, any "rationalism" in the work thus accomplished by St. Thomas : to recognize the value of reason or nature is not rationalism, or naturalism.

reason, and truths rationally separable from the principles of
faith, Christian reason was bound to arm itself with virtues
proportioned to the task of making discriminations and
acquiring knowledge. It was bound to be able to judge
demonstratively on that which is, in the pure light of intelligible objects and necessities ; that is to say, by a scientific
method. Theology, in the case of St. Augustine, by the very
fact that it was implicated in the discursive movement of a
superior wisdom which in itself was not discursive, was still
in its peculiar and human mode of science, in a state of
imperfection. With St. Thomas it was fully constituted in its
peculiar mode, which is the human mode of reason, and
attained its condition of human perfection. Put a scientist
before St. Augustine's doctrine and he is confronted with a
world of religious wisdom with which his own intelligible
universe cannot establish a living connection. If, as a believer,
he accepts this teaching, his thought is cut in twain. The
marvel of Thomist wisdom, of the metaphysic of being and
causes, of theology as a science, is that such knowledge, placed
at the topmost peak of human reason, conscious of its inferiority to infused wisdom, superior to all others, and distinguishing only to unite, establishes in the human soul,
without altering or diminishing by an iota, a rigorous
coherence and vital solidarity between such spiritual activities as touch the heavens and such as touch the earth.

It is related that, at Cologne, Master Albert advised his
great disciple always to follow Augustine in theology and
Aristotle in philosophy. Let us agree that this division is not
so much to be applied to the subjects dealt with as to their
formal aspects. So far as the aspect of *science* and the aspect
of *wisdom* are to be seen together in philosophy and theology,
we may say that Thomas Aquinas asked Aristotle for his
scientific equipment in order to deal with human and divine
matters, and received from Augustine, the other Fathers,
and Sacred Scripture, the substance of his wisdom. His

fidelity to the wisdom of Augustine is far more perfect than his mastery of Aristotle's technic. He corrected Aristotle ; he honoured Augustine as a son honours his father, and it is with filial piety that he offers him the support of his youthful strength in difficult passages (to be candid, there are plenty of them). Let us add that the more one shows the importance of St. Thomas's relation to Aristotle and Greek and Arab philosophy on the one hand, and to St. Augustine and the whole Christian tradition on the other, the more one will show, by the same stroke, the formidable originality of his genius.

Whether it is a question of the doctrine of beatitude or the Blessed Trinity, of the Eternal Law, of virtues and gifts, of contemplation,[1] evil, divine providence and foreknowledge, predestination, and, generally, the whole field of sacred theology, there is nothing more obvious than St. Thomas's perfect fidelity to St. Augustine in his theological synthesis. Everyone knows that the capital doctrine in which their agreement is most manifest is that of grace. We see, in St. Thomas, the coming to a perfect scientific formulation of the essential truths which affirm the distinction and union of the natural and supernatural orders, the sovereign liberty of creative love, the intrinsic reality and vital character within us of the infused gifts, which the wisdom of Augustine never ceased to assert against Pelagius, though in a language that had not yet found itself. When St. Thomas teaches the motion of free human will by grace and divine causality, in such a way that even the free mode of our voluntary acts is caused by God, and that all their goodness is derived both from God as first cause and from ourselves as second ; that we are a first (deficient) cause only for evil ; when he teaches us how liberty (in the sense of autonomy) is the work of the grace of the Holy Ghost, it is the very voice of Augustine, and of Paul, to which we are listening. It has rightly been

[1] Cf. Père F. Cayré's fine study, *La Contemplation Augustinienne*, Paris, 1927.

pointed out (and we are aware of the motive of the discrimi-
nation) that, in St. Augustine's " occasionally too literally
scriptural " theology,[1] the notion of nature has a much
more concrete and historical meaning than with St. Thomas.
" While the nature investigated by St. Thomas Aquinas is
a metaphysically indestructible essence, whose intrinsic
necessity resists even the corruption of original sin, abandoning to the latter only the graces of which it despoils the
former, and the powers which it diminishes or perverts,
Augustine describes under the name of nature the actual
state determined by sin, and what, in this state, authorizes
the hope that man may escape from it. There is no doubt
whatever in our mind that in the last analysis those two
attitudes are not dogmatically contradictory : St. Augustine
does not exclude St. Thomas in this centre of all Christian
philosophy, he rather makes ready for, and calls for, him ;
but in our opinion it cannot be maintained that the plan
of the two expositions is the same."[2] That, too, is our own
view. Still, it is well to add that the difference is purely
modal, that St. Augustine taught, as clearly as possible, the
ontological value of the distinction between nature and
grace,[3] that he clearly affirmed such a distinction, *even for
the state of innocence*[4] ; that, for him, grace is the root of
Adam's supernatural privileges as of his corporal immortality,
hence it is also supernatural[5] ; it is positively and intrinsically ordered to the Beatific Vision, which is not *due* to any
created intelligence, not even to the angelic[6] ; it is distinct
from nature, even in the case of the angels (*simul condens
naturam et largiens gratiam*).[7] Yet again, Thomist theology is

[1] Gardeil, *op. cit.*, p. xxx.

[2] Gilson, *Introduction à l'Étude de S. Augustin*, Paris, 1929, p. 298.

[3] *De Gratia et Libero Arbitrio*, xiii, 25 ; *De Prædestinatione Sanctorum*, v, 10 ;
Enarr. in Psalm., XLIX, ii.

[4] Garrigou-Lagrange, *Semaine Augustinienne* (Rome), April 24th, 1930.

[5] *De Correptione et Gratia*, xi, 29. " *Quid ergo ? Adam non habuit gratiam ? Immo
vero habuit magnam, sed disparem.*"

[6] *De Trinitate*, XIV, XV.   [7] *De Civitate Dei*, XII, ix.

here only making explicit in its own manner, and according to its own perspective, the substance of Augustinian thought.

But St. Thomas brought into his philosophical synthesis, and that in a far higher degree than is generally believed, if not the mode, at least the essential elements, of conceptualization.

It may be recognized, in that masterpiece of metaphysics —the Thomist doctrine of analogy and the divine names— defined, developed, and perfectly placed to produce the best effect ; for Augustine only Plotinizes here by manœuvring Plotinus in the direction of that " affirmative theology " demanded by revelation ; he does not merely teach that God is unchangeable, eternal, immense, infinitely simple, that He is all that He has,[1] Truth, Life, Beauty, Wisdom ; he knows that He is personal, conscious of Himself and of His own work,[2] *Deus non aliquid nesciens fecit*,[3] that he has done all things by his will, *causa omnium quae fecit voluntas ejus est*[4] and that He is being itself, *Ipsum esse subsistens*, as St. Thomas was to say : *Deum nihil aliud dicam esse, nisi idipsum esse.*[5] The Augustinian proof of the existence of God will be found equivalently in St. Thomas's *quarta via*[6] ; and he even seems occasionally to evoke it, under its own form,[7] although indeed, to be candid, we do not believe that its formulation would remain the same with St. Thomas (and that, no doubt, explains why, instead of developing this proof *ex*

---

[1] " *Quae habet haec et est, et ea omnia unus est* " (*De Civitate Dei*, XI, x). As Gilson rightly notes, this formula radically contains the medieval doctrine of the non-distinction, in God alone, of essence and existence. Cf. *De Trinitate*, XV, xiii, 22.

[2] Boyer, *L'Idée de Verité dans la philosophie de S. Augustin*, p. 108.

[3] *De Civitate Dei*, XI, x.   [4] *Enarr. in Psalm.*, cxxxiv, 10.

[5] *De Moribus Ecclesiae*, XIV, xxiv. Cf. *De Trinitate*, I, i, 2. " *Quae vero proprie de Deo dicuntur, quaeque in nulla creatura inveniuntur, raro ponit scriptura divina ; sicut illud quod dictum est ad Moysen : Ego sum qui sum, et, Qui est, misit me ad vos.*" Such texts as these, as also *De Trinitate*, IV, i, 2, and *Confessions*, XI, iv, 6 (see above, p. 208, n.), virtually contain the whole Thomist doctrine of the divine names and of analogy.

[6] Lagrange, *Dieu, son Existence et sa Nature*, fifth edition, p. 296.

[7] Especially this passage in the *Summa Contra Gentiles*, II, lxxxiv, whose importance Sestili rightly notes : *Veritates intellectae fundantur in aliquo aeterno. Fundantur enim in ipsa prima Veritate, sicut in causa universali contentivi omnis veritatis.*"

professo, he is satisfied with just alluding to it). Indeed, because of the very feature which constitutes, in the philosophical and noetic order, the chief difference between St. Augustine and St. Thomas – namely, as Father Gardeil has so well shown,[1] the substitution of the Aristotelico-Thomist dominant of *efficient causality* for the Augustinian dominant of *participation* – the eternal truths, whose value of ideal necessity and illuminating power Augustine indistinctly envisaged, caused him to move straight on to God, the first Truth and subsistent Light; whilst St. Thomas, in his search for their supreme reason in this same first Truth, and, thus, to conclude, from the truth in our own minds, to a first foundation in the order of reality, recognizing, as he did, in the active intellect (*intellectus agens*) the active light of our intelligence, was bound, as we think (if he wished to develop the Augustinian proof itself), to pass on from the created illuminating cause within us, and ascend to the First Cause in whose virtue the former participates.

Notwithstanding the fundamental difference of philosophical *sign*, of which we have just spoken, one is bound to say, in agreement with Père Boyer's fine study, that, by means of the general transposition and the manifold slight retouches consequently required, the whole substance of the Augustinian teaching on truth has passed into St. Thomas. Lastly, according to an idea, dear to our friend and colleague, M. Simeterre, it would even seem as if the Aristotelian construction of metaphysics and natural philosophy itself only found its completion in the Thomist synthesis thanks to an Augustinian corner-stone, I mean to say, thanks to the doctrine of Creative Ideas. For, it is in God Himself, in the Creative Ideas that enlighten the Angels before causing things, that the created world finds the supreme principle of its order

---

[1] Gardeil, *op. cit.*, II, Appendix ii. He here comments on and extends the scope of a thesis expounded in Gilson's *Pourquoi S. Thomas a critiqué S. Augustin.* Nevertheless, we think it would be well to do justice to Gilson's remarks (*op. cit.* p. 258, 3) especially in what concerns the notions of *creation* and *formation*.

and movement. Augustine not only set down the great outlines of a theory of creation, but his exemplarism supplies the conception of the world with a plenary consistency, a supreme metaphysical boldness, unknown to Aristotle's analytical cautiousness, and one which St. Thomas was to develop.

We have mentioned only a few characteristic traits. One should give an infinite number of examples, if one wished to point out all the Augustinian treasures assimilated by the thought of St. Thomas, and all the marks of veneration manifested by the Angelic Doctor — even in the minutest details[1] — for St. Augustine's authority. The more one studies both of those Doctors, the better is Father Gardeil's statement verified : " The positions on which they differ may be counted ; it is impossible to number those in which they agree. . . . The dumb ox . . . has devoured the whole spiritual substance of the eagle of Hippo . . . he has made it, as much as Aristotle, the very substance of his own mind."[2] If the *essential* values of Augustine's thought be considered in their integrity, it must be admitted, as we have already shown, that the sole metaphysical systematization of this thought which remains *essentially* Augustinian is the Thomist synthesis.

How foolish to oppose Thomism and Augustinianism as two systems (I mean the Augustinianism of St. Augustine himself) ! The first is a system, the second is not. Thomism is the scientific state of Christian wisdom; in the case of the Fathers and St. Augustine, Christian wisdom is still a mere spring. There is no opposition between the spring and the waters of the plain. It is not *à côté* of Thomist wisdom, and as if the spring had made the river overflow, that the unceasing flood of Augustinian inspiration reaches us in its purity. It presided over the formation of the Thomist

---

[1] It was on St. Augustine's authority alone that St. Thomas admitted that Moses had been raised by translation to the Beatific Vision. Cf. Lavaud, " *La Vision de Dieu ici-bas.*" *Revue Thomiste*, Jan.–Feb. 1929, pp. 75–83, May–June 1930, pp. 253–256.

[2] Gardeil, *op. cit.*, I, pp. xxix–xxx.

synthesis, passed into it, is bound to continue doing so, and urge it to fresh increases, because the doctrine of St. Thomas is bound to go on growing for ever. No doubt, tributaries from the source, after invisible meanderings, may spring up alongside the main stream : they are destined to increase its waters. No doubt, " Augustinian " systems will always continue to be elaborated in opposition to Thomism : to be candid, they will only bear witness to the sloth of Thomists, hindrances placed by them to the pursuit of that work of assimilation and universal elucidation so powerfully began by their master. Notwithstanding obstacles and delays, this work should normally go on. Those " Augustinian " philosophers who, despite the inconsistency of their systematic position, with some of Augustine's vigorous intuition, show forth the value of neglected truths or extend our knowledge of inner realities, will be unconsciously working for the philosophy of St. Thomas.

Augustine's inventive audacity, more disposed to take risks in the region of probability than St. Thomas's theological prudence, sought to obtain some understanding even of the mere succession of events in human history ; relying upon scripture, Augustine created the philosophy of history, let us put it more accurately (because the lights of faith are here necessary), the *wisdom of history* ; and the sentiment of irreversible historic becoming, of the world's movement and development in the sense of time is, in our opinion, one of the most precious jewels of our Augustinian inheritance. There is, we believe, a whole domain here, to be taken back from Hegel, and reclaimed for Christian wisdom. Will Thomist thought, stimulated by Augustine's spirit, some day enrich itself with those conjectures dealing with the exegesis of history, whose reflection upon culture can scarcely be ignored ? It would seem that the *Discours sur l'histoire universelle* should be rewritten, and that a modern continuation of *The City of God* would render much service.

At any rate, it is well to understand that the state of in-completeness in which we see the so-called Augustinianism in the course of its manifold attempts still remains is not of itself a promise of renewal and progress. Of itself, such incomplete-ness is rather a mark of imperfectibility. How can an organism, which does not succeed in establishing itself, grow ? It is precisely because Thomism has established itself as a science, with a well-defined systematic equipment, even though that too is unfinished (but in another sense), that it is capable of endless growth and progression. Far from telling us that everything has been done since St. Thomas, it says that as long as history shall last, and bring to light new problems, so long will more remain to be done than has yet been accomplished.

Let us recall what we already put forward regarding the wisdom of the Fathers and the wisdom of theologians. One might imagine that, by reason even of the height of its spiritual level, it was fitting that the Middle Ages should accomplish its millenary task under the primacy of the Fathers, and of St. Augustine in particular. Our age has a more re-stricted spiritual outflow, but more perfect instruments, more reliable means of verification and techniques. It has another task to accomplish. According to Leo XIII's pro-phetic intuition, it is fitting that Christian thought should put forth its effort under the still more direct primacy of the theologian *par excellence*.

Let men, if they will — definitions of names are free — call St. Augustine's wisdom *Christian philosophy*, and, more gener-ally, Christian wisdom, that is infused wisdom employing reason and discourse. Such a " philosophy," which essen-tially presupposes faith, charity, the gifts of the Holy Ghost, the whole supernatural order, is not the task of exploring the natures of things to which those who are usually called philosophers devote themselves, nor does it possess the means, once we rise above the spontaneous certainties of ordinary reason, of judging demonstratively, whilst assigning rational grounds for their existence, truths accessible of themselves to the unaided natural mental faculties. The peculiar philosophical instrument is not present. Once this instrument is begotten in the mind, it has its specifying object, which is the intelligibility of things, it has its own rules and light, which are those of natural reason and not of the infused gifts. If the names we employ are to correspond to realities, we should call *Christian philosophy* a philosophy properly so called, a wisdom defining itself as the perfect work of reason, *perfectum opus rationis*,[1] which will be found, in so far as the object is concerned, in harmony with revealed truths – and, as regards the subject, in vital connection with those supernatural energies whose philosophical *habitus* is distinct, but not separate, in the Christian soul. It is enough for such a philosophy to be true in its own order to find itself in harmony with revealed truths ; it will then form for itself, whilst manifesting " the rigour of its rational demands in all their integrity," and pursuing not a theological, but a purely and strictly philosophical, method, " a conception of nature and reason open to the supernatural,"[2] and confirmed by data, natural of themselves, and non-repugnant with data, of themselves, supernatural, which are contained in the deposit of revelation. But, because the human subject cannot, in fact, arrive at the whole body of the supreme truths naturally knowable if he be not aided from above, such a philosophy requires for its development, in the subject, in vital connection with faith, which, without entering into its texture or serving as a positive criterion, plays, in its

---

[1] St. Thomas, *Summa Theol.*, II–II, q. 45, a. 2.

[2] Chenu, *Bulletin Thomiste*, Jan. 1928, p. 244. By distinguishing what the notion of Christian philosophy implies *ex parte objecti* and *ex parte subjecti*, we think that Père Chenu's remarks may be reconciled with what is accurate in Gilson's observations (*op. cit.*, p. 302, i). As far as the order followed by St. Thomas is concerned, it is as a theologian and not as a Christian philosopher that the Saint follows the theological order. He had moreover an opportunity of following the philosophical order as a philosopher, and a Christian one at that, in his commentaries on Aristotle.

regard, the part of an extrinsic regulating principle, *veluti stella rectrix* ; and with theology, which, whilst employing it as an instrument, corroborates it ; and, lastly, with the wisdom of the Holy Ghost, who also supernaturally strengthens it in the Christian's soul. St. Augustine here reminds us of what Thomists, when they allow Thomism to decline, are tempted to forget : that Christian philosophy demands as conditions for its existence, to live and spiritualize itself in contact with the living faith and experiences of the Christian soul, to experience, in its own way, the anguish and peace of the work of redemption, and to be strengthened from on high by contemplation. St. Thomas reminds us of something that Augustinians seem from the start to forget : that Christian philosophy, in itself and in its intrinsic structure of rational knowledge, is rigorously independent of the subject's own dispositions, and wishes to be regulated only by objective necessities and intelligible constraints. What we have said of St. Augustine's wisdom, should be said also of the wisdom of the other Fathers, as has already been noted. If one wished to embark upon refinements, not without risk of presumption, it would perhaps be necessary to add that his special mark is to be found in the fact of his having an endowment of the *gift of science*[1] no less prodigious than of *the gift of wisdom*. From this special gift derives his privilege of such profound supernatural knowledge, not only of divine things, but of the human heart and of the complexities of the creature.

As to St. Thomas, it still remains to add that his fidelity, in nowise servile but filial, to the other Fathers of the Church, notably to the Greek Fathers, is no whit less than his fidelity to the greatest of the Latin Fathers.

---

[1] It is a matter here of mystical *science* which penetrates created things in a loving light due to connaturality with divine things by charity, and which corresponds to the blessed gift of tears. Cf. *Sum. Theol.* II–II, q. 9, and Jean of St. Thomas, *Les Dons du Saint Esprit*, trans. R. Maritain, ch. iv.

B. ROLAND-GOSSELIN

ST. AUGUSTINE'S SYSTEM
OF MORALS

TRANSLATED BY FR. LEONARD, C.M.

ST. AUGUSTINE'S SYSTEM OF MORALS

Has the twentieth century, which dreams of renewing the face of the earth, anything to learn from the past, and, in particular, from a great theologian who preached the Gospel fifteen hundred years ago in a remote corner of Africa ? No one of course thinks of contesting St. Augustine's exceptional gifts and the deep and wide influence which his genius exercised over the West ; his memory is honoured as that of a great servant of humanity. But can words of life be heard coming from a tomb for ever sealed ?

If it is true that the most spiritual human work is liable to decay at the point where it is touched by time, yet the breath of eternity, which gave it life and brought it into being, still endures.

Augustine, who was a past master in things of the mind, had a passionate love of truth, and served it with all his might. The point to be most admired in him is his persevering courage before the enigmas of nature and life : " What am I ? What is the universe ? What is God ? "

He was brought up in the Christian religion, but abandoned it in his impatience to shake off all that might hinder the free play of thought and action. He wanted to experience for himself the value of creatures and ideas, and gave himself up without reserve to sensual pleasures and intellectual curiosity. He was dazzled by the world and made drunk by success ; but he still remained discontented and felt an inextinguishable thirst in the bottom of his soul. In vain did he ask of reason and love a certitude he could cling to and a happiness he could enjoy.

At length he heard the divine call, but not the faint and

228 A MONUMENT TO ST. AUGUSTINE

far-off echo perceived by philosophers. He heard the voice of the living God of the Gospels. To all his doubts and agony it replied : " I am the Way, the Truth, and the Life." " Oh, Lord," he wrote in his *Confessions*, " Thou didst knock at my heart with Thy word, and I have loved Thee."[1] His whole moral system is contained in that sentence : " Lord, I have loved Thee."

(i)

Augustine did not believe that he was bound to repudiate his philosophical culture because he had recovered his faith, nor was he afraid to acknowledge the part played by Plato and Cicero in his return to Christ. He never showed himself ungrateful to his great educators, but took from them all that he could to strengthen the motives of his belief.

Moreover, his merits soon raised him to the highest rank amongst the Doctors of the Church. He had to confront opponents formidable by their talents and science, who tested his faith in the crucible of their criticism ; and in order to combat them effectively he never hesitated to meet them on their own ground, convinced as he was that as God is the author of reason as well as of faith, faith and reason can never contradict each other.

Hence his preoccupation to establish the natural foundations of morality, and to prove that Christ's message, far from being an unjust intrusion on man's conscience, supplied a decisive answer to the deepest aspirations of his nature.

What is the Gospel in reality ? The secret of happiness as revealed by God. Jesus, in the Sermon on the Mount, promises perfect happiness to all those who will follow Him in His progress towards the Father.

But does not reason in its own fashion tell us that God alone can satisfy the desires of the soul ?

[1] *Confessions*, X, vi.

No one has ever spoken of the soul like Augustine. If he experienced transports of joy and admiration at the sight of the riches, order, and beauty of the universe – that sublime poem to the glory of its Creator – he remained confounded before the human soul, which contains all worlds within itself. He was attracted, captivated, and held by that unfathomable abyss wherein the Blessed Trinity is mirrored.

And when he descends into its depths, he gives us, for a moment, a sensation of giddiness, so powerful is his intuition that God is to be found there, so strong is his desire to touch Him and help us to touch Him also.

Hence his contempt for Epicurus. How could a man calling himself a philosopher so misunderstand the soul, its greatness and dominion over nature, as to make it the body's slave? How could he maintain that happiness is the result of the play of sensual appetites, that the will is the sovereign good?

Experience, in the first place, shows that enjoyment does not bring happiness. The senses are never satisfied with what is allowed them. They always demand more, become irritated, and ultimately bring nothing but disgust and satiety. Augustine, unfortunately, was but too well aware of the fact; he had been only too faithful an Epicurean and had drained each cup of pleasure. He had sunk down into the most shameful bondage. " Wretched young man that I was ! From my earliest years, O my God, I had asked for chastity, but not yet awhile. I feared to be heard too quickly, to be cured too rapidly of this malady of concupiscence, which I preferred to see quieted rather than extinguished." Hence his struggles to overcome vice : " I was held back by these silly trifles, these foolish vanities, my ancient friends. They plucked me by the garment of the flesh and softly whispered to me ' Art thou about to leave us ? From this moment shall we no more be with thee for ever ? From this moment shalt thou no more be permitted to do this or that for ever ? '

And what things did they suggest to me under what I call
this or that – what things did they suggest, O my God ! . . .
What filth, what shameful things did they suggest ! . . . the
tyrannous voice of evil habit adding, ' Dost thou think that
thou canst live without these things ? ' " [1]

But it was not experience alone which condemned such
Epicurean materialism. It was clear to the eye of reason
that the body is not for the soul, but the soul for the body.
All the finest properties of the body, its activity, swiftness,
beauty, capacity for feeling, do not proceed from itself but
from life. And what gives it life but the soul ? The soul, then,
is the higher part of man, the source of all his qualities
and sentiments, the original centre of his well-being and
happiness.

But everything has not been said when Epicurus has been
refuted. For even if it is admitted that the soul is the principle
of the body's perfection it has not, for all that, been proved
that it is, of itself, capable of attaining happiness.

At this point we reach a delicate problem, which was
Augustine's main preoccupation during his sacerdotal and
episcopal life. It is easy to criticize Epicurean morality, for
it suffices to appeal to good sense and natural uprightness
to establish the spirit's primacy over the flesh ; but it is not
quite so clear that the soul itself can find happiness in the
exercise of reason and the practice of virtue.

The Stoics, as is well known, were the adversaries of the
Epicureans, and exalted the human will to such a pitch as
to turn it into a divine power. Their moral system consisted
essentially in the cult of virtue for virtue's sake : the disciple
of Zeno shut himself up in his own wisdom as in an impreg-
nable tower ; impervious to sorrow and weakness, he defied
fortune, despised riches, disdained honour and glory ; he
was without love or hate, but kind and just to all men ;
master of himself and of the universe, because he obeyed

---

[1] *Confessions*, VIII, vii, xi.

without demur the laws of nature, he declared that he was actually happy in the midst of sufferings and adversity.

This philosophical discipline had grown milder in the course of time, and became, under the Roman Empire, the religion of the cultured classes. Augustine heard echoes of it in the schools which he frequented, and learnt how to utilize it, even while fighting it to the death. It might serve against Epicurus, but at the same time it contained a poison deadly to Christianity, which it almost succeeded in infecting, in Augustine's own day, through the doctrines of the monk Pelagius.

There was, of course, no need to hesitate about taking sides with the Stoics when they affirmed the exceptional value of virtue and wished to separate it from pleasure and interest. But the question in dispute was : Can virtue make man perfectly happy? Augustine had no difficulty in showing that the wisdom of the Stoics is inhuman through being superhuman. The state of insensibility and apathy at which it aimed as man's supreme happiness is contrary to nature. Desire and fear, joy and sorrow, do not belong exclusively to the body, but have their roots deep down in the soul, which would destroy itself if it annihilated them.

So true is this, that the Stoic philosopher never existed save as an imaginary being. There is, in point of fact, no virtue capable of conquering and suppressing sensibility ; the perfectly just suffer as much, and often more, than other men – to such an extent, indeed, as to constitute a scandal for the impious, who take occasion of the fact to charge God with injustice.

Virtue, then, does not make the wise man perfectly happy ; and Augustine tells us the reason. Happiness implies the complete and permanent satisfaction of the whole man, body and soul ; a partial and limited happiness is not happiness, in the first place because it does not satisfy us absolutely, and next because the thought of its fleetingness makes us sad.

That, says Augustine, is the reason of our natural desire for immortality, which is the indispensable condition of happiness. Moreover, how can the human soul find complete satisfaction within itself, since its perpetual need of felicity is an evident proof of its wretchedness and instability? All is in vain ; neither knowledge nor virtue has power to extract from the soul what does not exist there.

It may be urged : If neither the goods of the body nor those of the soul are capable of fully satisfying our natural desire for happiness, then such a desire is vain. Augustine would not admit this, because in his eyes the order and finality of the universe were of such a nature as to constitute an irresistible argument for the intellect ; hence a universal natural tendency incapable of attaining its end would be a monstrosity.

Therefore, as man cannot find what will appease his desire for happiness either in himself or external objects, he should turn towards a higher, perfect, and eternal Good, which alone is capable of giving him complete and eternal happiness. In this fashion, then, does our love, when it does not suffer itself to be seduced by carnal pleasures with the Epicureans, or by the pride of virtue with the Stoics, lead us on to God. " This is eternal life," says the Gospel of St. John, " to know Thee, the one true God."

We desire to live, and to live happily : but we have two lives, one of the body and one of the soul ; and, as the soul is the life of the body, so is God the life of the soul.

" Too late have I loved Thee," cries Augustine, " O Beauty ever ancient and ever new ! Too late have I loved Thee ! And behold Thou wast within and I was abroad, and there I sought Thee ; losing my own beauty I ran after those beauties which Thou hast made. Thou wast with me and I was not with Thee ; those things kept me far from Thee, which could have no being but in Thee. Thou hast called, Thou hast cried out, and hast pierced my deafness.

Thou hast lightened, Thou hast shone forth, and hast dis-
pelled my blindness. Thou hast exhaled the fragrance of
Thy perfumes and I drew breath and panted after Thee. I
have tasted Thee and am hungry for Thee ; Thou hast
touched me and I am all inflamed with the desire of Thy
embraces. When I shall adhere to Thee with my whole self,
then shall I nowhere meet with sorrow or labour, and my
life will be fully alive when quite filled with Thee. . . . Thou
hast made us for Thyself and our heart is restless till it rest
in Thee."[1]

(ii)

When Augustine has shown that our nature tends naturally
to God he goes on to prove that we are morally obliged to
love Him. We are free : we can see quite clearly where our
happiness lies, and yet we voluntarily choose something else.
All morality reposes on liberty : morality is, properly speaking, the science of liberty ; Augustine wrote a book on free-
will to demonstrate this truth. On the other hand, we do not
think of a moral system without sanctions and obligations.
How then transform the proposition : " We tend naturally
to God " into : " We are bound to tend voluntarily to
God " ?

It is at this point that Augustine's superiority over the
greatest Greek philosophers is most obvious. Plato and
Plotinus, his former masters, also say that the human soul
desires God, that in Him alone does it find its just equilibrium
and perfect joy. God seems to them to be the sovereignly
desirable good, and the man who would turn away from
God, and allow himself to be taken captive by the attractions
of the sensible world, is utterly foolish. But one would seek in
vain amongst these thinkers for a metaphysical notion of a
real moral obligation, man's strict duty to accomplish his

[1] *Confessions*, X, xxvii ; I, i.

destiny along the lines indicated by his nature. Nature can only express a wish, an optative ; it can never utter an imperative.

No doubt a belief in divine laws and sanctions is to be found everywhere throughout Greek literature, in poets and tragic dramatists who mirror the soul of the people, and especially in their religious myths, which Plato utilized through lack of dialectical arguments. But philosophy called a halt when faced with the problem of moral obliga- tion and responsibility. Hence it always more or less iden- tified morality with justice, with the natural and positive law : it did, indeed, distinguish the one from the other, but it did not succeed in effectively establishing the concept of duty in the inner conscience.

The reason of this is that the ancients never made for themselves an exact representation of God. The idea of creation, so familiar to us, always remained perfectly strange to them ; matter, in their eyes, doubtless drew from God its motion, form, and order, but it had, like God, an inde- pendent and eternal existence. Hence there could be no question of God's absolute power over nature, or of an infinite, legislative will for men and society. Now it is this very notion of God as creator and lawgiver which is the most marked feature in the Bible ; thanks to this fact, Augustine was able to supply an unshakable foundation for those Platonist speculations which agreed so admirably with Christian dogmas. In the Old Testament God is revealed to us as the Absolute Being who made out of nothing the heavens and the earth and all that they contain ; He made man in His own image and likeness, and at once imposed a law on him in the Garden of Paradise ; later on He dictated His commands to the Patriarchs ; and finally He promul- gated the Decalogue on Mount Sinai. In the Gospels, the Son of God brings a new message, which again contains precepts coming from God. And all those laws are true laws, which bind men's consciences and are accompanied by sanctions.

What is the content of those laws, Augustine asks himself? And the answer is easy, being supplied by the Gospel : Jesus declares that the whole Law and the Prophets are summed up in the two commandments of the love of God and one's neighbour. Hence – and this point Augustine develops at length – the Decalogue and the Gospel are only a development and explanation of this universal decree, Do not do to others what you would not wish to be done to you ; do to others what you would wish them to do to you – or, more briefly, Give to each his due, to God, to self, to others ; and do this for the love of God.

The Old and the New Testaments thus agree with sound philosophy in directing man towards God. But whereas in the Bible the return to God is put before us as our good, and at the same time laid on us as a duty, we find that Plato, for instance, merely suggests it and cannot impose it.

Augustine, however, does not think for a moment that conscience places God before us as a desirable end without showing us, at the same time, that it is morally obligatory. Our reason, left to itself, does, in point of fact, judge that our end is to go to God, and also that this very end is willed by Him. This will of God, and this natural law which every man bears about within him, is known in the following manner.

When I look into my soul, I perceive two worlds, one which is my own self, my thoughts, memories, desires, tastes, temperament – all that goes to make up my personality – and another, made up of impersonal and universal truths, common to, and independent of, you and me. For instance, when I think of *Carthage* I evoke impressions that belong only to me, that live only in me, and that will disappear with me. I can share them with you, but I cannot make you know and feel them as they are in myself. On the other hand, take a mathematical proposition such as *Seven and three are ten.* I see that, of course, in myself; but still it is, in a way, foreign to me, in the sense that it has no need of me for its existence, and is to be found in the same fashion in all minds, in yours as well as in mine; nor is it tied, as we are, to space and time. Thus I see, and we all see, that seven and three are ten to-day, yesterday, the day before yesterday, always ; and you and I see that seven and three will be ten to-morrow, the day after, and always. Now just as we all necessarily see such theoretical truths, so also do we see certain practical ones : that life should be preferred to death, the soul to the body, strength to weakness, beauty to ugliness, happiness to unhappiness, eternity to time, and good to evil. There is, then, in man's mind a system of theoretical and practical principles which control his intellect and will, and which he may misunderstand but not suppress. Whence come those principles, those eternal reasons, as Augustine calls them ? Certainly not from ourselves, who are changeable, limited by life and death, and above all powerless against those truths by which we are dominated. They are therefore superior to us.

We are thus forced to recognize the existence of an immovable, rational, and moral order above ourselves, which logically and morally constrains us. But this rational order and this moral order are not mere abstract concepts, for abstractions have no hold on concrete living beings. We are, therefore, led to recognize the existence of an eternal Intellect and Will, the source and rule of all our theoretical and practical judgments, which imprints truth on our consciences like a seal on wax. In this way our idea of God is rendered more definite. Our desire for happiness leads us to God as sovereign Happiness. The law of truth, which rules our intellect and will from within, obliges us to recognize in God the Light that guides, and the Justice that commands us. God has created us for Himself; He cannot not wish that we should go to the confines of our nature, that is to say to Himself. Reason thus discovers in its own depths both the matter and form of morality, as they are taught in the Sacred Scriptures. If God thought fit to promulgate externally what we possess internally it was because the moral sense of the human race had been more or less obliterated by the corruption of sin.

To sum up : the ultimate basis of the moral law is the eternal law, which is nothing else than the divine reason or will issuing its commands to respect the natural order and forbidding it to be disturbed on pain of punishment.

We now see how Augustine's system of morality takes account of all the requirements of our nature. This many moralists omit to do. Some identify morality with the science of self-interest and happiness, entirely forgetting its sacred and disinterested character. Others identify it with the science of duty, forgetting that man cannot mutilate his nature, which is made for happiness. Augustine does not think that duty should be ultimately opposed to happiness. The law, in point of fact, no more exists for its own sake than a road leading from one place to another. Duty is unintelligible if it is a pure obligation, a categorical imperative leading nowhere. In other words, a precept has no justification other than the realization of an end, and that a good and happy one. God is not an autocrat who governs, like a tyrant, by caprice or whim. He wills only one thing : that we should realize the order imprinted on the very foundations of our nature, which is created in His image and likeness. On the other hand, Augustine did not admit that morality should be assimilated to the pure and simple search after one's own interest. For if the moral law finally tends to realize our nature and happiness, it still imposes on us a choice of means that proves costly in this present life, the chief means of all being a humble submission to the will of God. The moral act is, therefore, a mixture of spontaneity

238 A MONUMENT TO ST. AUGUSTINE

and constraint, disinterestedness and higher interest, as
Augustine admirably perceived. His morality is a morality
neither of happiness nor of duty, but a morality, if one may
say so, of God ; it sets out to leads us, by the sole act of love, to
God, the supreme Order and supreme source of Happiness.

We have now a clearer grasp of what Augustine meant by
the love of God, which has nothing in common with a vague
sentiment of the divine, or a more or less sensuous sympathy
with nature and humanity that springs rather from instinct
than right reason. In his eyes God is the first Truth, first
Justice, Beauty, and Goodness. To love God is to love truth,
justice, beauty, and goodness. Now what are truth, justice,
beauty, and goodness, but different expressions of measure,
proportion, and order ? The best way, then, to represent
God is to look on Him as Absolute Order ; to love God is,
ultimately, to love order – hence Augustine's definition of
virtue as the order of love.

Our conscience tells us of the order of love : God, the soul,
the body. The love of God consists in the submission of our
senses to reason and of our reason to God : this law we are
bound to establish in ourselves, in society, and wherever our
will has power to act. The universal command to render to
everyone what is his due has no other meaning, for God is
worth more than the soul, and the soul is worth more than
the body. Augustine did not doubt that reason's submission
to God takes precedence of the senses' submission to reason :
in the first place, the worship of God is the chief virtue and
the source of all others ; secondly, reason does not command
the senses properly unless it is first submitted to God. Hence,
in Augustine's eyes, a morality without religion is essentially
immoral, and purely human virtues, which take no account
of God and are devoid of his love, though they may have
a certain value for temporal society, remain without any
effective worth for the Kingdom of God.

" Woe be to those who hide away from Thy guidance, O

Divine Wisdom, sweet light of the purified soul ! Woe be to those who wander away from Thy paths, who love Thy footprints rather than Thyself, who forget what Thou wouldst have them hear ! Like listeners who retain nothing of a discourse but the harmony of its words, who take no thought of the ideas of which they are but the symbol, they turn their backs on Thee and shut themselves up in darkness. The elements of happiness which they still find in their works of the flesh they owe to the radiance of Thy light, but the darkness they love weakens their eyes and renders them incapable of supporting Thy sight. The night of sin gradually enfolds their conscience. Through no longer regarding as an evil what flatters and enchains them, they at last cease to be willing to recognize either the True or the Good."[1]

(iii)

Since the vital act of morality consists in loving God, in uniting our will with His, the question now arises, How can we unite our will with the will of God ? Here we enter the very heart of the Christian religion ; here is the great mystery that was hidden from the Greek philosophers and even from Plato. Augustine, in order to set it forth, now bids a definite farewell to the Academy and seeks his inspiration in the Scriptures, especially in the teachings of St. Paul and St. John.

As we are made for God, the law of our being is to love Him. But God is not what some philosophers imagine Him to be, an idea to be assimilated, a virtue to be acquired, a rule to be imposed, a harmony to be attained. The God of the Christians is a loving, personal God, the greatest of all personalities, whose liberty cannot be encroached on, whose goodwill cannot be won. We cannot even have an effective will to love Him if He does not first come, by His grace, to

[1] *De Libero Arbitrio*, II, xvi, 43.

arouse our love, to strengthen it, increase it, and raise it to Himself. St. Augustine never loses sight of the fact that, despite the undoubted affinity between God and man, the relation of man to God is a relation of the creature to its Creator, of a finite to an Infinite Being. However urgent the call of the infinite nature to the heart of the finite, there exists an abyss between them which the latter is incapable of transcending without the loving help of the former.

God granted this grace to our first parents, and from Him they received a good will capable of loving Him. But, as the bad angels, at the instigation of their leader Satan, had done already, our first parents preferred to love themselves by wishing to live, not according to the law of God, but according to a law of their own, thereby establishing themselves at the same time in pride and falsehood. A being, created to do the will of God rather than its own, that does not live according to the law of its creation is a lie. What can be more false than a will seeking happiness through a life not according to the manner of its being? And, if pride is the perverse appetite of greatness, what can be more proud than to desert, of one's own accord, the principle to which the soul is bound to adhere, that it may become, and be, in some sort, its own principle, by complacency in itself? What, in the case of a spiritual creature, really constitutes the evil will, or sin, is for it to take delight in itself, as if it were the light, and to turn away from that Light which, if It were loved, would really transform the creature into light.

When, with Augustine, we consider the drama of sin in the history of the world and the human race, we are far removed from cold, grey, philosophical analyses. He fully understood the part played by mysticism in the life of men and nations, and his genius enabled him to draw magnificently on the Scriptures, which give such tragic meaning to human existence. Who does not know that moving sketch of his masterpiece, *The City of God*, in which his whole philosophy of history is condensed ? " Two loves have built two Cities : the love of self, which reaches even to contempt for God, the earthly City ; and the love of God, which reaches even to contempt for self, the heavenly City. One glories in itself, the other in the Lord. One seeks its own glory amongst men ; the greatest glory of the other is God, witness of its conscience. One, swollen with pride, uplifts its haughty head ; the other cries out to God with the Psalmist : ' Thou art my glory, it is Thou who dost lift up my head.' "[1]

These two loves, one of which is pure, the other impure, one of which is founded on egoism, the other on charity, divide the spiritual world into two societies : the society of good and the society of evil. The first is predestined to reign with God for all eternity, the second to undergo eternal punishment with the Evil One.

Augustine does not fail to assign a very important place to society in his moral and religious conception of the universe. No doubt the individual soul of every man is definitely the sole substantial value in humanity. But there is such human solidarity in good and evil, such an interchange of ideas, sentiments, and influences, that it is impossible not to consider each man as forming part of a social whole that transcends the individual. Here, indeed, he follows Christian tradition, and, more especially, St. Paul's profound conception of the mystical body of Christ.

The City of God, then, is at war with the City of the Devil to the end of time. Its King is the Son of God, the Eternal Word, Uncreated Wisdom. Since the fall of the angels and of the first man He is building up His City out of all souls of good will. He enlightened the Patriarchs, gave the Law to Moses, guided the chosen people to the Promised Land. But He has done much more. In order to snatch men effectively from the power of Satan, from the power of pride,

[1] *De Civitate Dei*, XIV, xxviii.

QA

which raised up a wall of brass between God and the human
race, " the Word was made flesh and dwelt amongst us."
In Him mankind was reconciled with God ; and He sealed
the eternal alliance of heaven and earth in His blood. The
human race, which had been kept apart from heavenly
justice by earthly injustice, needed a justice that would take
account both of time and eternity, that would unite by an
unbreakable bond the Supreme Riches with human misery.
Hence Christ is called the Mediator. Man-and-God between
God and man, He has given back God to man and man to
God, and has by His Incarnation and Redemption merited
for men a divine adoption. The Son of God, by taking the
form of a slave and humbling Himself even to the death of
the Cross, not only caused a fount of living waters to gush
forth for all eternity, but taught the world how to obey and
love.

Love : such is the message of Him who came not to destroy, but to fulfil, the Law. The Divine Physician bent over
the despoiled human race, which lay stretched in its sickness from East to West. He took it by the hand and mur-
mured mysterious words in its ear : " I am the Way, the
Truth, and the Life. No one cometh to the Father save by
Me." With what delicate forethought did the Good Samari-
tan take possession of the grief-stricken soul ! What balm
did He not pour over its wounds ! How He helped it to
awake, teaching it to love what slumbered in its own deepest
depths ! Regenerated by His Holy Spirit, embraced by His
charity, it no longer desires anything but to attach itself to
the good, has no other hope than to participate in the truth,
no other joy than to owe its happiness to Him who gave it
being.

The grace of Christ, far from supplanting or destroying
nature, repairs and sets it to work ; it restores to man God's
justice, and His image which was lessened and deformed
by sin. It brings him good things in abundance : " I will be

their God and they shall be My people." Is there any greater or more perfect felicity than to live by God " the fountain of life," in whose light " we shall see light."[1]

This is the life promised by Jesus to His friends : " He that hath My commandments and keepeth them ; he it is that loveth Me. And he that loveth Me shall be loved of My Father ; and I will love him, and will manifest myself to Him."[2] And again : " Dearly beloved, we are now the sons of God, and it hath not yet appeared what we shall be. We know that when He shall appear we shall be like to Him, because we shall see Him as He is."[3]

The life of grace is, then, says Augustine, the universal way of justification which alone leads to a free, peaceable, and immortal City. The Kingdom of God, which, in the course of its foundation, was the appanage of the Jewish race, is, now that it has been established, the birthright of all nations. It is God's Church, the mystical body of Christ, the temple of the Holy Ghost, which has received the mission of spreading through space and time the good tidings of salvation and redeeming grace. It is the incarnation of the City of God, and gathers together, one by one, predestined souls, bearing them to the throne of God.

In the course of her earthly pilgrimage the Church appeals to all men without exception, taking no account of diversity of manners, laws, and institutions, which, provided they be not opposed to her divine apostolate, she neither outrages nor destroys — rather does she observe them and conform herself to them. She desires and promotes the harmony of all peoples, temporal order being, for her, a prelude to the eternal. But though she labours for unity of faith and the brotherhood of souls, in which, as St. Paul says, every distinction of sex, social condition, and nationality is effaced, she knows that perfect communion of minds and wills is realized only in Heaven. As she forms part of human society,

---

[1] *Psalm* xxxv, 10.   [2] *John*, xiv, 21.   [3] *I John*, iii, 2.

she respects its organization, as it has been established by God, the author and master of nature and grace.

We may note here, once again, how he knows how to harmonize the Gospel with reason. In every age there are minds – some generous if not clear-sighted, others erratic – which set out to interpret the Gospel literally and use it as a leaven of rebellion and anarchy. Under the pretext of universal liberty and charity – the law of Christ is liberty and charity – they condemn, in the name of Jesus, all social hierarchies, the organization of justice and coercive power, private property, force, even when placed at the service of right, and the state itself. The most remarkable representative of such dangerous exegesis in our own times was Tolstoy, one of the fathers of the Russian Revolution.

St. Paul had, even in his days, to warn some Christian communities who wished to shake off the yoke of obedience to the laws of the Empire. Augustine, in the fifth century, had to deal with sectaries who were the heirs of this intellectual anarchy, which seemed to him to be all the more dangerous for its attempt to prove that Christian morality was incompatible with the normal life of the state. Hence he set out to prove that charity, rightly understood, not only is not opposed to the legitimate demands of politics, but is also the firmest support of society.

Men object, he says, that the teaching of Jesus is not adaptable to social order. Not to resist evil, to turn the right cheek after one has been struck on the left, to give six to him who has asked for five, to let go one's cloak to him who has taken one's coat, would be the ruin of right and discipline. But, then, how was it that the Romans who, as Sallust says, preferred to forgive an injury rather than avenge it, were able to govern their land and turn a poor country into a rich empire? Cicero praises Cæsar for never forgetting anything but insults and outrages. When pagans are found to be magnanimous, men cry out in admiration. That, they say, is what raised the glory of Rome to such a pitch and rendered it worthy of ruling so many nations. Is it because divine authority imposes on all men a precept of loving-kindness that religion should be accused of being an enemy of power ?

The divine law, if it were understood as it should be, would give states a cohesion and prosperity unknown to the Romans, even in the days of Romulus, Numa, and Brutus. What is the *respublica*, as the Romans called the state, except the public, common, thing – the affairs of the city? And what is the city except a society of men united by concord ? And what better guarantee for concord than the charity preached by Jesus Christ ? To turn the other cheek, to let one's cloak go, is to overthrow egoism and hatred before love and sacrifice. To oppose malevolence to malevolence is to plant more deeply the roots of discord.

Furthermore, benevolence does not always exclude rigour. There are times when men should arm themselves with severity to chastise, even in spite of themselves, those whose interests are to be consulted rather than their will : a line of conduct which the Romans praised very highly in the case of one of their leaders. When a father chastises his son severely he does not renounce his paternal love : he strikes only to heal. Even in war itself there is a place for charity. Nothing is more evil than the prosperity of the wicked, which nourishes the sentiment of impurity and strengthens the will to commit crime. That victory is salutary which snatches from the vanquished the power to do evil, and lets them live in a society to which peace has come by justice and piety.

In conclusion, Augustine desires that statesmen doubtful of the political value of the Christian religion should give their countries an army, governors, husbands, sons, masters, servants, kings, judges, taxpayers, and teachers according to the spirit of the Gospel. They might then say whether Christian doctrine is harmful to the public good. Actually, if they are loyal and sincere, they will admit that Christ's moral teaching is the salvation of society, because it bears within it treasures of human and divine wisdom. All the social virtues exalted by Cicero – economy, continence, chastity, fidelity to the marriage bond, uprightness, and honesty – are taught by the Church, the saintly educator of nations, not merely in word but in deed. Besides, what laws or philosophies are comparable to the two precepts of Christ : " Thou shalt love the Lord thy God with thy whole heart, with thy whole soul, and with all thy mind ; and thy neighbour as thyself "? In them the whole moral life is summed up, since the good life consists in loving what should be loved, in the way it should be loved – that is to say, God and men – and also the whole of politics, since neither States nor societies can live without concord – without a love of the common good of which the origin and end are God, in whom and for whom all men should be loved.

(iv)

Hence we cannot win God if we are not united by the life of grace to the mystical body of His only Son, Jesus Christ, the source of truth and charity. The real obstacle to our salvation is egoism, the spirit of independence – in a word, pride.

Augustine saw quite clearly that the first, fundamental, gospel virtue is humility. He had personal experience of those uncharted seas in which the proud soul suffers ship-wreck. As a young man he set out to be his own guide, to make his own truth, as men say to-day, to do without an intellectual and religious discipline. And he knew what all that cost. Hence what attracted him most strongly in the Christian mystery was the humility of the Son of God made man, the humility of His condition, life, and doctrine, and the supreme humility of His death. In Jesus Christ, he loved to salute the Doctor of humility, certain that no philosopher would dispute this title with the Saviour of humanity. To be proud is to be false, to close the mind and heart to the light, to hand them over to falsehood and covetousness. To be humble is to be true, to throw open the soul to light and love, to call aloud to God.

With what accents and fervour did not Augustine sing of the soul's meeting with God ! It was not for him a lesson learned from a book, to be repeated before cold listeners. If, when we now read his homilies on St. John, we feel a divine flame penetrating our very bones, what must not have been the ardour of his words, the conviction of his faith !

To the Christians of Hippo he says that those who take delight in God experience unspeakable joy. If Virgil could say that every man is drawn by his pleasure, what are we to think of those who place their delight in justice and truth, which are nothing else than Jesus Christ Himself? Are the senses to have their pleasures and the soul none ? How, then, explain the Psalmist's words : " The children of men will be filled with hope in the shadow of Thy wings ; they will be inebriated with the abundance of Thy house, and Thou wilt quench their thirst in the torrent of Thy delight. For in Thee is the fountain of life and in Thy light we see light."

" Give me a man who loves, who desires, who hungers and thirsts in this desert of the world, who sighs for the fountains of his heavenly fatherland ; he will understand me, he will know what I mean."

God deigns to abide in us by charity, and we become His temple. Jesus Christ is the great high priest who inclines God towards us. When we are inflamed in His presence with a pure and holy love then we burn sweet-smelling incense in His sight, sacrifice holocausts when we fight to the death on behalf of Truth.

Let us run in the paths of our return to God ! Let us sigh after the ineffable peace of the City of God. If only our groaning spirit felt the weight of its exile, if only we ceased to love the world, and, in a transport of love, knocked without ceasing at the door of Him who calls us ! Desire is the depth of the heart, and God will enter into us if we put no bounds to our desires. The Sacred Scriptures, Church councils, the celebration of the divine Mysteries, the hymns we sing to God, instruction and theological discussions, all tend to that one end. It is their function to sow the seeds of desire, to help it germinate, to enlarge its bounds, until it becomes capable of attaining " what the eye of man has not seen, nor his ear heard, nor hath it entered into his mind to conceive." Augustine reached the final conclusion that the whole Christian life is a divine hope, a blessed love.

Men of this twentieth century, then, who wish to renew the face of the earth, have much to learn and re-learn from this great fifth-century theologian. We are aware of many things of which he was ignorant : we have discovered infinitely great and infinitely little worlds at the ends of our telescopes and microscopes ; we have torn many secrets from the heart of nature, and we shall tear many more. We rule earth, water, fire, and air with more and more success.

But are we any better than our fathers ? Are we any happier ? Have we not forgotten the only knowledge that makes for happiness : the Knowledge of God ?

ERICH PRZYWARA, S.J.

ST. AUGUSTINE AND THE MODERN WORLD

TRANSLATED BY E. I. WATKIN

ST. AUGUSTINE AND THE MODERN WORLD

Hegel, in his *Lectures on the History of Philosophy* (*Vorlesungen über die Geschichte der Philosophie*) – which are of the first importance for the understanding not only of Hegel but of modern philosophy in general – introduces the period opened by Descartes with the following passage : " In this new age the leading principle is thought, the thought which originates from itself, that interiority which is a universal feature of Christianity and the distinctively Protestant principle. It is now the principle universally admitted, to hold fast to interiority as such, rejecting, and regarding as impertinent and lifeless, externality and authority. In accordance with this principle of interiority, thought, thought for its own sake, is now the pure quintessence of inwardness, interiority which posits itself for its own sake."[1] When, further, we remember that for Hegel the portal through which this period is entered is formed by the unity of two antitheses, Bacon's realist empiricism and the tragic-dialectic of Jacob Boehme's theosophy, the issue between Augustine and modernity is revealed in its main outlines.

As in his religious and theological aspect Augustine was claimed by the Reformation, so the modern philosophy which began with Descartes seems likewise the understanding (*intelligere*) of that belief (*credere*). It is thus, in the first place, the progressive working out (to use Hegel's terminology) of the Protestant interiority until it becomes the interiority of the " pure intellect," from the Cartesian *cogito* to Kant's "synthetic unity of the ego " and on to Hegel's "self-conscious intellect." But the process is at the same time the

---

[1] *Werke*, Stuttgart, 1928, xix, 328.

working out of the inner logic of that interiority. For on the
one hand it is the radical laicizing of the secular sphere – that
is to say, the installation of the " inward " in the realism of a
purely secular world – and on the other hand this takes
place as the logical result of the Reformers' doctrine of
Original Sin : it emphasizes the transcendental significance
of this world as manifesting the irresolvable conflict between
God and the Devil, or, more fundamentally, the contrast
between a demonic God of wrath and a truly divine God
of mercy. This "laicizing" is realized in the new philosophy
on the one hand by the tendencies that originated with Bacon
and reached their climax in Locke and Hume, the realism
which renounces an " unreal ideality," on the other by the
" theo-logic," as we may term it for brevity's sake, which
carrying through the theme which Jacob Boehme decisively
marked out, passes through Pascal's *extrémités* to Kant's " anti-
nomies," Schelling's " indistinction of opposites," Hegel's
" contrast in unity and unity in contrast," and Kierkegaard's
" dialectic of equivocality." Thus the problem, " Augustine
and the modern world," appears in its full stringency. For
the " and " in this title we might, it would seem, substitute
to a very large extent " in," if not indeed " as." But as we
proceed it will become evident that a deeper point of view
demands an " above " and an " against." The modern
world is indeed the advent of Augustine, but an advent to
overcome it from within.

(i)

A comparison between the openings of Descartes's three
principal works, the *Discours de la Méthode*, the *Méditations*, and
the *Principes de la Philosophie*, and Augustine's earlier writings
might well lead us to see in " the true originator of modern
philosophy" (as Hegel termed Descartes) an immediate resurrection of the father of all Christian philosophy. The subject

of the first *Méditation*, abandonment of all things in the depth
of the mind's interiority, is the venerable prescription of
Augustinian introversion : "*relinque foris et vestem tuam et
carnem tuam, descende in te, adi secretarium tuum, mentem tuam* –
leave without thy garment and thy flesh, descend into thyself, enter thy secret place, thy mind."[1] If after this stripping
and turning away nothing remains for Descartes save the
ego as " an object which thinks," this seems identical with
Augustine's goal, the "mind itself" (*ipsa mens*), in its solitary
independence. Descartes proceeds to argue the existence of
God as the inner presupposition of his *chose qui pense*. But
that also is precisely Augustine : " God and the soul,"[2] and
that in the sense of an immediate inner relation between God
and the soul : " not in his body but in his mind itself was
man made in the image of God. In His likeness let us seek
God, in His image recognize the Creator."[3] Descartes's object in thus setting out from this tie between the *chose qui
pense* and God was to find the way to a certain knowledge of
things. But that also is exactly Augustine's object : " Commit to the Truth whatever thou hast from the Truth . . . and
they shall remain with thee and abide unto the ever remaining and abiding God."[4]

Nor yet would it be possible to differentiate straight away
between the more distinctive positions of Descartes and
Augustine. For Descartes's "universal doubt" discovers,
precisely as Augustine's doubt discovers, in the doubt itself
the indubitable reality of thought: "Whosoever apprehends that he doubts, apprehends a truth, and is certain of
that which he apprehends, is therefore certain of truth."[5]
And no less than Augustine's great pupil Thomas Aquinas
speaks of the internal connection between the universality
of philosophy and universality of previous doubt. " As to
it (philosophy) belongs the universal survey (*consideratio*)

[1] *In Johann. Tract.*, XXIII, x.   [2] *Solil.*, I, ii, 7.   [3] *Ibid.*
[4] IV, xi.   [5] *De Vera Religione*, XXXIX, lxxiii.

of truth, so also to it belongs universal doubt of truth." [1]
Even Descartes's alleged subjectivism is no ground for reproach. For Augustine also, indeed he particularly, not only
attains insight into truth in his seven steps of the soul, [2] but,
in the last resort, wisdom or truth (" what think you is wisdom save truth ") is precisely a condition of the soul . . .
whereby the mind ponders itself (*sese librat*). [3] And finally that
Descartes's Mathematicism, which makes him doubt the
reality of concrete objects but regard everything mathematical as "something certain and indubitable," [4] does not
divide him from Augustine is evident to anyone who has an
ear for the Augustinian note, the " unchangeable truth of
numbers." [5]

Nor should we be too hasty in urging that throughout
Descartes lays the emphasis on thought, Augustine on
truth, and that to that extent Descartes gives precedence
to the subjective, Augustine to the objective aspect of truth,
" which you cannot call mine or thine." [6] For that would be
to lose sight of the thoroughly Augustinian fashion in which
the *Discours de la Méthode* understands by *penser* my thought
as a participation of the divine thought and overcomes
doubt by " the greater perfection of knowing than doubting." [7]
It would be to forget how the *Méditations* lead up to " the
admiration and worship of the incomparable beauty of this
infinite Light," [8] so utterly abandoned to, and lost in the objectivity of, the very Truth that its incomprehensibility is
exaggerated into the (late Scotist) doctrine of the Divine
Will as an arbitrary fiat. [9]

But, when all these similarities have been admitted, there
remains the fact, of decisive significance, that Augustine,
when he deals with the question of doubt, says " apprehends

---

[1] *In Metaph.*, III, i.
[2] *De Quantitate Animae*, XXXIII, lxx–XXXVI, lxxx.
[3] *De Beata Vita*, XXXIII, *sq.*   [4] *Œuvres*, Paris, 1824, I, 171.
[5] *De Libero Arbitrio*, XI, xi, 30.   [6] *Ibid.*, XII, xxxiii.
[7] *Œuvres*, I, 159.   [8] *Ibid.*, 291.   [9] I, 279 ; III, 78, 81, 119.

the truth," whereas with Descartes it is " think," and not only that (which indeed Augustine also can say[1]), but understood in the sense " that I, who thought it, was something,"[2] and further as giving precedence in " think " to " I am." For the *Méditations* treat " I am," " I exist," as, strictly speaking, the first indubitable truth. [3] This attitude is clearly expressed by the fact that for Descartes the object of the entire meditation is "to walk securely"[4]; it is a search for assurance by " a man walking alone and in the dark " who must therefore take care " to go forward so slowly, and to be so circumspect in all things, that though I make but very slight progress, at least I keep myself from falling."[5] It is a search for assurance against malicious deceptions from without, includes indeed a lengthy consideration of the possibilities of such deception on the part of God, or at least of some demonic power. That is to say, we recognize every feature of that terrified longing for assurance characteristic of Luther's religious attitude, here transferred to the domain of philosophy and therefore producing the same results, the same exclusive trust in the individual's interior experience : " the man who walks alone," " to study . . . in myself."[6] That which is unconsumed in the furnace of doubt is not truth in itself, but "conceiving very clearly and very distinctly,"[7] that is to say, subjective "certitude . . . in the understanding alone when it possesses clear perceptions."[8] It is not an objective " first principle," as understood by Plato and Aristotle, Augustine and Thomas,[9] but the "*je pense, donc je suis* " which is here " the first principle of philosophy," understood, moreover, as "thought which conceives itself "[10] It is not even thought in the sense of objective thought (a noematic thinking, as Husserl would express it), but as self-

[1] *De Trinitate*, XIV, vi.   [2] *Œuvres*, I, 155.   [3] *Œuvres*, I, 248.
[4] *Ibid.*, I, i.   [5] *Ibid.*, I, 139.   [6] *Ibid.*, I, 139, 132.
[7] *Ibid.* I, 159.   [8] *Ibid.*, III, 15.   [9] *Ibid.*, III, 14.   [10] *Ibid.*, III, 71.

consciousness : " to think is not only to understand, will, and imagine, but also to feel."[1] Hegel was therefore right when in reference to Descartes he says, " it is the Protestant principle that in Christianity interiority should universally become conscious of itself as thought."[2]

But with Descartes opened that fatal perspective which in part Hegel himself shared. This assurance of truth consisting in the conviction of the subject may take an active or a passive form. Passive when this subjective conviction is regarded as the immediate efflux of the divine Truth ; active in the doctrine that the intelligence of the subject is as such and in its finitude the seat of truth, the " epistomological God in the world." As representatives of the former standpoint Hegel sharp-sightedly designates Spinoza and (with limitations imposed by his Christianity) Malebranche. For Spinoza, whom Hegel considers " the complete logical fulfilment " of Descartes[3], " infinite and finite are one in God "; that is, he holds the Oriental doctrine of " absolute identity,"[4] inasmuch as " the world [possesses] no genuine reality, but everything is absorbed in the abyss of the sole Identity . . . nothing [exists] in finite reality, for that is devoid of truth."[5] For Malebranche, " whose system takes its place beside Spinozism and is also a complete development of the Cartesian philosophy,"[6] this identity appears in a modified form : " the Cartesian doctrine of God's assistance in the act of knowing,"[7] or as Gratry, Malebranche's fellow Oratorian, put it later, " according to Malebranche God produces in us directly and immediately all our ideas and all our sensations. He produces them by His presence and touch after the same fashion in which He produces in us His own Idea of the Infinite."[8] Alike in Spinoza and Malebranche this is the Lutheran mysticism of possession, in

[1] Ibid., III, 67–8.   [2] Werke, XIX, 331.   [3] Werke, XIX, 368.
[4] Ibid.   [5] Ibid., 408.   [6] Ibid., 411.   [7] Ibid., 412.
[8] Philosophie de la Connaissance de Dieu, Paris, 1854, I, 401.

which the arms outstretched in self-surrender have become arms outstretched to embrace.

The second, the active, form of the conquest of truth by the subjective conviction of the unaided self began with Kant's categories and attained its completion in Hegel's triad. Here the very form of our thought is in and by itself the bearer of absolute truth. In his account of Kant, Hegel reproaches him with a shallow finitizing, whereas Spinoza represents for him an impracticable infinitizing. But this very criticism reveals plainly the gigantic strides with which the deification of thought has advanced from Kant to himself. For Kant the absolute reality of truth is still finite. For Hegel, on the other hand, to attain truth is to take forcible possession of the living God in the pure concept. In the form of the judgement which is at once unity and differentiation he sees the form of the divine Idea in its unity and internal dialectic. From Kant to Hegel speculation follows the road of that forceful Lutheran defiance which seeks to take the world and God by storm. It is evident that the goal to which this path between Scylla and Charybdis leads is but the return in an aggravated form of that confusion which the method of " assurance " attempted to overcome – uncertainty of life, a restless dissatisfied motion hither and thither as Descartes depicts it so vividly in the opening pages of his *Discours de la Méthode*. The pit opens deeper still : the demonisms of West and East are combined – the demonism of the West, self-conquest by defiant force ; the demonism of the East, self-conquest by magic absorption. So is reached the more abysmal demonism which lies between both : selfcombat to blood, self-generation in the process of selfcombat. More terribly true than he knew had now proved Descartes's description of man : " I am, as it were, a mean between God and nothingness "[1] – willing to be God, and being nothing.

[1] *Œuvres*, I, 295.

RA

But Augustine's attitude to this line of development, the message he addresses to it, is clear : " Hope not in thy-self, but in thy God. For if thou hope in thyself, thy soul is troubled within thee, since it hath not yet found that whereby it may be confident concerning thee."[1] The only right path for the soul is fundamentally the path of decisive self-surrender to God, not a forcing of God but the worship of Him as one " always greater " ; above all, no subjective state of any kind whatsoever, but " the praise of God " as " the highest work of man."[2] It is, moreover, the path of self-surrender, in view precisely of the demonism to right and left : " even when a man confesses his sins, he should confess them with praise to God."[3] It is the radical trans-cendence of " clearness " " evidence," as a subjective prin-ciple in " evident knowledge of the Divine Majesty " ; that is to say, an evidence or sure knowledge, which can so little become a possession that it bows in adoration the knee of the seeker awed by its remoteness : *I* am the Truth.

Gratry sees in Pascal the opposite pole to Malebranche, in whom the mysticism of Descartes found its complete expression. " Malebranche . . . rendered to philosophy the imperishable service of proving . . . the presence of God in reason. In the seventeenth century this fundamental truth needed as powerful affirmation as the impotence of human thought when isolated from its Divine Source . . . these two truths, one of which Pascal and Malebranche each upheld, sometimes even to excess and disharmony."[4] With this dictum we can agree, but must then maintain as an explicit thesis what Gratry merely implies, when he traces the problem of modern philosophy to its source in Descartes, to show its inner contradictions worked out in Pascal and Malebranche (to be reunited, in Gratry's opinion, by Fénelon, and so through Petavius Thomassin

---

[1] *Enarr. in Psalm.*, XLI, xii.   [2] *Ibid.*, XLIV, ix.   [3] *Ibid.*, CV, ii.
[4] *Philosophie de la Connaissance de Dieu*, I, 405.

and Bossuet to culminate in Leibniz). Descartes and Pascal
permeate each other. Behind all Pascal's apparent scepticism
lies Descartes's preoccupation with *la chose qui pense.* " Man
is obviously made to think. It is his entire dignity. And his
entire merit and duty is to think correctly. But the order of
thought is to begin with himself, his Maker, and his end."[1]
It is no objection to this that Pascal's doctrine of thought
issues in the polarity between the geometrical mind (" *esprit
de géometrie*") and the intuitive mind (" *esprit de finesse* "),[2] or
more emphatically expressed between " *mind* " and " *heart.*"
For in the first place this polarity hardly amounts to more
than St. Thomas's distinction between " apprehension of
first principles " and " rational deduction of conclusions "
(" *intellectus principiorum* " and " *ratio conclusionum* ") ; the
" intuitive mind," like the " heart," is concerned with the
" first principles," the " geometrical mind," like the " reason," with " proofs,"[3] – that is to say, with the entire process
which links principle and deduction. And in the second
place Pascal's concern – in the close relationship between
" heart " and " love " – is the stronger assurance of truth
through " God experienced by the heart,"[4] the saving
apprehension of the *Deus Veritas* in contrast with the God
" of the philosophers and men of learning." We might
indeed describe his attitude as " an epistemological Jansenism." Truth, which is God, is attainable solely through
the free " irresistible " grace ; conveyed in " God experienced by the heart." That is to say, Pascal in his relationship
to Descartes signifies unmistakably the Protestant desire
for assurance of salvation manifesting itself as the desire for
assurance of truth. The reverse aspect, however, is thereby
revealed ; for the cleavage of which there is barely a hint
in Descartes becomes Pascal's peculiar theme. It appears in

---

[1] Brunschvicg, larger edition, Paris, 1904, IV, 146 (*Pensées*). [I have taken
this rendering from the English version of M. Chevalier's *Pascal*, Sheed &
Ward, 1930. – Tr.]

[2] *Pensées*, 1.   [3] 282.   [4] 278.

a still relatively neutral form in Pascal's tense polarities. It is not simply or principally a " polarity at rest " which manifests man's inner breadth; Pascal's concern is rather with the constant movement thereby set up between the poles, and, moreover, with that movement as a dialectical conflict. " In disputes men love the conflict of opinions, but the contemplation of truth in no wise. To enjoy the sight of truth, it must arise out of a dispute. . . . We never seek things but the search for things."[1] Indeed, his final refinement is the æsthetic delight of the unconcerned spectator : " to laugh at philosophizing is the true philosophy."[2]

He discovers thus the deeper form of the polarities, the real cleavage. Practically and in the concrete they are mutually destructive : " these two principles of truth, reason and the senses, are not only deceptive in themselves, but mutually trick each other."[3] No doubt " to depart from the mean is to depart from humanity,"[4] but this mean (*milieu*) signifies on the one hand that the roads to every extreme lie open before man, and on the other that the circumscribed territory between is the sole ground he can occupy. " For us the extremes are as though they were not, and in respect to them we are not : they escape us or we them. . . . We behold ourselves on a vast territory in the midst, always uncertain and unsteady, pushed from one end to the other. . . . We are on fire with the longing to find a firm site and an ultimate fixed base whereon to erect a tower that shall rise to the infinite, but our entire foundation gives way, and the earth opens to the abyss. Nothing can fix the finite between the two infinites which enclose and escape it."[5] The Cartesian " mean between God and nothingness," has been developed to the utmost. Man is that " incomprehensible monstrosity "[6] a " mean between nothingness and the all," " a nonentity in relation to the infinite, a whole in

[1] 135.   [2] 4.   [3] 83.   [4] 378.
[5] 72.   [6] 420.

relation to nonentity."[1] He is the " chimæra," the " chaos," the " subject of contradictory attributes," at once "judge of all things " and "feeble earthworm," "depository of truth " and " a mass of uncertainty," in very truth " the pride and refuse of the universe."[2] In other words, the restlessness of his constant movement between the opposite poles is his " epistemological concupiscence," to will to be God and to eat the dust of the earth. " It is a remarkable fact ... that the mystery most remote from our knowledge, that of the transmission of original sin, is a thing without which we can have no knowledge of ourselves."[3] And therefore "our true and sole virtue is to hate ourselves, for concupiscence has made us deserving of hate, and to look for a truly lovable being to love."[4] " It was necessary that Truth should come, that man might no longer live in himself."[5]

If, however, invincible epistemological concupiscence (a thoroughly Protestant conception) is the epistemological original sin, then by an internal necessity the last word must be the " hidden God " of unconditional predestination. The " epistemological cleavage " leads with logical inevitability to the inscrutable darkness which conceals God : Pascal approves the doubt which complains, " I look on all sides, and everywhere see only darkness."[6] " I know not who has brought me into the world, nor what the world is, nor myself. I am in a terrifying ignorance of all things."[7] "That God should exist is incomprehensible, and that He should not exist is incomprehensible."[8] Hence the situation presents itself in which man must " take a certain risk for an uncertain gain."[9] But the personal presupposition of this is affirmed by that " true and only virtue – to hate oneself and to seek a truly lovable being to love." This, however, is already " God experienced by the heart " – that is to say, by free choice. The final conclusion is thus inevitable in which the

[1] 72. [2] 434. [3] Ibid. [4] 440. [5] Ibid. [6] 229.
[7] 194. [8] 230. [9] 233.

Reformation enters the sphere of epistemology, and the Cartesian Truth, God of arbitrary will, finds complete expression : " there is sufficient light to enlighten the elect and sufficient darkness to humble them ; sufficient darkness to blind the reprobate, sufficient light to condemn them and render them inexcusable."[1]

There can be no question that Pascal in this his most distinctive position expresses in unprecedented fashion the Augustine who, combating the Pelagian doctrine of the sound reason and will, and also in opposition to the tone of his own early writings, tears the mask from human nature, and reveals man as the victim of unending restlessness and futility : " every day in this time of ours so cometh into being that it may cease to be "[2]: " these . . . days are not : they depart wellnigh ere they come, they join themselves one to another, follow one after another, and abide not "[3] : man, whose life is an incurable disease : " who is not ill in this life ? Who does not endure a lengthy sickness ? To be born here in a mortal body is to fall ill. . . . Whatsoever relief be given to weariness, another weariness follows "[4] : man therefore a creature of the night : " it is night because here the human race wanders blindly."[5] " Someone loves thee, and thou thinkest that he hates thee, or hates thee and thou thinkest he loves thee, but whichever it be, it is night."[6] " Is not man's heart an abyss ? For what abyss is deeper ? Can you believe there is in man a depth so profound that it is unknown to the man himself in whom it is? "[7] "In the pilgrimage of our life in the body each bears about with him his own heart, and every heart is closed to every other heart."[8]

But in all this realistic philosophy of " night " we nowhere catch sight of Pascal's sinister gleam, or hear his harsh cry.

[1] 578.
[2] Enarr. in Psalm, CI, v, 2, 10.
[3] Ibid., III, viii, 7.
[4] Ibid., CII, vi.
[5] Ibid., CXXXVIII, xvi.
[6] Ibid., CIII, xii.
[7] Ibid., XLI, xiii.
[8] Ibid., LV, ix.

However Augustine may exaggerate his contrasts, in the depth there is as it were a soft calm smile. " Yes, that is how it is. What would you then ? " There is no anxious search for assurance. On the contrary, he lies quietly down to rest in the night. " The good heart is hidden, the evil heart is hidden, in the good and the evil heart alike there is an abyss, but they are open to God, from Whom nothing is hidden."[1] There is here no anxiety, and this is but the logic of the Catholic denial of an absolute assurance of salvation, to know in what state I may really be. I must forget myself completely in the praise of God. " Alike when this night is light, and when it is dark . . . be His praise always in thy mouth."[2] Thus all ends beyond every radical contrast, in that humble charitableness upon which Augustine in his controversy with the Donatists (the predecessors of Jansenism and Pascal) is never weary of insisting. " It is God's will that these things of time should be of mingled nature."[3] " Thou blamest enviously and dost praise rashly. Thou who dost praise, make mention of the evil intermingled with the good ; thou who dost blame, see the good there also. . . . If you would not be deceived, and would love the brethren, bear in mind that every vocation in the Church hath its hypocrites."[4] " So long as we live as members of the human race we cannot forsake human society. We must endure the wicked with whom we must live, even as the good, when we ourselves were wicked, endured us."[5] Thus he attains to that holy calm above the world which proceeds from the sublimity of adoration, the *laus Dei* : " wouldst thou be long-suffering ? Behold the eternity of God. For thou lookest to thy few days and wouldst have thy few days embrace all things. God embraceth them in His time. . . . He is eternal, let Him deliver [what thou canst not seize]. He is long-suffering. . . .

[1] *Ibid.*, CXXXIV, xvi.   [2] *Ibid.*, CXXXVIII, xvi.   [3] *Ibid.*, LXVI, iii.
[4] Ibid., XCIX, xxi, xiii.   [5] *Ibid.*, L, xxiv.

Unite thy heart to the eternity of God, and with Him thou shalt be eternal. Unite thyself to God's eternity, and with Him await the things that are beneath thee, for when thy heart shall have cleaved to the Most High, all things mortal will be beneath thee."[1] In this calm the night which draws into the deep and the longing for the light which attempts wild flights are overcome : " His darkness doth not overwhelm me, for His light doth not exalt me."[2] Above all sharp contrasts Augustine has found the " ever wakeful rest,"[3] the " old age that is childhood, and the childhood that is old age . . . that your wisdom may not be proud, or your humility unwise."[4]

(ii)

The Cartesian " clear and distinct " expresses almost verbally the tendency which was to give birth in the modern world to what is known as the Enlightenment and Classicism. Pascal's man of " contradictions " (" *contrariétés* ") and his " hidden God " herald, on the other hand, their irreconcilable antipodes, Romanticism. No doubt in Descartes himself the enlightening, the clarifying, clear thought yields finally to the darkness of faith, which he particularly emphasized. Nevertheless, Hegel's description of the Cartesian method is correct : " we must reject every prejudice – that is, every presupposition accepted immediately as true – and set out from thought in order to reach thus by way of thought something certain, and so make a clean start."[5] For Hegel is here abstracting from Descartes the individual the historical type, and this, there can be no doubt, seeks to replace all first principles by thought as the absolute principle. *Hegel is thus the fulfilment of Descartes.* For thought is for him not only act, but itself object, as the *System der Philosophie* pointedly

[1] *Ibid.*, XCI, viii, 10   [2] *Ibid.*, CXXXVII, xvi.   [3] *Ibid.*, CXIV, vi.
[4] *Ibid.*, CXII, ii.   [5] *Werke*, XIX, 335.

states it. " The free act of thought consists in placing itself at the point where it is for itself, and thereby itself produces and makes its object. . . . In this fashion philosophy is shown to be a circle returning upon itself." [1] Descartes has found his fulfilment : thought is the first and the last – that is, God. Thereby the object of philosophy becomes identical with that of religion. Truth is the common object of both, and that in the highest sense, since God is Truth and He alone is Truth. [2] But philosophy as " absolute knowledge " transcends religion, for the latter conveys, through " feeling," only the " inconceptual form," philosophy, on the other hand, the " concept," and therefore the form in the concept. The concept is the understanding of itself and of the inconceptual form ; the latter, however, does not from its inner truth understand the former. [3] The classical clarity of clarifying or enlightening thought is therefore the clarity of God Himself. Thought is " God as thought."

And on the other hand, no doubt, not only is Pascal's doctrine of contrasts, with its issue, the " night " of the " hidden God," crossed by the metaphysician's interest in reasoning, but that interest at least attempts to refashion the doctrine of contrasts, by giving it an unmistakable direction towards the Aristotelian " mean," which is not simply an internal harmony of the contrasts, but their accurate determination in reference to their middle point, their " mean," and setting out from it. Nevertheless, the primary concern of this doctrine of contrasts is to unmask human nature – superficially a harmony in the classical style – and uncover the abyss of original sin in man, that the gulf which divides " deceitful man " from " God the Truth " may be plainly revealed. In Pascal's epistemology, reason must indeed accept its own humiliation, on this account alone, that comprehension of any kind, in virtue of its " ideal concepts," is incompatible with the *homme chaos*. But this humiliation is,

[1] *Werke*, VIII, 63 *sqq.*   [2] *Ibid.*, 41.   [3] *Ibid.*, 24.

strictly speaking, an end in itself; the reason which renounces itself is through that renunciation, and thus alone,
the " worship in fear and trembling " by " deceitful man "
of " God the Truth," as the " hidden God." It is this, however – as we should already have guessed from these
characteristics of Pascal's thought – which makes Hegel's
most irreconcilable opponent, Kierkegaard,[1] Pascal's peculiar
fulfilment. The typically romantic " Irony of Longing " and
" Longing of Irony," which in Pascal does little more than
colour his language, becomes in the hands of the Danish
genius a fully developed epistemological method – not only
the logic which with every affirmation pronounces the corresponding negation, but the logic which strips off masks, the
logic of double aspect, which can so little issue in that
" unity of contrasts " which is Hegel's last word that on the
contrary it regards the " cleavage " as the ultimate reality,
"that the two halves of an idea are held asunder by something
foreign intervening,"[2] " that an unsatisfied craving has
called it into being, yet has failed to find satisfaction in it."[3]
Longing taken by itself might yet signify that the infinite and
eternal God was a goal attainable by the man who longed.
Irony taken by itself would be but "longing reversed," that is
to say, despair of this goal, a despair, however, which does not
renounce the claim to it. But where both interpenetrate we
have the attitude which affirms most inexorably the infinite
difference of nature[4] between God and man, who in irony
unmasks his own claim. The understanding decisively
apprehends God as " absolute Majesty," in proportion as He
is for it the " Unknown " " against which man beats in his
paradoxical passion, and which moreover prevents him truly
knowing himself."[5] " Irony in longing " and " longing in

[1] See the Author's *Geheimnis Kierkegaards* (The Secret of Kierkegaard),
Munich, 1929.
[2] *Tagebücher* (Haecker, München, 1923), I, 47.
[3] *Ibid.*, 48.   [4] *Ibid.*, 30.
[5] *Ges. Werke* (Schrempf, Jena, 1909), VI, 36.

irony " thus signify not merely the romantic direction " to the infinite," but glimpses of the rigid " boundary " which separates us from the " otherness," the " absolutely different."[1] Here there is no classic " circle," no closed movement returning upon itself. There is only the cleavage by which the movement is broken and despairing bursts into flame. Here, therefore, is no place for any philosophy which would comprehend and so find room for religion. On the contrary, philosophy in its classical acceptation is the mask of man guilty of original sin, a mask which must be torn off. And the contrast-cleavage of romantic thought is precisely this unmasking. Thought, therefore, is so far from being " God as thought " that it is the opposite extreme, the mask or unmasking of original sin, its " ye shall be as gods, knowing . . . "

Hegel and Kierkegaard, therefore, agree in holding that man's faculty of knowledge must be regarded as a relationship between thought and faith. But for Hegel faith is but the preliminary to the " revealed religion " of thought. It is the emotionally experienced form which must be translated into the corresponding concept. For Kierkegaard, on the other hand, faith is the " totally different " other world beyond thought. Between it and thought lies the " paradox," the " reversal," the " scandal,"[3] for faith is the " power of the absurd."[2] Hegel and Kierkegaard also agree that dialectic is the " nature of thought."[4] But for Hegel it is the dialectic of thought which transcends faith, the dialectic of the divine idea in its triple movement from " pure idea " : logic, corresponding to the Father, to its " otherness " in the form of exteriorization,[5] nature, corresponding to the Son, and so to its return to itself, spirit, corresponding to the Holy Spirit. For Kierkegaard, on the contrary, dialectic is the " epistemological original sin,"

[1] *Ibid.*, 41.   [2] *Ges. Werke*, VI, 8–100.
[3] *Ibid.*, III, 29.   [4] Hegel, *Werke*, VIII, 55.   [5] *Ibid.*, 65.

thought which passionately clutches at God to lay hold, not
simply of darkness, but of the storm-cloud which enwraps
the God of Judgement. Lastly, Hegel and Kierkegaard alike
perceive that the ultimate problem is that of becoming, and
therefore of the relation between essence (what a thing is)
and existence (the fact that it is) ; and is, moreover, already
involved fundamentally in thought itself, since thought is
itself movement. But for Hegel existence passes over into the
ideality of essence, existential into essential becoming, as
Kierkegaard truly and acutely observes.[1] It becomes the
ideal " logical movement " of the idea. Being " is " this
movement, and therefore thought is simply the consciousness
and awareness of it. It is " essential " thought, absorption
in the structure of the idea in its movement. For Kierkegaard, on the other hand, every ideal property of the essence
is stripped off in the real existence of " fear," " guilt,"
" despair," and " death." Here, too, thought is " consciousness of being," but consequently " absorption in existence,"[2]
this existence of fear, guilt, etc. If Hegel's " essential "
thought ascends to the height of " God the Truth," to be
not only a participation in His thinking but that thinking
itself, Kierkegaard's " existential " thought can be nothing
but the complete expression of the nature of man under
original sin : fear, guilt, despair, death as thought.

Thereby is carried to its utmost conclusion what Hegel
says of modern thought, that it is " the pure culmination of
the most interior " in the Protestant acceptation of interiority ; in other words, Protestantism as thought. When Hegel
identifies thought with " God as thought," he expresses the
ultimate logic of the fundamental Lutheran axiom : " the
finite is capable of the infinite." And when Kierkegaard
maintains that thought is " original sin as thought," he
carries to its climax the fundamental axiom of Calvinism :
" the finite is incapable of the infinite." The philosophy of

[1] *Tagebücher*, II, 127 *sq.*   [2] *Ges. Werke*, VII, 215.

both thinkers receives its distinctive form from theology, and from Protestant theology. In their irreconcilable opposition to each other the opposition between the two leading varieties of Protestantism reaches its climax, and therefore its most comprehensive and most uncompromising presentation. Both, moreover, display a conscious theological orientation.

In Hegel this is shown not only by the avowed aims of his early writings, which draw the outlines of a theology which is to vanquish the theology of original sin, a " reassuring " theology of simple union with God. It is as plainly visible in the prefaces to the *Enzyklopädie*, whose dispute with the theologians has but one object – to base theology on the doctrine of the Trinity instead of on the doctrine of original sin. Hegel is thus from a twofold point of view the most extreme representative of the distinctively Lutheran[1] principle as opposed to the distinctively Calvinist. In the question

[1] " Lutheran " here means Luther-Melanchthon, as opposed to the earlier Luther, whose guiding principles were identical with Calvin's. The element common to the earlier Luther and Calvin was that which is specifically Protestant as opposed to Catholic. Objectively it was the denial of indwelling grace which resulted from the denial of the removal of original sin in justification (baptism). Subjectively it represented the self-assertion of " interiority." But the two axioms mentioned above (whose formulation was a result of the controversy between Lutheranism and Calvinism) gave expression to the two subtle distinctions which it already contained implicitly. *Capax infiniti* (as distinctive of Lutheranism) signifies indeed *incapax*, as far as indwelling grace, considered as created grace, is concerned – that is, in practice a " grace for good works " (which makes good works possible). It signifies, however, *capax* in inasmuch as the *incapax* results in God working " all in all " in the incapable man. The self-assertion of interiority (in the " Protest ") is, therefore, based on the ground of this sole agency of God apprehended as " interior." *Incapax infiniti*, as distinctive of Calvinism, stresses on the contrary the fact concealed in this point of view, that this " in " is essentially the " in," the negation of God in the *homo incapax*, that is to say in the persisting gulf between the man guilty of original sin and the Majesty of a Holy God. Here the only *capax* is the fact that this Holy Sovereign takes possession of the sinner to use him as His " obedient tool " ; not for " good works " of which he is *incapax*, but for " the discharge of the Lord's incomprehensible will." The self-assertion of " interiority " is now based on this employment as the tool of His activity Who is the Sole Agent. Distinctive Lutheranism is dominated by the contradiction of a " transcendent immanence," distinctive Calvinism by that of an " immanent transcendence," both, that is to say, by the wresting of the mystery enclosed in God alone to " comprehensibilities," expressed in assurance of salvation. *Cf.* the author's *Ringen der Gegenwart* (Augsburg, 1929), II, 543–78, also *Das Katholische Kirchen Prinzip* (*Zwischen der Zeiten*, July 1929, 277–302).

of grace (God's ontological sole agency) he completes the doctrine that " the justice of Christ is formally ours " by making " the justice of God formally ours." In the question of faith (God's epistemological sole agency) he improves upon justification by faith only with his doctrine that God " alone thinks " in us. Thus the Lutheran " lumping " of grace and faith is exaggerated into an " identification." " God's thought in us " is " God's being in us," immanence carried to identity. That Kierkegaard is first and foremost a theologian is sufficiently proved by the order of subjects which his writings follow, from the erotic-æsthetic – *Enten Eller Oder (Either Or)*, etc. – to the philosophic – *Philosophiske Smuler (Philosophical Bits)* – and finally to the formally religious and theological, which constitute the majority. He can say of himself not only " I am and have been a religious writer," but that " the Christian religion is the centre of my entire work as a writer."[1] His aim is that which to-day in Protestant Germany dominates the work of Karl Barth and his friends, to overcome Lutheran immanentism by an uncompromising doctrine of God's transcendence. His profoundest note is Calvin's – the exclusiveness of the glory of the Divine Majesty. Thus, in the question of grace, it is not " sole agency " as the blissful inner consciousness of Lutheranism, but " sole agency " as unlimited readiness to be employed by the Divine Master in a service of conflict and sacrifice. So also in the question of faith : " faith only," not as conscious union with God, but as blind loss of self in unconditional obedience. As with Hegel grace and faith are exaggerated in an immanence which has become " identity," so with Kierkegaard in transcendence pushed to " paradox." As, however, in the actual Reformation Luther and Calvin interpenetrate, so is it with their fulfilments, Hegel and Kierkegaard. Hegel's " identity " is itself identical with " contradiction " ; creation as the contradiction of

[1] *Ges. Werke*, X, 3.

God is the form of His exteriorization in the Son. But this contradiction is not only " out " of the identity, but also " in " it, and again, in the Spirit, " to " it. That is to say, the formal principle of Calvin and Kierkegaard, transcendence even to paradox, enters indeed into the formal principle of Luther and Hegel, immanence even to identity, but moulded into conformity with the latter as the superior form. Similarly in the depth of Kierkegaard's paradox sounds the note of "love" as the true "prime mover,"[1] and "sacrificial obedience " is not demanded by the " Law " which prescribes " Thou shalt mortify myself," but by the Love which asks "Dost thou not love Me then?"[2] But this immanence is not simply (as Luther, and Hegel also, would say) " from above alone," but, further, it is as such never strictly speaking " experienced." " Experience " is always experience of the " paradox," and of that alone. " Out " of this paradox, " in " it and " to " it, this is love.

We have thus reached a double conclusion. On the one hand, that Hegel and Kierkegaard in themselves denote the bankruptcy of Protestantism. Of Hegel this is obvious. For his philosophy of religion is the substitution of philosophy for religion. Immanence is carried to such an extent that man is God. God is thought, in the sense that thought *qua* thought is God. But Kierkegaard's paradox involves the consequence that thought when its object is God is doomed of its very nature to encounter in solitude the " Unknown."

If in Hegel an " absorption of God " issues in atheism, in the logic of Kierkegaard's paradox, when unswervingly carried through, atheism proceeds from "despair of God." But on the other hand both thinkers (though in entirely different ways) surmount the Protestant position to attain the Catholic. In Hegel, it is true, the process is unconscious, disguised from himself by wholly different aims, the result of his struggle against the Protestant doctrine of original sin.

[1] *Tagebücher*, I, 126.　　　　[2] *Ibid.*, II, 291.

The treatment adopted in his *Systeme der Philosophie* does not only hark back unintentionally to the form of the mediæval *Summas*, to the principle which determines their method, "God the starting-point and goal"; it also represents a return to the patristic mode of thought, which regarded the history of man's salvation as the revelation of a process within the Trinity, the "economic" Trinity of the "supereconomic." That is to say, the characteristic tendency of Lutheranism to make everything centre in the salvation of man, soteriological anthropocentrism, is overcome by the fundamental Catholic orientation, God in Himself and His glory. With Kierkegaard also the Protestant standpoint is surmounted, but here the process is a profound penetration, conscious and deliberate, of the Catholic scheme. Kierkegaard carries to its utmost point the Calvinist heroism of " the pure tool " of " God's glory," to discover in it what he terms the " erotic equality " of the tool-hero with God,[1] by which he means a self-sufficiency, consisting in freedom from needs of any kind, which claims the self-sufficiency of God. He thus discovers for the first time how beneath the apparent theocentrism of the Calvinist " glory of God " lurks an anthropocentrism, of the more dangerous passive type which speaks of a " mere tool," but in so doing usurps the divine dignity. But in the second place he perceives how everything depends upon a " positive difference " between man and God ; it is God's " almightiness " as " His goodness " which can " confer independence, and bring out of nothing what has existence in itself."[2] The former insight produces Kierkegaard's deliberate and damning criticism of Luther. The latter obtains his assent to that position of the traditional pre-Reformation philosophy and theology which the Reformation most passionately rejected – the doctrine of the independent activity and agency of creatures, the doctrine

[1] *Tagebücher*, I, 415 *sq.*   [2] *Ibid.*, 292 *sq.*

of secondary causes. While the Hegelian transcendence of soteriological anthropocentrism awoke the Catholic spirit of objectivity, so from Kierkegaard's transcendence of heroic anthropocentrism rose again the Catholic spirit of childlike detachment.

But it is an awakening and a resurrection on the brink of the abyss, in face of that atheism of the " absorption of God " which stares from Hegel's countenance, or that other atheism, the " despair of God," which never ceased to threaten Kierkegaard. With the contrast between Hegel and Kierkegaard the intellectual movement of the modern world is completed in this awful " sign of judgment," the alternative, atheism or Catholicism. And when we consider the dizzy audacities of Hegel's conceptions and his increasing outbursts of irritation, and the admittedly neurotic atmosphere which surrounds Kierkegaard, we realize that the alternative is also the alternative between neurotic introversion and Catholicism. The " self-indwelling of the intellect " which Hegel praises as " the principle of the Reformation,"[1] has become the " self-indwelling " of introversion, from the very fact that it was the assertion of self ; " a Reformer, determined to shake off the yoke," as Kierkegaard pointedly remarks.[2] Thus is fulfilled our Lord's saying, " Whoso holdeth fast his soul, loseth it."[3] But the Catholic principle unfalteringly repeats in sacrifice in and for the Church the Gospel text, " Whoso loseth his soul, gaineth it."

These lines have already sketched Augustine by implication as the internal reconciliation of the opposition between Hegel and Kierkegaard. There can be no question that the Augustine represented by Descartes achieves his most complete expression in Hegel, the classical Augustine for whom " understanding " (*intelligere*) is the peculiar " gift . . .

---

[1] *Werke*, XIX, 262. [2] *Tagebücher*, II, 153.
[3] *Matthew*, x, 39, and parallels. [The Authorized and Douay Versions have " life " : the Greek is *psyche*. – Tr.]

SA

which God was to bestow on believers,"[1] and "the advance
of the intellect to understand what it believes,"[2] is the
very purpose of faith, " we believed...that we might know."[3]
– and its inner effect – " every believer thinks, and by
believing he thinks, and by thinking he believes "[4]; the
Augustine who finds an essential correspondence between
the threefold interior process of this understanding (memory, understanding, and will) and the triple process of the
Divine Intellectuality (the Father as memory, the Son as
understanding, the Holy Ghost as will,) so that in the very
act of advancing from faith to understanding the Abyss of
the Godhead is revealed. But it is equally beyond doubt that
the other Augustine who reappeared in Pascal is completed
by Kierkegaard, the romantic Augustine, for whom faith is
" to submit the soul to God,"[5] and therefore understanding
the supreme self-surrender to God – " what God sees, do
thou believe "[6] – the righteousness or justice of faith is " to
believe what thou seest not,"[7] understanding, therefore,
" to find for further search,"[8] " to find how incomprehensible
is that which it sought,"[9] so that this act of understanding is
not only the experience of a God " always greater, however
much we grow,"[10] not only the realization of an inevitable
ignorance (which cuts across all analogies between the
mind [mens] and the Trinity) – " What is in thyself thou
canst know. But what is in Him Who made thee, whatever it
be, when canst thou know? Even though hereafter thou
wilt be able, thou canst not yet. And yet when thou wilt be
able, never wilt thou be able to know God as He knoweth
thee "[11] – but also, in and besides these experiences,

[1] *De Libero Arbitrio*, II, ii, 5.
[2] *In Johann. Tract.*, XXVII.
[3] *De Agonia Christi*, XIII, xiv.
[7] *Ibid.*, CIV, viii.
[9] *Ibid.*, XV, ii, 2.
[3] *Enarr. in Psalm.*, CXVIII, xviii, 3.
[4] *De Prædestinatione Sanctorum*, II, v.
[6] *Enarr. in Psalm.*, XXXVI, ii, 2.
[8] *De Trinitati*, IX, i, 1.
[10] *Enarr. in Psalm.*, LXII, xvi.
[11] *Sermo*, LIII, x, 23.

experience of the gulf which divides the " true God " from " deceitful man."[1]

But however these two points of view may appear to contradict each other (and that precisely in Augustine himself) in the contrast between Augustine as he expresses himself in his early writings and Augustine writing against the Pelagians,[2] they nevertheless contain from the outset that internal unity which we have detected above in the final accents of Hegel and Kierkegaard, and which completes the Augustinian transcendence of Descartes and Pascal – " Abide not in thine own sight ; thou mayst be in the sight of God."[3]

The Augustinianism of Hegel and the Augustinianism of Kierkegaard alike are arrayed against the lowliness and humility of man's existence in the flesh, and in the flesh of the visible " Head and Body, One Christ." For the Augustinianism of Hegel it is a stage of childhood unworthy of the adult, which must therefore give place to " pure intellectuality." For Kierkegaard's Augustinianism it is the " scandal of the flesh " which is opposed to the Holiness of the Divine Majesty. The real Augustine shares the feelings of both. He feels the craving to get away from " the transience " (*transitorium*)[4] of " the Word made Flesh "[5] " that we may be fed with milk,"[6] " to the inward divinity of Him who has deigned to offer to us, who need to be fed on milk, His outward Humanity "[7] ; and he feels a still keener suffering, " the disgust . . . which arises from the bitterness of all earthly things,"[8] until he can ask himself, " Must we despair of the human race and say that every man is already doomed to damnation ? "[9] – for it cannot be denied " that in the Church hypocrites are to be found in every vocation."[10] But he is aware that the impatience of this craving expresses the disobedience of pride, and therefore needs to be humbled by

[1] *Enarr. in Psalm.*, CVIII, ii.　　　　　　[3] *Retractationes*, I, i, 2.
　[2] *Enarr. in Psalm.*, CXXII, iii.　　　[4] *Enarr. in Psalm.*, CIX, v.
[5] *In Johann. Tract.*, XIII, iv.　　[6] *Enarr. in Psalm.*, CXVII, xxii.　[7] *Ibid.*
　[8] *Ibid.*, LXXXV, vii.　　　[9] *Ibid.*　　[10] *Ibid.*, XCIX, xii, 13.

patient obedience : " Dost thou desire wisdom ? Keep the commandments, and the Lord shall grant it thee ; but let not a man reverse the due order, and expect, before he possesses humility and obedience, to reach the height of wisdom, for he cannot possess it, unless he proceed in the right order."[1] He knows that this impatience reveals the unlessoned stubbornness of a child ; it is sufficient proof that the time of weaning is not yet. " Grow on milk, that thou mayst become able to eat bread. . . . The bread from the table must pass through the mother's breast if it is to be food for an infant."[2] He is even more strongly convinced that the bitterness of the complaints is the clearest evidence of such immaturity. For, " if the fruit is already in thee, thou under-standest that thou must tolerate tares among the good."[3] He is therefore the more insistent : " We should take the utmost care lest anyone be weaned before the time. Let him fulfil the commandments of humility. He hath wherewith to practise ; let him believe in Christ, that he may understand Christ. Let him believe . . . and suck."[4] But it is an even more important truth " that Christ always gives faith, to make a man a Christian by giving it . . . that Christ should ever be the origin of the Christian, that in Christ the Christian should strike root, that Christ should be his head."[5] True also that " you are sons of the Church. In the Church you have progressed ; in the Church you will progress who have not yet progressed, and in the Church you must make fur-ther progress who have already made progress."[6] That is, our entire growth and development is never out of Christ, but deeper into Christ ; all our progress is never out of the Church, but deeper into the Church. " Thou goest not through one thing to another "[7] ; " thou goest through Me, thou goest unto Me."[8] For this " visibility in the flesh " is the visible presence of God in the flesh. But in relation to

[1] *Ibid.*, CXVIII, xxii, 8.   [2] *Ibid.*, CXXX, xi.   [3] *Ibid.*, xiii.
[4] *Ibid.*   [5] *Contra Litt. Petiliani*, I, v, 6.   [6] *Enarr. in Psalm.*, LXII, xvi.
[7] *In Johann. Tract.*, XIII, iv.   [8] *Enarr. in Psalm.*, CIII, iv, 6.

God we are always " babes at the mother's breast."[1] " Then shall we be always great in Him, if we are always tiny beneath Him."[2]

Thus is the sharp discord between the Augustinianisms of Hegel and Kierkegaard resolved in the " beauty of a contrast of opposites."[3] Hegel's Augustinianism is dominated by Spinoza's " love of God." But this " love " has a double aspect. If on the one hand it exhibits the Augustinian unity of " truth and love," at the same time there burns in it a sublimated " lust (*concupiscentia*) of the intellect " to make God captive in the concept, and thus to manipulate Him. Here, accordingly, the inner victory consists in the character which Augustine demands for love, the " chaste heart " which " loves chastely." This, however, does not simply mean that man should love God alone and for His own sake : " God wishes to be loved disinterestedly, that is, to be loved chastely, not to be loved because He gives something besides Himself but because He gives Himself."[4] He also protests against an " absorption of God " within the boundary of the subject : " Love God disinterestedly, grudge Him to none. Seize Him as many as can, as many as shall possess Him. He grows no smaller, you will not limit Him thereby."[5] He therefore deliberately emphasizes the " disinterested worship "[6] of " divine praise."[7] In other words, for Augustine " chaste love " is not only pure in the sense that God is its exclusive object ; it is also pure because it is the reverend awe which worships a transcendent Deity. It is the " chaste love " of the " disinterested worship " expressed by the psalmist's words, " I will freely sacrifice to Thee."[8]

But this " chastity " also overcomes, in Kierkegaard's Augustinianism, the paradox of the fear of God. There is, no doubt, in this paradox a vision of the absolute transcendence of the Divine Majesty and its unconditional claim upon

---

[1] *Ibid.*, XXX, xiii.   [2] *Ibid.*, LXII, xvi.   [3] *De Civitate Dei*, II, xviii.
[4] *Enarr. in Psalm.*, LII, viii.   [5] *Ibid.*, LXII, xxxiv.   [6] *Ibid.*, LII, viii.
[7] *Ibid.*, LIII, x.   [8] *Ibid.*

man. But at the same time there looms darkly a negative
concupiscence, the reverence which "maintains its distance"
from God in order to " safeguard self." Augustine, therefore,
says without hesitation that " the fear lest He come " is
the fear of " the adulterous woman " . . . whereas the sole
" fear of the chaste woman " is the " fear lest He forsake
her."[1] The fear of which God approves is chaste fear, the
fear which is aware of the presence of love within, but for
that very reason utters its awestruck " *non sum dignus*." It
is a " fear lest He delay," as it is a "fear lest He depart,"[2]
because love's knowledge of the infinite distance between
God and man always trembles with the knowledge that God
in no way comes within the scope of man's calculation, far
less can be held in his grasp. It is thus " chaste fear," not
only in the sense that it is the awe of " chaste love " and
therefore a sign that every " flight from God " is the effect
of a previous " flight to God,"[3] but in the distinctive meaning of " chaste," the chaste delicacy of feeling which is
ever aware of " God as always the greater," Whose reply
to every attempt to grasp Him is, " *Noli me tangere*." Since,
then, in " love " and in " fear " alike, " chastity " is all in
all, they become identical with each other. There is the one
intimate presence of God, Who is deeper within me than my
inmost self (" Thou art more inward than my inmost "),
because in any relationship of love He is the Master, Who from
the outset owns His child as His creature but will now possess
him in the " free servitude "[4] of love " Thou hast inscribed
Thy law in my heart with Thy Spirit as it were with Thy
Finger." Therefore this intimacy with God is at once fearing
love and loving fear : " that I might love Thee with a chaste
fear and fear Thee with a chaste love." "Thou Who art
more inward than my inmost hast written Thy law within
me in my heart with Thy Spirit, as it were with Thy Finger,

[1] *Ibid.*, CXVIII, xii, 3.   [3] *Ibid.*, CXXVII, viii.
[2] *Ibid.*, II, i, 8.   [4] *Ibid.*, XCIX, vii.

that I should not fear it like a slave without love, but love it with chaste fear as a son, and with a chaste affection fear it."[1]

Thus is the fearful alternative overcome between a comprehended Hegelian God, Who therefore is not God, and the unattainable God of Kierkegaard, of Whom therefore man must despair. It is overcome by the unity of the " God Who is at once without and within." " But what do I love when I love Thee ? Not the beauty of the body, not the fair adornment of time, not the bright light so dear to these eyes, not the sweet melodies of all kinds of song, not the sweet scent of flowers, unguents, and spices, not manna nor honey, not limbs pleasant to the embraces of the flesh. Not these do I love, when I love my God. And yet there is a light, a song, a fragrance, a food, an embrace, which I love when I love my God – the light, song, fragrance, food, and embrace of my inner man, where there shines in my soul that which no place contains, where there sounds that which time bears not away, where there is a fragrance which the breeze does not disperse, a taste which no greed makes less, and an embrace which no satiety puts asunder. This it is that I love, when I love my God."[2]

From this inner correlation between the unity of fear and love and the one God exterior and interior – the final position in which Augustine decisively overcomes the Augustinianism of modernity – it should be obvious where alone in this modern age his spirit finds its perfect reincarnation : in Newman.[3] For this correlation is precisely the quintessence of his work, that " fear and love must go together "[4] ; in more explicit terms, " that we fear Him while we love Him."[5]

[1] *Ibid.*, CXVIII, xxii, 6.   [2] *Confessions*, X, vii, 8.

[3] For a more detailed exposition see the author's *J. H. Newman, Christentum*, I–VIII, Freiburg, 1922 *f.* (English translation in the press, Sheed & Ward) ; also *Ringen der Gegenwart*, Augsburg, 1929, II, 802–879.

[4] *P. S.*, I, 303. The abbreviations are those of the Index to the Uniform Edition.

[5] *P. S.*, V, 28.

This is the distinctive spirit of his "real" God and Kingdom of God ; God in apprehensible reality, God "in real thought," God in the organ which apprehends reality, the conscience. But this very apprehension is the experience of His incomprehensibility : "In all such real apprehensions not only do we see Him at best only in shadows, but we cannot bring even those shadows together."[1] There is the intimacy of love in the "real" experience of the Augustinian "light, song, fragrance, food, and embrace," but then precisely does the soul experience fear as awe of "the true God."[2] "All is but a whirling of the reason and a dazzling of the imagination and an overwhelming of the feelings, reminding us that we are but mortals and He is God."[3] Augustine sinks to his knees : "If thou hast understood, it is not God ; if it is God, thou hast not understood."[4] In the same spirit Newman prays, "Unless Thou wert incomprehensible Thou wouldst not be God. For how can the Infinite be other than incomprehensible to me !"[5] But as in theology Newman completes that conquest of Protestantism contained in the ultimate logic of the contrast in unity of Hegel and Kierkegaard, so in philosophy also his victory over the modern age does not consist in simply holding together the tendencies which we have contemplated hitherto. In theology he settles accounts with the Reformation more thoroughly than Hegel and Kierkegaard, inasmuch as by his refutation of his own *via media*, the unrelenting realism of the *Twelve Lectures* addressed to the Anglican Party of 1833 and *The Present Position of Catholics in England*, and by his rejection of the optimistic hope of a "corporate reunion," he prophetically anticipated the conviction, born of the fiascos of Lausanne, Stockholm, and Malines, that the Reformation cannot be overcome by "negotiations" of any kind, but only by a thoroughgoing reversal of "first principles." It is

[1] G. A., 131.   [2] Mix., 309–320.   [3] Ibid., 320.
[4] Sermo LII, vi, 16.   [5] M. D., 308.

this cold realism of the English thinker which in philosophy also utters the decisive word. The tendencies expressed by Descartes, Pascal, Hegel, and Kierkegaard are counterbalanced, in Newman, by the " British realism " of Bacon, Locke, Berkeley, Hume, and Butler. It was no less a man than Hegel whose keen vision observed this " counterpoise of the English " (as he expresses it in his *Vorlesungen über die Geschichte der Philosophie*) in the contrast between Bacon and Jakob Boehme at the opening of the modern age [1]; in Locke as the counterweight to Descartes, Spinoza, and Malebranche [2]; and finally in the famous opposition between Hume and the Leibniz-Wolff alliance [3] which gave birth to Kant.

For Newman no doubt this factor represented in the first instance a further complication. This is shown by the way in which his philosophic wrestling, even to the late period of his life when the jottings in his diaries were set down, [4] is always with Locke, Berkeley, and Hume, while there is no doubt that Butler's *Analogy* was the medium through which St. Thomas's classical *Analogia* reached him. The influence is threefold. In the first place, British realism stresses the bond with the world visible to sense ; this, however, involves the danger that the spiritual world may appear unreal. Secondly British realism sets a special value on the knowledge conveyed and increased by practice ; this is all too easily accompanied by a distrust of theoretical knowledge, knowledge of the object " in itself." Finally, British realism is inclined to emphasize strongly the boundaries which confine the individual consciousness and render doubtful the existence of a world in itself common to all ; this, however, leads to that peculiar solipsism which may be regarded as the epistemological version of " my house is my castle." In this respect Berkeley is not the antithesis of Locke and Hume, but their inner and necessary fulfilment, to which

---

[1] *Werke*, XIX, 278. [2] *Ibid.*, 417 *sqq.* [3] *Ibid.*, 493 *sqq.*
[4] *Cf.* the author's *Ringen der Gegenwart*, II, 815 *sqq.*

the entire movement of sceptical realism must lead. But he introduces into the workaday pedestrianism of Locke and Hume an element of "sentimental romanticism" – his characteristic doctrine that the material world is an appearance of the world of spirit – and thus becomes, precisely by this aspect of his system, the British version of Descartes in his doctrine of God's immediate relation to the *chose qui pense* : the " pre-Raphaelite of philosophy."

There can be no doubt that Newman not only grew to his full philosophic stature by wrestling with all these three forms of British realism, but that the struggle left permanent traces. Not only does the *Grammar of Assent* sharply portray the dilemma between knowledge of reality (real apprehension) and knowledge of ideas (notional apprehension),[1] but notional apprehension threatens to fade into a background of unsubstantial wraiths. Moreover, by its emphasis upon the factor of " decision " in real assent (assent in the strict sense) the *Grammar of Assent* does but continue in a quieter vein the more passionate but naturally more one-sided argument of " The Tamworth Reading Room " – the defence of " action " against theoretical " inference." And that through the entire body of Newman's writing flow powerful currents whose source is Berkeley everyone knows who has felt the pendulum-swing in his words whenever he speaks of the reality of the outer world. It is Newman's most intangible, but perhaps most " English " quality – on the one hand mistrust of the " notional " by comparison with the solid earthbound " real " ; on the other the dream of the Sermon on the angels, preached in 1831, which remained his dream to the end : " every breath of air and ray of light and heat, every beautiful prospect, is, as it were, the skirts of their garments, the waving of the robes of those whose faces see God in heaven."

But this extreme fragility of problematic speculation,[2]

[1] *G. A.*, 33–39.   [2] *P. S.*, II, 362.

which reflects " his sensitiveness," becomes, under pressure
of this same mental environment, with all its additional
difficulties (the inner debate with Locke, Berkeley, and
Hume), the secure step, wellnigh as assured as a somnambu-
list's, with which in awe-inspiring boldness and calm he
treads the knife-edge stretching between the opposite abysses.
Indeed, it is not a strictly determinable mean. It is a
" poise." For it is mastery of the tension between the opposites, " singing strings," the epistemological equivalent of
his touch on the violin when he played Beethoven. This he
accomplished because, and so far as, he did not " nurse "
that " extreme fragility," but suffered it to break down
completely in the unreserved " surrender " which no longer
admits the least desire to " see " anything, not even self,
which God alone keeps and guides. " My unchangeableness
here below is perseverance in changing. Let me day by day
be moulded upon Thee, and be changed from glory to glory
by ever looking towards Thee and ever leaning on Thy arm."
From this root sprung his inner victory over that in which
Hegel saw the fundamental orientation of the modern
world : " pure interiority," of which " thought " is the
" culmination." That victory consists in what, taken by and
for itself, might be regarded as Newman's particular brand
of individualism – what has indeed been interpreted by
modernism in that sense – his doctrine of " conscience."
Continental modernism understands Newman's " conscience " as " consciousness," and by this alone reaches a
" pure interiority." Conscience, however, belongs to the
domain of ethics, and ethics simply as such lies within the
sphere of " practice," that is to say of " action " which
" resists." But for Newman conscience has a further significance peculiar to himself. It is essentially the Newmanic
form of Augustine's " God and the soul," the immediate
immanence of God in the soul. But whereas for Descartes

¹ *M. D.*, 508.

and Malebranche this immanence leads to a dangerous blurring of the distinction between God and the soul, a confusion of God with thought, it is precisely Newman's "conscience" which reveals most emphatically the interval between God and the soul, the interval which divides the master from the servant, holiness from the sinner, the judge from the prisoner at the bar, unfathomable mercy from the recipient of its free pardon. And since all self-sufficiency of the *ego* is thereby fundamentally eradicated by unreserved self-surrender, at this point also Newman's system decisively opens to consciousness the world outside itself, indeed "delivers" consciousness "up to it," in virtue of its "mission in the world," a penitential mission which admits neither the attitude of Hegel and Descartes, the superiority of the intellect, nor yet the attitude of "indignant suffering," as in Pascal and Kierkegaard.

This final combination – "fragility even to failure" and "irresistibility in failure" (the Pauline "when I am weak, then I am strong") – is also the basis of Newman's inner transcendence of the irreconcilable contrasts of the modern age (between Descartes and Pascal, Hegel and Kierkegaard). The decisive step is taken in his theory of "real" apprehension (*Grammar of Assent*). This "real apprehension" signifies (as is demanded by the logic of Newman's doctrine of conscience which we have just described) the definite installation of the intellectual interiority of consciousness in the unbounded and unattainable world of reality, the radical renunciation, therefore, of the self-contained intellect of Descartes and Hegel. But on the other hand, caught as he is in the flux and pulsation of the imponderable, Newman stresses man's unswerving orientation towards knowledge of an ultimate structure of this world, though it be such that it issues in the darkness of God's mysteries ; and thereby he destroys that "tragic agnosticism" which gnaws at the heart of Pascal and Kierkegaard.

The second step – the logical consequence of the former – is Newman's doctrine of the " Idea in history " (expounded in *The Development of Christian Doctrine*). Hegel, true to the dialectic of the Cartesian " pure intellectuality," saw in history only the logical presentation of the idea; for him, therefore, it is not the history of creatures, but the history of God's becoming. This involves the complete naturalizing of the historic revelation, because already, on the purely natural plane, history is, as such, the history of God. Kierkegaard, however, carrying out Pascal's *homme chaos*, cannot make the gulf wide enough between history, a resistant chaos for ever incomprehensible, and an ideal significance. So far from being " idea " history is, on the contrary, a mere " instant," that fragmentary, accidental thing, that alluring flash, the " instant." If, then, it is to be an " instant " of the " idea," it must be so in sheer contrast with its nature, not as an " instant of time " but only as an " instant of eternity." As an " instant of time " it is always simply that chaotic instant of temporal nothingness. Revealed history, therefore, can, as such, never be temporal, it can only be, in contrast with temporal history, eternity under the form of history, the " instant of God " cutting vertically across the time series like a lightning flash. Temporal history is of its nature a book closed and sealed to God. Newman's philosophy of history overcomes this dilemma, inasmuch as it carries over into history that vibrating tension between " idea " and " reality " which constitutes " real apprehension." History is the unfolding of the idea, not, however, as the logical deduction of reality from the idea, but in and by the forces of reality, as it apparently serves itself alone. Almost every event can be referred to purely real ends, but nevertheless it accomplishes such an unfolding of the idea that the immanent logic of the idea is revealed in those unfoldings. Moreover, revealed history is consequently, on a higher plane, the miracle of this interplay of contrasts. Human history, whose course is to all appearance purely natural, which indeed so often actually opposes God, and even appears to exclude His providential guidance altogether, nevertheless in all its stages subserves the unique historic revelation, unfolding with an awe-inspiring logic the fundamental ideas of God's Word.

Thereby, however, a third and last step is taken, and the antithesis between the optimism of Descartes and Hegel, in their judgement of the world and history, and the pessimism of Pascal and Kierkegaard, is radically removed. For God's greatness is revealed precisely in the fact that He reveals Himself in an opposing world. " The whole course of Christianity from the first . . . is but one series of troubles and disorders. Every century is like every other, and to those who live in it seems worse than all times before it. . . . Troubles . . . have ever been ; they ever shall be ; they are our portion. ' The floods are risen, the floods have lift up their voice, the floods lift up their waves. The waves of the sea are mighty and rage horribly ; but yet the Lord, who dwelleth on high, is mightier.' " [1] The sublimity of this conquest is the sublimity of Augustine. " God, by Whom was made the universe even with the evil it contains." [2] It was in presence of the fall of the old world that Augustine rose to this ultimate and most sublime vision. Newman saw man, the world, and history from the already almost prophetic perspective revealed to him by that final struggle between Christ and Antichrist legible on the countenance of the modern world. He is thus the peculiar and unique *Augustinus redivivus* of modern times, and that because, amidst the torrent which bears all things to their doom, his gaze is calmly fixed upon the God of the end. DEUS *omnia in omnibus.*

---

[1] *V. M.*, I, 354 *sq.*   [2] *Solil.*, I, i, 2.

ETIENNE GILSON

THE FUTURE OF
AUGUSTINIAN METAPHYSICS

TRANSLATED BY EDWARD BULLOUGH

THE FUTURE OF AUGUSTINIAN
METAPHYSICS

The fifteenth centenary of the death of St. Augustine will not fail to concentrate once again the attention of historians and philosophers upon his work. Many books have already appeared in honour of the occasion, and the present year will see many more. There will never, it is true, be too many ; in the first place because the immensity of the task exceeds the efforts of any single individual writer ; secondly and especially, because the very character of his work is such that it cannot live without the collaboration of interpreters who study it, assimilate it, and transmit the results of their labours to others. But this work of interpretation, a work of fundamental importance, would avail nothing without the complementary work of appreciation and assessment. Will this fifteenth centenary, we wonder, rest content with the historical statement of the existence, once upon a time, of a doctrine belonging to the past, classified and superseded, or will it mark a fresh outburst of vitality of Augustinian thought, a third or fourth renascence, heralding a new period of life ? This is the question that we propose to consider, by asking ourselves whether the thought to St. Augustine retains still to-day something of its original fertility, or whether it is now nothing but an object of curiosity for the diversion of the historian.

i. THE OBSTACLES

We may well ask ourselves whether Augustinianism has any future before it. In the first place, it is a Christian philosophy : this expression does not simply mean that his was the philosophy of a Christian, for a man may be a Christian and a philosopher without holding a Christian philosophy ; such a thing has happened – Réné Descartes would be a quite good instance. What, on the contrary, is characteristic of the thought of St. Augustine is that, in his case, revelation is the source, rule, and even the very food of his rational thought ; he holds faith to engender reason, and dogma, taken as such, to engender philosophy. Not by any means that he confuses belief and knowledge, or even philosophy and theology, for to believe in the dogma, and to deduce from it the consequences it implies, is, for him, no more philosophizing than it would be for any of our contemporary positivists. But to let reason go out to meet faith, to account rationally for his faith to himself, to construct, under the influence of a supernatural and transcendent light, a system of ideas which, though purely rational in themselves, would yet be impossible without this light, is what he had always meant to do, and what he did with wonderful success.

At the same time we cannot but recognize that his very success is one of the most serious obstacles standing in the way of Augustinianism to-day. *Nisi credideritis, non intelligetis* is and will always remain the charter of every Christian philosophy. It is what distinguishes a Christian system not only from anti-Christian systems, but even from systems merely compatible with Christianity. Now, in proclaiming this principle and repeatedly asserting it with his well-known emphasis, St. Augustine appears to cut himself off from the communion of philosophers whose fundamental principle is that every philosophy, properly so called, is amenable to reason only. When we ask St. Augustine to prove to us the existence of God, he asks us in his turn first to believe in it ; can we make the same request to our contemporaries without losing our qualification to be philosophers ? And if Augustinianism presupposes Christian faith as a necessary condition, are we not driven to the conclusion that, at best, it is but a philosophy good enough for Christians ?

But there is an even more serious question : we may well ask whether even for Christians, and more especially for Catholics, such a philosophy is still good enough. There has been a good deal of talk about " St. Augustine's exile " – wrongly, we hold, for there have always been, and there will always be, Augustinians among us ; but we should fail of the most elementary intellectual honesty if we hid from ourselves the suspicions and the sort of disfavour of which St. Augustine, *qua* philosopher, has been the butt in the minds of many Catholic thinkers. The causes of this situation, which, unless we are much mistaken, is a patent fact, are complex and numerous. A complete history of Augustinianism – an ocean added to the ocean of Augustinian study itself – would be needed to disentangle these causes ; but we may at least try to define the main causes, or at least those most directly accessible to observation.

Taking the question as a whole, it would seem that the principal difficulties confronting the progress of Augustinianism spring from one of its essential characteristics : its fundamental condition of incompleteness. Considered under this aspect, it appears, compared with Thomism for instance, as structurally quite different. All those who have had to teach the philosophy of St. Thomas know how little margin he leaves to the imagination of his interpreter. In expounding him, almost everything we may add of our own invention is false ; interpreting him means essentially to get to know him, to understand him ; it means never, or hardly ever, to complete him. If we venture to do so, we learn sooner or later to our cost that whatever we attribute to a master like him rarely amounts to more than an average intelligent misunderstanding. Hence the remarkable stability of Thomism in the course of history : its teaching has developed but little, fixed as it is by its very perfection, resting upon the evidence of its principles and rounded off by the rigorous completeness of its deductions. The history of Thomism up to the present is indeed the history of the thought of St. Thomas Aquinas, whereas the history of Augustinianism is by no means the history of the thought of St. Augustine.

However great St. Augustine is – and St. Thomas himself would have been scandalized at being placed above his master – he is far from having left us a complete system of philosophy. Neither he nor his time felt the need of it, and the character of his teaching can be understood only if we put ourselves back into the conditions under which it was conceived. It is difficult for us nowadays to realize St. Augustine's starting-point, and what a prodigious effort he had to put forth to set himself free from difficulties which, thanks to him, had ceased to exist for a man of the thirteenth century : the refutation of radical scepticism ; the discovery of spiritualism in opposition to the Manichæan materialism ; the solution of the problem of the existence of evil. We must never forget that St. Augustine took years before he came to conceive the bare possibility of a non-material reality and the compatibility of an imperfect universe with a perfect God. Little wonder that the painful conquest of these fundamental principles should have appeared to him, for the very reason that it allowed his reason henceforth to move freely within his Christian faith, as the equivalent of a complete philosophy. Once in possession of these key-positions, he clung to them with the full conviction that reason under proper guidance would have no difficulty in finding its way, provided it followed the light of faith.

In fact, as St. Thomas has justly observed, St. Augustine had but re-thought and deepened, from the point of view of a Christian, the essential elements of Platonism. He had done so with genius, but with an intuitive rather than systematic genius. By putting into circulation principles without the series of consequences which explain but at the same time limit them, he left behind him a philosophy rich in undefined possibilities, but incomplete, poorly protected, and for that reason exposed to all sorts of deviations. It is a fact of experience that Augustinians are rarely disciples of St. Augustine, and yet if it is made a matter of reproach against them they do not protest without reason : for they indeed begin with him, but are compelled to leave him, since he himself so often is content to make no more than a beginning. Augustinians are always conscious of having set out along the master curve, but they sometimes forget at what moment they went off at a tangent. Jansenius, Malebranche, Gerdil, are so many tangents of Augustinianism ; they are not St. Augustine.

To limit ourselves here to the sphere of pure metaphysics, we should say that the two most dangerous temptations imperilling the integrity of its essence to which Augustinianism has yielded are Cartesian idealism and modern ontologism.

Whether Descartes did or did not come, directly or indirectly, under the influence of St. Augustine, is a purely historical question, which in the present state of the texts cannot perhaps be wholly solved. Personally, we believe in the existence of a direct influence, but it matters little as far as the question we have raised is concerned. Whether Descartes did or did not study St. Augustine, the fact remains that his method condemned him to follow in metaphysics the road of St. Augustine. We hope to show that the converse is not true, and that the metaphysic of St. Augustine does not condemn the Augustinian to follow the Cartesian method. Herein lies, if we may say so in passing, the justification of Cartesian Christian thinkers, at whom it is fashionable to be scandalized, although they flourished not so very long ago. If we take the trouble to examine their manuals used for instruction in seminaries without any scandal, and, as far as we know, without any harm being done, it will be seen that not one of them followed the method of Descartes ;

but what they all find behind Descartes and cling to is St. Augustine. St. Augustine is Descartes *minus* the " Method " and the impossibilities which it entails ; Descartes is the attempt to invest the "Method" with the very substance of St. Augustine. Hence strange deformations inflicted upon Augustinianism, which are all the more dangerous as their principles are rarely apprehended.

It is a remarkable fact that scholastic philosophers to-day are constantly mistaken concerning the meaning of the Cartesian method. They usually do not penetrate beyond the appearances, and when a right feeling for what is foreign to them in Descartes's system leads them to attack it, they aim, by preference, in the first place at his methodical doubt. Kleutgen and Zigliara, so acute when they are dealing with St. Thomas, are guilty of surprisingly naïve mistakes in this matter. They insist upon proving that the first principles of knowledge, such as the principles of causality or of identity, are inaccessible to methodical doubt, as if Descartes had not proclaimed this fact before them. Mistaking entirely the Cartesian meaning of the term *principle*, they fight with shadows and win but the shadow of a victory. Perhaps this explains why, convinced as they are, they have been so little convincing. In reality, it is necessary to go farther back and to deal, behind the *cogito*, first principle of the Cartesian metaphysics, behind even the doubt which prepares it, with the mathematical method that demands both and justifies them to Descartes's satisfaction.

Descartes is essentially a man who attempted and carried through an experiment on the following notion : What happens to metaphysics, if we apply to it the mathematical method ? In our opinion, what happens to it is that you destroy it. Descartes did not hold that view ; on the contrary, he believed himself to be the first to save it ; but his very illusion was possible only because, under certain aspects, Augustinianism lent itself to the experiment.

If there is an incontestably Thomistic and, generally speaking, mediæval, principle, it is the principle " *a posse ad esse non valet consequentia.*" But the mathematician, as such, is convinced that "*a posse ad esse valet consequentia.*" Not only does the consequence hold for him, but it is the only consequence that holds ; nor can anything be more natural, since he works only upon ideas. There is no difficulty about it, as long as he confines himself to the strictly mathematical order. Applied to that aspect of the real for which it is designed, his method yields full results ; but as soon as he universalizes his method and decides to apply it to the totality of reality, Descartes entangles himself in singular difficulties. To start with, he wagers, without a shadow of possible justification, that there is nothing in things that escapes the mathematical method ; then, bound to model reality on his ideas, instead of modelling his ideas on reality, he is driven to recover the things only through concepts and to have no other starting-point but thought. There precisely Augustinianism presented itself for the Cartesian mathematical method as the only road opening out upon metaphysics.

St. Augustine too had a method, quite different, we believe, from that of Descartes, but it had led him to results which could be utilized by the new philosophy. Like Descartes, he had at first relied on pure reason ; again like Descartes, he had doubted, not only as a matter of method and exercise, but really and painfully ; again like Descartes, he had issued from his doubt, thanks to the triumphant evidence of his " *si fallor, sum* "; like Descartes, finally, he had from the evidence of thought, held by direct grasp, drawn the certitude of the spirituality and immortality of the soul, as well as the proof of the existence of God. Why should not Descartes, when by his method he had closed for himself the Thomistic road, have taken that of Augustinianism, which asked for nothing better ? By setting out upon it, he, who had no right to start from anything but t hought, recovered, without leaving for a moment the sphere of thought, all the conclusions of the traditional metaphysics, even, as he believed, the existence of the external world. That is the reason why the philosophy of St. Augustine, passing over into the system of Descartes and profiting by the new glory shed upon it by this genius, came to make common cause with a method which was not its own, joined forces, willy-nilly, with idealism, and, by losing its essence in such an apparent triumph, lost at the same time its fertility.

The second metaphysical tangent of Augustinianism is ontologism. Zigliara, who has done more than anyone to discriminate between these two doctrines, has nevertheless not hesitated to write with his customary loyalty : " That St. Augustine has very often used expressions which at first sight seem to favour and even openly to affirm ontologism, I would certainly not deny, for it would mean denying a very obvious fact." Perhaps something that goes deeper than mere expressions may be here in question, and without believing, any more than Zigliara does, in an, even moderate, ontologism of St. Augustine, we believe that we must go back to the very structure of his teaching in order to explain this fresh contamination and to purge his doctrine of it.

Once St. Augustine, for reasons which we shall have to state more in detail, had chosen as his starting-point the evident fact of the existence of the soul, he was bound to pass through the soul in order to reach all other spiritual substances, and more particularly God. His position is, therefore, from the very start very different from that which was later to produce the metaphysics of St. Thomas. It is true that, in both doctrines, it is by the analogy with the soul that God is best known ; but the point of bifurcation between Thomism and Augustinianism lies farther back, at the point where the knowledge which the soul has of itself is defined. According to St. Thomas, the soul is, for man as he is in this life, less known than the body ; for St. Augustine, even in this life, the soul is better known than the body. When, therefore, his thought attempts to rise to God, it will quite naturally find its starting-point or its footing in the soul, for the consideration of the body only serves to lead the soul to itself, whence it can then attain to God.

One consequence of this initial position, which in its turn rests upon the Augustinian conception of the union of soul and body, is that on such a theory every proof of the existence of God must rest in the last resort on a certain content of thought. St. Augustine has no other way open to him, but he sees in this direction a short and effective means of reaching his object. One of the possible contents of thought, capable of supporting a proof of the existence of God, might have been the very idea of God, considered as an effect, the cause of which required to be discovered. St. Anselm, Descartes, and even Hegel were later to take that road ; St. Augustine had the presentiment of it, even prepared it, but did not himself tread that path, for a reason perhaps deep enough to warrant our attempt later to determine it. The fact on which he fastened as the witness in ourselves of the existence of God was the true judgement. His analysis, often repeated, of the characteristics of necessity, immutability, and eternity, which formally define truth as such, is well known ; the antinomy between the contingency of the subject as the vehicle of truth on the one side, and the necessity of truth itself, whatever its object, on the other, can only be solved by the admission of a subsistent truth, the cause of all truth, which is God.

Nothing could be more impressive than such a metaphysical analysis, especially if followed through the meanders of his closely packed argument in the actual text of St. Augustine ; yet it is burdened with a heavy load of epistemological difficulties. Those who endeavour in all conscience to reconcile the Thomistic with the Augustinian theory of knowledge fail to observe that at the end of their efforts they have either eliminated the Augustinian proof of the existence of God, or have introduced into Thomism a proof which cannot find room there without changing the whole structure of the system : the proof by the truth, not in things (which St. Thomas admits) but in thought (which Albert the Great still admits, but St. Thomas admits no longer). And the reason for this is clear. For the Augustinian proof to have its full effect, it is necessary that, somehow or other, the human intellect, which conceives the truth, should not be the immediate sufficient cause of its truth ; if it is, there is no necessity for it to affirm the existence of God as cause, and then the way opening through thought is blocked at the very entrance. Doubtless there would remain the search for God in the order of causality, as cause of the intellect itself (which Albert the Great was to attempt), but St. Augustine does not even try this, because the only operation of the intellect which requires the affirmation of God as its sufficient reason is the conception of truth. He has, therefore, always to come back to the true judgement, or, what comes to the same thing, the intellect, so far as it is capable of conceiving truth. Unless, therefore, the immediate presence of God is imprinted as, so to say, a negative impress, on our judgements, there is no proof of His existence. In writing these lines, we are trying to keep as close as possible to the thought of St. Augustine, and we certainly use terms very much less forcible than the expressions he uses himself.

The essential feature of such a position, whatever its ultimate interpretation, is a definition of the human intellect which leaves us nothing wherewith to account for the existence of truth. If St. Augustine had simply held that man cannot know truth without an intellectual light given him by God, his analysis of the contingency and insufficiency of human thought would be lacking in a precise object ; but if, as the consensus of the most important texts shows, this is the point on which his proof rests, it must necessarily follow that Divine illumination (to give it its traditional name) must reach thought directly. For either it reaches it directly, and in that case we grasp at the same time the sufficient reason of truth and God who is its foundation ; or it reaches it indirectly, and in that case we are equally incapable of attaining to the existence of God and of accounting for truth.

This is both the central and the vulnerable point of the Augustinian metaphysics. Precisely because St. Augustine was at the very antipodes of ontologism, he is poorly protected against it. He never dreamt of restraining those who might attempt to go off at the tangent followed later by Gerdil and Gioberti. It occurred to him so little that, as Zigliara himself admits, he calmly supplied them with the weapons, or at least with the pretexts. To say that we " know in God," or that we see His hidden light, is this not tantamount to inviting the metaphysician in search of a mystical intuitionism to treat God as the very light of our thought, as the natural and first object of this thought, so that, instead of knowing Him through things, we know things through Him? This deviation begins from the end of the twelfth century onwards, under the influence of Arabic neo-Platonism, and especially of Avicenna ; dammed in by the efforts of St. Bonaventura and of St. Thomas Aquinas, it spreads in the seventeenth century with Malebranche, thanks to the influence of Cartesian idealism, and reaches its height in the nineteenth century under the impulse of German idealism.

In these circumstances, it is not a matter of surprise to observe the unexpected and yet undoubted phenomenon described as " St. Augustine's exile." It is certainly an unexpected phenomenon to find St. Augustine an object of suspicion within Catholicism itself, where everyone respects and loves him to an extent that makes him almost indistinguishable from it. It is no less a painful fact because it gives the impression of an inner disruption of that Christian thought whose indivisible unity is a matter of daily experience for all those that live it. To remedy the situation, the

Thomists try with as much persistence as ingenuity to bring St. Augustine over to them. Nothing can be more legitimate as long as it is a matter of showing that Thomism accounts equally well, or better, for all that is true in Augustinianism. But it is an operation not without danger for Thomism itself, if carried out by hands other than the infallible hands of St. Thomas himself, for Thomistic thought is sometimes contaminated in its essence by contact with a thought other than its own; and it is always fatal to Augustinianism, which, if the operation is successful, disappears by assimilation in an essence different from its own.

Augustinians have another remedy. They protest; they attack; they denounce the situation. Yet it is they who are responsible for it. The true Thomist has at his disposal a complete, coherent Christian philosophy; he lives in an atmosphere where his metaphysical thought and his religious life can expand and grow in perfect freedom. It is his duty to join the Augustinian in conclusions common to both, but it is also his right to do so by ways which are peculiar to him. As to the legitimacy of the ways preferred by the Augustinian, it is for the Augustinian, not the Thomist, to prove it. All that he needs do to succeed, it seems to us, would be to be not less, but a little more, Augustinian. In face of this negligence of the philosophers to take in hand the task which is theirs, the historian, whose proper function is merely to preserve intact the deposit of tradition, has the impression of a dangerous abstention; he hopes, therefore, to be forgiven for doing what he can to palliate it.

ii. THE MEANING OF AUGUSTINIANISM

The difficulties which at the present time beset Augustinianism are not an ill for which we need to find remedies, for St. Augustine himself is not affected by any ill; all that is needed is to return from the Augustinianism of the

Augustinians to that of St. Augustine. This task is not easy. There is room for asceticism even in the most abstract metaphysical thought, for a change in point of view means a change in habits. We have, therefore, by no means the pretension of convincing the reader of the true meaning of Augustinianism by simply setting before him what we believe it to be, not only because with the best will in the world we may be mistaken, but also because, even if we were right, we should have to let time do its work and allow ideas to come to maturity of themselves. The real question is, whether at this time of the day we can reverse the engine and find St. Augustine as he was, before three centuries of idealism had passed over his teaching. If it is possible at all, the essential operation, in order to do so, consists in eliminating the method of Descartes from the system of St. Augustine.

The important point before all else is to understand that the two philosophies have no essential relation, and altogether, if there is any relation between them, that it is, so to say, unilateral, not between St. Augustine and Descartes, but between Descartes and St. Augustine. While admitting that the first principle of Cartesianism is the universal application of the mathematical method, with the resulting idealistic method, we can admit as equally evident that nothing of the sort is to be found in St. Augustine. Now, it follows therefrom, on further reflection, that even when the two philosophies employ the same concepts and arrange them in the same order, they do not mean the same things. Whether the *si fallor sum* of St. Augustine has or has not led up to the *cogito ergo sum* of Descartes, it cannot be charged with the same implications. Pascal congratulates Descartes on this fact. One might feel disposed, perhaps, to congratulate St. Augustine.

By placing the *cogito* at the beginning of his metaphysics as fundamental basis of the entire edifice, Descartes is committed beforehand, in the name of his mathematical method,

to attributing to thought whatever is contained in his clear
and distinct idea, and, correlatively, to attribute to it only
what is thus contained in it. In this sense, the *cogito* is as
rich in exclusions as in affirmations ; it is but the first of
that series of conceptual snippets which substitutes progressively a mosaic of abstractions for the continuity of reality,
digs impassable trenches between the aspects of the concrete,
and requires the invention of illusory bridges for the attempt
to cross them again. This is not the place to set out the
numberless difficulties in which the *cogito* entangles metaphysics ; what matters is to observe that the very *cogito* of
Descartes, that is, the one of all Descartes's steps which we
would most certainly expect to furnish a concrete reality in
all its proper substantiality, furnishes actually only that part of
the reality which can be retained in idea, for whatever part
of the *ego* the idea does not contain it denies : *a non nosse
ad non esse valet consequentia.*

When, on the contrary, we consider the attitude of St.
Augustine, it appears as very different from that of Descartes,
and each of his theses displays a fruitfulness which Cartesianism destroyed by its very rigidity. To begin with, instead
of being a method practised upon ideas, Augustinianism is
an enquiry concerning the concrete content of thought. It
is true that, for St. Augustine as much as for Descartes, man
apprehends himself only through his ideas, but St. Augustine
does not hold in anticipation that his inner experience will
divide itself into a certain number of simple natures and
defined essences ; taking man altogether, he observes him,
and while he formulates him in ideas, he models his ideas
on the empirical content that he has observed. Hence the
fundamental character of his work, which, it must be said,
Cartesianism has not only not safeguarded, but systematically destroyed. In proportion as the teaching of St. Augustine
aimed at being a metaphysic, it is a metaphysic based upon
a psychological empiricism, or, if preferred, a metaphysic

of inner experience. Hence its extreme suppleness, its power of rebirth, and the very incompleteness which left a permanent possibility of progress open before it.

This essential characteristic is displayed in the thought of St. Augustine from its very beginnings. It too opens with doubt ; but this doubt is not methodical or intentional, still less a pretence, like that of Descartes ; St. Augustine is the prey of doubt, uncertain and almost despairing of finding truth. What is, for the French philosopher, but the initial step in a regulated order of thoughts is for St. Augustine a concrete and painful experience, an illness from which he has suffered and of which he has cured himself. Hence the remedy he has discovered and now offers us is no more necessary than the illness itself : his *si fallor sum* appears in its place whenever sceptical uncertainty threatens him as a possible danger, but its place is not at the beginning of a general exposition of his teaching, because the radical preventive of doubt is much less the *cogito* than the act of faith. Whoever believes in God and His word holds a truth infinitely richer and more fruitful than the *cogito* : " I believe, therefore I know " is better as a first principle than " I think, therefore I am."

For the same reason, the Augustinian empiricism discovers in the *cogito* something very different from what the mathematical method of Descartes discovers in it, for Descartes is committed once and for all to find in it nothing immediately but the essence of thought to be defined, whereas St. Augustine finds in it the whole of man to explore : man, that is, the body, the soul, and grace. The point is of such importance as to warrant special emphasis.

Three centuries of idealism have produced in us so intimate an adaptation to the Cartesian method that, wherever we observe its absence, we seem to observe an empty gap. Here, however, we encounter a solid. What St. Augustine discovers is, in the first place, his thought ; but instead of denying – even provisionally – what it is *not*, in order to define it better, he takes together with it all that it is not, and wherein he finds it, to compare it with and locate it in. Thus, his thought is that of a man who thinks, and a man is a body among other bodies, just as much as a spirit among other spirits. Analysing his thought means for him analysing the beings which are presented in it quite as much as analysing it itself. He finds there all the degrees of reality taken in its complexity and its hierarchic order : inorganic being which only is ; the plant which is and lives ; the animal which lives and feels ; finally man, who lives and feels and thinks. Thought as it apprehends itself directly is, therefore, in this case a life of a higher order than the others, and it apprehends consequently the others in itself, not in the manner of Descartes as something foreign to its essence, but as inferior virtualities which it cannot but have realised, since it apprehends itself as occupying the highest degree. The *sum* of St. Augustine affirms at one stroke the existence of man – not only of one half of him, destined to struggle desperately to rejoin the other half.

It is at this point, it seems to us, that the original deviation inflicted by modern Augustinianism on the authentic Augustinianism must be sought. There is a great temptation to see in it nothing more than an inconsistent idealism. Yet, if we may be allowed to use an expression unknown to St. Augustine, his philosophy is fundamentally just as realist as that of St. Thomas Aquinas. It is possible to read St. Thomas though the spectacles of Hume ; the thing has actually been done. It is also possible to read St. Augustine through the spectacles of Descartes, and the St. Augustine obtained in the second case is about as good as the St. Thomas obtained in the first. We confess to disliking the word *realism*, though it is often difficult to avoid using it ; perhaps some day, when it has been purged of certain meanings, it may be used without fear. What cannot in any case admit of the slightest doubt is that every substitution of abstract concepts for reality, and of a geometrical analysis for the investigation of concrete experience, is repugnant to the very essence of authentic Augustinianism. Another method may be preferred, but in that case we ought to realize that we are no longer Augustinians.

If this matter had been fully appreciated, the illusion of an ontological St. Augustine, or a St. Augustine tending to ontologism without fully committing himself to it, would never have arisen. Malebranche (whom we do not, by the way, consider as an ontologist), Gerdil, Gioberti, and many others, believe they can justify their point of view by a skilful exegesis of Augustinian texts on divine illumination. The Thomistic interpreters, like the eminent Zigliara, attempt the opposite operation by the same method. This method may have to have its day, but in the last resort it is worth only as much as the whole ideology on which it rests. All that such analyses establish is that at times the letter of St. Augustine invites ontologism and at others rejects it. But what is the significance of the letter? To discover it, we have to deal with his ideas. And here again it seems to us that every ontologism presupposes an idealist interpretation of Augustinianism and falls to the ground together with that interpretation.

Assuming it be admitted that St. Augustine's method is as we have described it, what do we find as the necessary starting-point of our search? Facts, and nothing but facts. These facts may be, and often are, facts of inner experience, they may be ideas – but ideas taken not as principles of deduction, but as the basis of induction. The problem of the existence of God enjoys no privileged position in his teaching. It is, indeed, a unique case in respect of the reality at stake and consequently also in respect of the nature of the datum which allows us to attain to it, but this datum differs from other data only in content, not in nature. Like being, like life, like

U A

sensation, like thought, truth is a fact ; like other facts, it is presented to our empirical observation ; like other empirical observations, it demands of metaphysics the discovery of its sufficient reason ; and if God alone can furnish its sufficient reason, we shall have proved the existence of God. Nothing here ever leaves the strictly philosophical order to pass over into mystical intuition and to substitute it for philosophical thought. The mystical order is certainly anticipated, hoped for, prepared for, but we have not got there yet ; we are even still so far from it that it is never by pure philosophy that we can reach it : the order of knowledge has first to be superseded by the order of charity.

Every ontological interpretation of St. Augustine presupposes, then, a more or less complete misunderstanding of his radical empiricism. This explains also why such an interpretation believes itself able to introduce idealism into it. The *primum cognitum* of St. Augustine is not God ; it is man within the universe, and, within this universe and this man, the experience of a true judgement. But it must be added that this *primum cognitum* is not even the *primum reale* ; on the contrary, it becomes intelligible only on condition of finding its sufficient reason in a transcendent fact which provides its explanation. It is of the very essence of Augustinianism to affirm that this transcendent fact has left on man its mark and impress, that this impress is decisively legible for us only in true thought ; but an impress is not the seal, and to forget that is the sure way of destroying Augustinianism. Far from taking his starting-point, like Gioberti, from a *primum cognitum*, which is, *pro tanto*, the First Being, St. Augustine starts from a complex *cognitum*, in which he distinguishes by analysis an order of reality which postulates in its turn that of the First Being. Once this Being is apprehended and posited, it becomes possible to set off into an order which is not that of deduction, but rather of production ; and even then it must be remembered that the start is taken not from a principle, but from the consequence, since we ourselves are only a consequence. Whatever, then, the letter of St. Augustine may be – and we have tried elsewhere to explain what it signifies – it cannot signify ontologism, unless it implies the negation of the entire thought of St. Augustine : the doctrine of divine illumination is not the vision of the First Cause, but the induction of the First Cause, starting from an effect, namely truth.

But we have to proceed, we think, even farther on that road in order to give back to the Augustinian empiricism its proper character. Among the losses it has suffered in the course of history, perhaps the most surprising loss is that of its religious inspiration. An Augustinianism without grace is surely a strange metaphysical monster. Yet it has seen the light of day, and again we owe it to Descartes. Not by any means that Descartes ever dreamt of denying grace, but since it eluded the grasp of the mathematical method he had to relegate it to an extra-philosophical order and had to isolate it as another piece of that conceptual mosaic which for him was reality. For St. Augustine, on the contrary, the initial *sum* contains the supernatural order given in his experience and his being, as well as the natural order into which the supernatural is inserted. He cannot forget in his philosophizing that his first attempt to attain to truth and beatitude ended with an appeal of the reason to faith and of the will to grace. The congenital impotence of our intellectual light to apprehend truth, a correlative impotence of our will to compass the good until truth and goodness are accepted as the gifts of God, instead of being conquered like the spoils of the victor, had been St. Augustine's experience, undergone with an inner clarity of evidence unparalleled by anything else. Why, then, should a consistent psychological empiricism refuse, how could it avoid, to take this fact into account as much as the others ?

St. Augustine never dreamt of avoiding it, any more than

Maine de Biran, one of the most authentic of his race, while
under the threat of his approaching death he felt the sting of
his conscience and found in it an unimpugnable sign of the
presence of grace. He felt it as soon as it was there and immediately surrendered to it. More fortunate, St. Augustine
surrendered earlier ; that is why the supernatural order by
which he had access to truth was for him always an integral
part of his philosophical inquiry. It is grace which turns
knowledge into wisdom and moral effort into a virtue, with
the result that instead of regarding Christianity as a belated
crowning of philosophy, he sees in philosophy an aspect of
Christianity itself, since it is the Way, the Truth, and the
Life. Considered under this aspect, Augustinianism is something else and something more than a Christian philosophy ;
it is its very charter and enduring model. Beside it there
are anti-Christian philosophies to be found, or philosophies compatible with Christianity ; but to be Christian
qua philosophy a philosophy must be Augustinian or nothing.
His metaphysic of nature completes a metaphysic of grace,
because nature is given to the Christian in grace, which,
working in him inwardly, manifests itself there in the manner
of a cause revealed by its effects.

Thus restored in the purity of its essence, the philosophy of
St. Augustine seems to us capable of setting out upon a new
and fruitful course, but only on condition that those who
undertake to promote it exercise care not to betray it. To
put a stop to the painful sense of St. Augustine's exile all
that is needed is that those who have exiled themselves from
him should return to him ; they will find him where he has
never ceased to be – at the very heart of Christian thought,
side by side with St. Thomas Aquinas, who may have
differed from him, but has never left him.

The fact is that both are indispensable. Those who judge
of the history of Catholic thought from the outside may see
in the present-day triumph of Thomistic philosophy nothing

more than an accident of history or an incident in the ideological game. But, if we admit that a sole religion is bound
to find expression in a sole *magisterium*, and ask which
metaphysician can be regarded as the model and norm of a
Catholic philosophy, whom could we choose but St. Thomas?
Him and no other ; not even St. Augustine. The perfection
and completeness of his work protect it against the ceaseless
deviations to which Augustinianism remains exposed. Considered in its living workings, Thomism is completed ; the
framework within which its future progress can be realized is
set up. Augustinianism has yet to be completed, and by reason of its very nature will always remain in that condition.
Nothing could be more logical and even necessary than that
the Catholic Church should have chosen St. Thomas as her
official Doctor, but we should fly in the face of facts and of
her spirit in thinking that the choice of St. Thomas meant
the exclusion of St. Augustine. Far from contradicting each
other, the two doctrines complete each other, and their complementary nature does but indicate the infinite wealth of
the religious reality whose rational exploration they attempt. God alone is necessary, and numerical diversity
emerges simultaneously with the emergence of the contingent. All that matters is simply to know whether Augustinianism is something contingent that Christian thought can
easily do without. We do not think so ; it remains to give
shortly our reasons for thinking so.

Like the work of St. Augustine, the work of St. Thomas is
that of a saint. For a variety of reasons, some of which are
co-essential with his work, it takes longer to become aware
of this in his case than in the case of St. Augustine. Still, of
all the discoveries we enjoy by living for a long time in
close contact with him, one of the most certain is, that of
him, as of his master St. Dominic, it is true to say " *aut de
Deo, aut cum Deo.*" What is apt to disguise in part this obvious
truth is partly St. Thomas's intellectualism and partly what

might be called his " physicism." The famous utterance of
St. Paul about the *invisibilia Dei* has become for him, as
it were, the programme which philosophy has to accomplish. Watching him in his exploration of the nature of
ea quæ facta sunt, we are apt to forget what he is searching
for. Yet it is equally true to say that it is nothing but God
that he searches for and that it is there that he is searching
for Him. Taking man as he conceives him within nature as
he finds it, St. Thomas asks himself the question, before all
else, whether a universe like ours carries with it its own
sufficient reason, and, if not, where it is to be found. Hence
his entire theodicy is essentially cosmological. Search is
sometimes made for a key to the system of St. Thomas, and
after having conscientiously explored the *Summa Theologica*
its supposed discoverer generally offers us a concept. But the
object of Thomistic philosophy is not ideas ; its object is
things, for a real philosopher always speaks of things ; it is
the professors of philosophy who talk of ideas. The fundamental object, the primary experience on which St. Thomas
continually bends his exploring gaze, is the fact of physical
change. He wants to know its nature, its conditions, its
causes. Convinced as he is that here is, not the only reality,
but the most obvious reality for man as he is, the philosopher
selects this as the best starting-point because it is the most
evident and accessible. Not that St. Thomas has any illusions
as regards the knowledge of God that such a metaphysic can
give us. If we start from the most crudely sensible fact in
order to attain to the purest intelligible, no wonder that in
such circumstances we end in a *quia est* whose *quid est* escapes
us. But at least this *quia est*, and the little we induce concerning the *quid est*, cannot elude our grasp ; they participate in the evidential and solid nature of the initial fact on
which the entire structure rests. It would be rather naïve to
ask on what grounds St. Thomas selects this philosophy ; for
a philosopher does not select his philosophy, he accepts the

only philosophy he holds to be true. At best we might perhaps take into consideration the circumstances in which he found himself, the contamination which Augustinianism had undergone, and the state of confusion that its teaching presented, but these would be in the last resort merely accidental reasons which would make no difference to the essential question. If St. Thomas had thought that the philosophy of St. Augustine were the best, it would have been easy for him to restore its essence ; if he preferred to do something else, the reason was that he visualized the possibility of a truer system.

Having said that much, the fact remains that by the very act of choosing the way he considered best he precluded himself from at the same time following another. St. Thomas was not an eclectic, ready to stitch together pieces borrowed from different philosophies to give them the external appearance of a system. He was a true philosopher, and though agreeing with St. Augustine on the meaning of the problems as well as on the formula of their solution, he yet did not consider himself justified in adopting it for the technical proof of these solutions when this seemed to him unsatisfactory. Every choice implies a limitation. Basing his efforts strictly upon the cosmological foundation of his theodicy St. Thomas was precluded from basing it upon its psychological foundations. It is a question not merely of the practical difficulty of exploring two such different fields of research, or the difference of aptitude required for the task, but of the divergence of the roads followed by St. Augustine and St. Thomas. They can meet again in the same conclusions, but the roads leading to them, though constantly crossing, never follow at any point the same direction. All that immense field of inner observation, wherein St. Augustine has no rival, would remain fallow if he were to be abandoned ; none of the tracks he has started would be pursued ; those ascensions that God has prepared for the heart of

man would cease to be an object of meditation by the
philosopher as such ; all sorts of possible ways to God would
be definitely closed which it is perhaps better to keep open
for the greater good of Christian thought.

What it is consequently important to grasp is that the programme of Christian philosophy is the same for both St.
Thomas and St. Augustine : *invisibilia Dei per ea quæ facta
sunt*. It is in no case possible for man to start from God to
deduce from Him the creature ; on the contrary, he must
mount from the creature to God. The course recommended
by St. Augustine – and herein lies his personal contribution
to the treasure of tradition – is the path to God, leading
through this particular creature which is man, and in man,
thought, and in thought, truth. But this means, quite beyond
speculations about the nature of truth and its metaphysical
conditions, a sort of moral dialectic that, taking as object of
its search the search itself by man of God, endeavours to
show the presence in the heart of man of a contingency much
more tragic and disturbing than that of the universe, because it is the contingency of our own beatitude. Even when
we know how and why we are capable of truths, we still need
to know why we are capable of the desire of truth ; we need
to understand the presence in us of an appeal by God who,
working in our soul, creates in us a fruitful restlessness, moves,
stirs our soul, and leaves it no rest until it has finally put
itself into His hands. That this opens a field of inexhaustible
fertility to analysis and metaphysical reflection is sufficiently
proved by the recent controversies about the possibility of a
natural desire of God in man. St. Augustine opened the
way, but the Augustinians mistook it when, setting out on
it themselves, they mistook his description for a demonstration and their emotions for proofs. It is for them to create
an entire technique, to set up a metaphysic of charity able
to meet the strict demands of Thomism ; to give to nature
what belongs to nature, and to grace what belongs to grace ;

able to discriminate between moral asceticism and the knowledge which it conditions ; and, while observing better than hitherto the distinction of plans and orders, to *verify* Augustinian teaching, in the full sense of that word : adding to its truth in the future the truth which it contained in the past, instead of merely confirming, and sometimes of diminishing, that truth. One of the great features of superiority in Thomism is that it possesses enough creative power to assimilate the results of Augustinianism ; the only question of the moment is whether Augustinianism has retained enough creative power to assimilate, without destroying itself, the decisive advances made by St. Thomas Aquinas.

We venture to hope so. We are personally convinced that other ways may be possible, and even that they may have advantages over that followed by St. Augustine ; but we are not prepared to assert that that of St. Augustine is impossible, or that it offers nothing but disadvantages. It is impossible not to be struck at once by his extraordinary philosophical vitality. St. Anselm left, in our opinion, the right road, when, abandoning the fundamental problem of the origin and of the ontological foundation of the idea of God, he shifted the burden of proof to the inner necessity of the concept itself. His mechanism for deducing God carries no conviction, and gives the impression that what is of value in it lies rather in what it hides and neglects than what it places in the forefront and shows. It is not in the *Proslogion* but in the *De Veritate* that he lays his hand upon that secret door behind which God stands. Yet St. Anselm is an outstanding witness to that tenacious conviction in the heart of man that there is a divine sign by which the creature can recognize his Maker : *signatum est super nos*. By following on the footsteps of St. Anselm in their turn, Descartes, Malebranche, Leibniz, Hegel, bear each one witness in his own manner to the persistence of this sentiment. Pascal and Maine de Biran, on the other hand, attest the vitality of the moral and religious dialectic. Philosophical thought does not usually pursue with such pertinacity roads leading nowhere. It may grope, it may err and lose its way, but, if need be, it is capable of turning back, to make a fresh start and recover itself.

This is, we think, what Augustinianism can and ought to do, and the progress of Thomistic thought is vitally interested in the doing of it. It would be easy to show how much Augustinianism could gain in precision, in discipline, and enrichment of every kind by contact with Thomism, but St. Thomas himself is there to prove that a St. Thomas is impossible without a St. Augustine. All that the Master has gathered from his illustrious predecessor, not by way of an external eclecticism, but by a real absorption and assimilation, disciples could gather in their turn, if a renewed Augustinianism offered them something to assimilate. But to do that, Augustinianism itself would have to become assimilative and creative, as it was in St. Augustine. It is capable of so becoming ; it will so become, once it realizes that its function is to do well what has been badly done by modern idealism, to re-establish it on the foundations of a psychological realism which is its natural basis, alone capable of bearing its erection. If it is thus assimilative and creative, an immense future opens out before it. It can secure to contemporary thought the legitimate possession of truths whose presence this thought feels confusedly without being able to grasp them, because it grasps them together with errors ; by means of Augustinianism, Christianity can once more accomplish its purifying, liberating, creative task. Everything invites it to this task ; everything is waiting for it. Let Augustinianism embark upon this task, and in proportion as it will be true, it need fear nothing from anyone, from the Church less than from all the rest. The unity of Catholicism is not at stake ; it is not waiting to be brought about ; it exists. For the last six centuries Thomism and Augustinianism have gone side by side ; six centuries – fifteen centuries : it counts for little in the life of the Church. They may still go for long together in exile ; what they cannot prevent is that every one of their successful efforts to be more completely themselves will bring them more closely together, for their source is at the same spot, on Calvary ; and their goal is at the same spot, on Thabor.

MAURICE BLONDEL

THE LATENT RESOURCES IN
ST. AUGUSTINE'S THOUGHT

TRANSLATED BY FR. LEONARD, C.M.

THE LATENT RESOURCES IN
ST. AUGUSTINE'S THOUGHT

The study of St. Augustine raises problems peculiar alike to his method and his doctrine.

The fundamental originality informing his whole philosophy is what in the first place is of the greatest importance to grasp, and we shall be able to grasp it only by realizing the reasons for the perennial fertility of his philosophy and the high promise the future holds for it. Leaving out of account the enduring causes of success and influence common to it and other great systems of the past, we propose in this essay to try to ascertain why this ' Catholic philosophy ' —as profoundly philosophical as it is profoundly Christian – offers us – over and above the rich abundance of particular truths which it contains – something more than one system among many – a unity of thought and life, a novel and superior kind of philosophy in close relation to the aspirations and needs of many contemporary minds. The time has, no doubt, come for the more explicit realization of what may hitherto have been but obscurely felt, desired, or practised, and now needs to be more fully understood, more amply justified as regards both the method itself and the solution of the problems which still continue to perplex many minds.

We may begin by admitting the reasons – they may be described as commonplace – for the perennial interest attaching to the author of the *Confessions*, *The City of God*, so many admirable treatises, letters, and sermons : the moving tones, the glowing imagery, the charm of expression, the vigour of dialectic, the splendour of spiritual vision, all combine to form a whole which, viewed from without, impresses the spectator as something unique, like the beauty of a masterpiece of art.

But there is more – ever so much more. If philosophies survive, it is because of the element of truth they convey, or, rather, which conveys them.

The philosophy of St. Augustine combines, more intimately, perhaps, than any other system, two very distinct elements : on the one hand, an intellectual structure, subtle and rigorous analyses, a warp and woof of logic, a perpetual insistence on clarity, and a generally successful effort to achieve such intelligibility as might satisfy a mind possessed of the highest degree of acuteness and perspicacity ; on the other, an impetuosity which masters every detail and seems to transport the whole soul far beyond the regions where dialectic, however vivid and swift, seems a mere bloodless and desiccated assortment of bones. In proportion, therefore, as its teaching reflects that " beauty ever ancient and ever new " which Augustine regretted that he had come to love so late, a philosophical system enjoys a share of the permanence of the ideas it radiates. And yet this is an inadequate explanation – and particularly inadequate where Augustine is concerned – of a persistent survival which makes him almost a man of our time, a man of all times, and preserves his identity in the presently nameless multitude of so many pioneers of learning and expositors of truth. Augustine always remains himself.

He has been compared to a great, living stream, an Amazon among rivers. But the current in this case is so overwhelming that men in every age, in every crisis of the Christian conscience, have striven in vain to draw off its waters and mingle them with those of other streams, or turn them to a thousand uses ; the immense volume is only increased by tributaries, recovers the waters drawn off, and purifies them once more. And, whatever it may carry with it, the river Augustine still preserves its own name, its freshness, its impetuosity, its " seminal virtues," its dynamic, fertilizing energy. And although the truths involved are quite impersonal, it is not the truths alone which give Augustine his perennial value : he has made them so completely part of himself that to attain them we must return to, and pass through, him.

Yet even such a simile as this gives us no true idea of Augustine's originality. We must go on to still stranger paradoxes – for instance :

Most of the particular theories or fragmentary truths which disciples, more or less faithful in intention to Augustine, have borrowed from him in the course of centuries have been not so much a translation of his real thought as a deformation. His disciples, so far from interpreting their master, have, even more than is usually the case, done him a positive disservice. So far from enriching, they have not only impoverished but also occasionally misrepresented him. And it is his opponents in the end who will be considered as having contributed most to the discovery of his secret and the renewal of his influence.

There is a paradox still more surprising :

When Augustinianism seemed to be resulting in dangerous confusions or encouraging perilous tendencies, there was no lack of opposition, reprisal, and effort to restore the balance. And it so happened that his adversaries, by their very criticisms, secured a more penetrating knowledge of the real Augustine. They thought they would confine the current, stem the tide : in reality, they merely encouraged the taking of fresh soundings and thereby showed that the Augustinian waters rose from depths still deeper than had thitherto been suspected. The course of our study will doubtless show, by a few significant examples, the practical verification of this law of interpretation, which is only applicable to such a doctrine as his. And this very originality may in the end strike us as a powerful confirmation of the vitality no less than the truth of such a philosophy, seeing that it shows itself capable of

WA

absorbing and assimilating what appeared to be opposed to it.

But there is still another and final peculiarity to be observed. For – supreme paradox – not only does Augustine's doctrine not lightly tolerate biased expositions and derivations which in most cases are mere distortions : not only does it reduce into its own power and subject to its own authority speculative innovations which appeared to be in contradiction to it, even though they derived from the salutary shock which it administered, but the very internal strains from which it appeared to be suffering, and which seemed to prevent it attaining the completeness of a systematically constructed edifice, ultimately serve to assure its profound cohesion, to revive its interior power of unity, and enable such a plastic force to assimilate further elements, because of one same dominating idea. And this is perhaps the way in which we shall most clearly perceive the secret of the ever-fruitful youth of Augustinianism, and that Augustinianism offers us the pattern, though it be only a rough sketch, of a truly integral philosophy, not only directed to a definite end, but also susceptible of unlimited adaptations and developments.

To speak of his influence in the past and make no mention of the message he brings us to-day and the help we expect from him for to-morrow would be to betray him, to treat him as a corpse, whereas he is, in fact, the most alive of the living and has no need of our purple cerements. All that he asks is that he may continue to help us, and he has more to give us than ever.

(i)

One preliminary point, however, should give us pause, and really deserves a critical examination : is the doctrinal claim we have just put forward realizable ? Is it possible to combine permanence and perpetual renewal ; and, if Augustine remains plastic, is it not because he is, in point of fact, wanting in systematic rigour ?

This is a preliminary objection which has, often implicitly, prevented many historians from giving Augustine a place amongst the ranks of professional philosophers, so to speak. It is an act of injustice which should now be put an end to.

Moreover, it is worth remarking that in the past, for want of sufficient care for historical exactitude, borrowings from previous doctrines have, as a rule, been partial, accessory, concerned with special theories or subjective and utilitarian interpretations, careless of any thorough understanding of the spirit animating the philosophy before judging and exploiting it.

If the still very recent science which goes by the name of the history of philosophy has made any progress at all, the reason is that instead of confining themselves, in the endeavour to compass it, to fragmentary theses which they were liable to run counter to and misinterpret so completely as to see nothing but chaos in the doctrines of the past, the march-past of all the errors ever committed by the human mind, which is the opinion of Brucker, the author of the first great general history of human thought, historians of philosophy have increasingly devoted their attention to grasping the deep-lying unity and mutual relations of systems ; for they can only be understood and judged by adopting provisionally their own various points of view. [1] Augustine, more than any other, calls for the application of such a method, because every single one of his statements, as his most recent and, perhaps, most penetrating historian, M. Étienne Gilson, has remarked, implies the whole body of his doctrine. [2] They cannot, therefore, be interpreted with any degree of precision unless apparently alien or even mutually contradictory assertions

[1] See the articles by V. Delbos on the " Conception of the history of philosophy, its object and methods," in *Revue de Metaphysique et de Morale, 1920,* etc.

[2] Gilson, *Introduction a l'Étude de S. Augustin.*

are brought back to one common standpoint. Pascal formulated the rule that, to understand an author well, the reader must succeed in taking a point of view at which the most different, the most contrary, truths come together in the most natural fashion. And it is from some such point of view that one may speak, in Thucydides' fine phrase, of "eternal possessions." This could not possibly be the case if it was a mere question of material inventions, which are so quickly superseded, or abstract ideas, which, as Bossuet says, are "always inadequate in some respect." But once a living, concrete truth is involved, it may grow indefinitely, like a tree ; and partial prunings do not prevent the dominant idea from always remaining the same, or merely make its significance and range all the more manifest.

It is, no doubt, more difficult to succeed in making such an exact description of one same spiritual organism than to construct formulas absolutely static within the limits of their artificially rigorous definitions. If Augustine ever showed any intellectual antipathy, it was for such an absolutely static conception, and because he was concerned to defend a true dialectic and a precision which is one of the chief characteristics of his acute mind. We shall find the confirmation of this statement in studying the single but still complex method he employs and the conception he formed of truth and philosophy.

(ii)

The attempt has only too often been made to limit the value of Augustinianism by representing it as merely one aspect, merely one method, of philosophical and Christian thought. It has been repeatedly stated that St. Augustine offers us rather a collection of vital examples than rational demonstrations. He is said to have been not so much a lucid expositor as a fiery enthusiast, a soul aflame with charity rather than a spirit of pure light and scientific precision.

Even historians who, in other respects, have a lively sense of the intellectual character of the Christian Plato have, with unconscious inconsistency, opposed St. Augustine to St. Thomas, as though the latter had the sole prerogative of technical demonstrations of a properly rational science and an impersonal and logically compelling method ; St. Augustine, they declare, not only followed a different method, but even pursued a different object ; St. Thomas established a formal science, whereas St. Augustine pursued a vital work perpetually inspired by the experience of his conversion under the influence of grace.

Nothing could be more artificial and disfiguring than such an unjust parallel between the two doctors. The two paths which some would have separate and distinct meet and mingle in both, but not to the same extent and in very different ways. Even in passages where, according to William de Tocco, the first historian of St. Thomas, the Angel of the School expresses himself with the utmost possible precision, and, so to say, with the utmost rational impassivity (*semper formalissime loquitur*), St. Thomas is making a secret but none the less genuine reference to an entirely personal and concrete experience, to an interpretation of Tradition and social life, to that profound dynamism of which the third part of the *Summa Contra Gentiles* describes the itinerary. And, symmetrically, in passages where St. Augustine seems to be recalling only his own pathetic history, his personal conflicts with his passions or with grace, it is not simply an individual case, an emotional impulse, some urge of life or generous gesture of charity that he describes, but a work of light, a craving for truth, a teaching of universal value, a discovery of inward reality, an illuminating solution of which he is giving us the benefit. It is odd that it could have been so much as said of the doctor *par excellence* of interior illumination that his philosophical method has not really an intellectual character or any scientific value when, in fact, no one

ever loved the light of intelligence more than he, or pene-
trated so far into the recesses of truth. But what he saw, and
what he tries to make us see, is that truth is never a thing
which it will be sufficient to consider from without, to view
in its abstract outlines, to deal with as something to which
access is forever denied.

Now if, in our own time, there is one thing needed, it is
surely the combination of the two methods of thought of
which St. Augustine offers such a marvellous example.
How often, in these last years, have men discussed what
Newman calls notional and real knowledge, what Pascal calls
the geometrical mind and the intuitive mind, and what
ascetical and mystical authors have to tell us about the
degrees of the spiritual life from the discursive phases of
Knowledge and laborious meditation up to the summit of
contemplation and union ! We should fail to recognize one
of the greatest services which Augustine has rendered us, if
we omitted to take to heart the lessons, not always immediately apparent, but always thrilling and illuminating,
which he offers us, in theory and in practice, on the continuous degrees and the ultimately indissoluble union of
knowledge and wisdom, of didactical method and the illumination which attains its perfection in charity.

As a sort of counter-proof which will enable us to realize
more fully not only the expediency but also the urgency, so
to say, of returning to a more vivid appreciation of the lesson
we can learn from St. Augustine, we may consider for a
moment the error committed and the risks run by those who,
during the last few years, have professed to oppose what
Augustine unites, to deprive the philosophy of St. Thomas of
the inspiration it drew from Augustine himself, to separate
the intellect from the other faculties of the soul, to turn
wisdom into a purely theoretical science. A strict, dry,
rational process ends in such static concepts, in a dialectic
so firmly riveted in concatenations of immovable ideas or

mere verbal formulas that minds, grown callous in such an ideological casing, become impervious to any form of correction, reject any suggestion of a less rigid attitude, and, self-confident and infatuated, oppose their dense mass of abstractions even to the living authority of the Church or the teaching of real life. All such novelties, which have resulted at times in the setting up of false masters as enthusiastic exponents of a political Positivism and counsellors of insubordination where religious authority is concerned, proceed from an error in method against which St. Augustine offers a sovereign antidote. What better proof of his ever-recurring vitality ?

But in other matters, also, we can perceive his importance at the present time, and the as yet unacknowledged service he has rendered the world.

(iii)

There is still a rich store of philosophical doctrine, hitherto unbroached, from which he can make a generous contribution with regard to the very conception and function of philosophy, the relation between rational speculation and the Christian order. And we shall certainly be able to find in doctrines apparently opposed to his the means of surmounting such oppositions.

The following two propositions have often been contrasted : in one sense, everything is philosophical in the doctrine which tends to identify Reason with the Divine Word which enlightens every man that comes into the world. But, in another sense, everything is pure religion, pure Christianity, wherever Christ is the sole light of men's minds, the sole strength of their will to do good, the one goal of human destiny.

To take one or other of those aspects by itself is to run the risk of grave misunderstandings, and even to incline towards

dangerous errors – to the error, in the first place, of a
" separate philosophy." Rational speculation has, indeed, at
one time, been exalted to the point of turning it into a sort
of Illuminism, lacking both the definite data of revelation
and the discipline of the Church's authority. At another time
it has emerged in the form of an Ontologism, allowing our
minds the intuition of Being while dispensing us from the
necessity of alleging any proofs of the existence of God in
virtue of an intuition which would give us at a glance the
certitude and, as it were, the presence of God. At still another
time, all human philosophies, and even the natural virtues,
have been relegated to the rank of arrogant illusions or, to
employ once more a phrase of Augustine's, " *splendida vitia.*"
Now, all such deformations of the authentic doctrine are
attributable to the fact that the master's thought has been
reduced to a system of abstractions, without taking any
account of the compensating inspirations which we are now
about to bring forward. And, that we may be successful, let
us first recall how those doctors who seemed to contradict
St. Augustine have, in the end, prepared the way for a
better understanding of his real doctrine. St. Thomas maintained an absolutely fundamental and indispensable distinction between the data of experience, science, and metaphysics in the natural and rational order on the one hand,
and the supernatural domain and the order of grace – that is
to say, the data of faith and the whole structure of theology –
on the other.

Such limitations seem at first sight to create a gulf between
two systems which, considered historically, are, according to
M. Gilson, heterogeneous, irreducible, and even incompatible, even though their respective authors possess and
represent, each in his own way, a plenitude of Christian life.

May I venture to contest a judgment which seems to me,
at least in certain respects, too absolute ? For true doctrines are never embalmed, like mummies, in the past, and,

wherever there is a plenitude of Christian spirit, oppositions are only so many stimulations to a more perfect knowledge of the one truth, ever ancient and ever new.

It is nevertheless true that, taken literally, from a static and logical point of view, the two conceptions referred to do seem incompatible. They are like two cliffs with a gulf between them, but it is through them, nevertheless, that the current of history flows. They are equally useful for embanking turbulent waters ; and not only do they serve to guide the current on to plains which are to be fertilized, but one balances with, and follows, the other in a course which we must now endeavour to make comprehensible.

It would be an error to think that the ambiguity referred to resulted, in the case of Augustine, in a twofold, alternative confusion ; philosophy does not lose itself in theology, or theology in philosophy. If he did not specify the distinctions which were subsequently drawn, he had a livelier and deeper sense of their heterogeneity and solidarity, as will presently appear, than was manifested by those who, coming after him, attempted to discriminate between and contrast, the respective capacities of each.

It would be a symmetrical error to think that St. Thomas has, contrariwise, established a separate philosophy, merely reserving the right to subject such provisional autonomy to a theology making a belated appearance in a rational order already self-sufficient and stabilized. Those who so interpret Thomism do it an injustice, and we must strenuously repudiate such a manner of perverting and ossifying a philosophy which has not ceased, through salutary distinctions, to maintain such contacts, such compenetrations even, as were necessary.

Nevertheless, how are we to reconcile or, rather, reunite in one and the same doctrine, Augustine, and such original disciples as St. Bernard and St. Bonaventure, with St. Thomas Aquinas, whose undertaking, as we are so often told, was directed against the growing menace of thirteenth-century Augustinianism and remains more indispensable than ever against contemporary Idealism and Semi-Rationalism ?

The solution can only be found in such studies as have, for some time past, succeeded one another in rapid succession on the limits and scope of philosophy. Cardinal Dechamps, Archbishop of Malines and one of the draughtsmen of the Constitution *de Fide*, had already based his great, apologetical work on this fundamentally Augustinian principle that the profound unrest which gives rise to philosophical inquiry ultimately issues, not in rational and richly satisfying solutions, but in problems which philosophy propounds without being able to solve and so opens its doors, in religious expectancy, to admit teachings of a superior order. More recently, amongst many other publications relating to this question, Père Guy de Broglie has shown that, " in the philosophy of St. Thomas " – that is to say, in even the rational aspect of philosophy – there is " a place for the supernatural." [1] Dom Laporta [2] and Fr. O'Mahony, [3] in works which have attracted considerable attention, have still more profoundly investigated, by a study of less familiar writings or an analysis of the inner life, this conception at which the apparently parallel or divergent lines of Thomism and Augustinianism will ultimately meet. There is in the nature of a spiritual being a desire to see God, an aspiration towards beatitude, and there is no other beatitude than that granted by God. It is an obscure and ill-defined desire, as St. Francis de Sales observed, a disciple in this respect also of St. Augustine, a desire which sets our mind and will in motion towards a

[1] Père Guy de Broglie, S.J., "*De la place du surnaturel dans la philosophie de S. Thomas,*" *Recherches de science religieuse*, vol. xiv. (1924), pp. 193 *et seq.* ; pp. 481–496.

[2] Dom. G. Laporta, O.S.B. "*Les notions d'appétit naturel et de puissance obédientelle chez St. Thomas d'Aquin,*" *Ephemerides theologicæ Lovanienses*, Ann. v, Fasc. 2, Apr. 1928.

[3] James E. O'Mahony, O.S.F.C. *The Desire of God in the Philosophy of St. Thomas Aquinas.* Cork University Press, 1929.

goal inaccessible in the order of nature, whereas our reason is sufficient for a knowledge of the existence of God, but a God whose mystery it would be unreasonable to attempt to violate or attain to by the unaided powers of the intellect or will. The alleged ambiguities, the oppositions between various aspects of the Augustinian doctrine, then disappear. Everything is explained.

(iv)

There is yet another domestic quarrel, and the complaints against Augustine are legion. His theory of knowledge, they say, is equivocal, and opposed to the thesis of the school which maintains that the datum of sense is the sole source and necessary vehicle of all our further knowledge : *omnis cognitio a sensu externo initium habet.* St. Augustine, on the contrary, in his *Retractations*, as in the course of many of his other works, declares that the soul has its own sense, *sensus et mentis*, that the soul is the certain principle of our most incontestable, most original knowledge.

Again, his doctrine of interior illumination shows us the light of the Word as the unique source which illuminates all knowledge. From the psychological point of view, no doubt, and in the order of duration, we have a primary knowledge of ourselves which disposes us to seek God ; but in a still more profoundly true perspective our illusions with regard to ourselves, the meaning of our existence, and the destiny of our being, would appear to us only through an illuminating knowledge of God. In so taking, not only a speculative, but also a moral and religious point of view, he repeats and, in a manner of speaking, lives, the doctrine that to know oneself one must know God, put God, so to speak, within oneself, and discover in Him one's own image : *noverim me, noverim Te.*

How is all this simultaneously possible, and is not the

scholastic thesis more coherent in granting us only a preliminary knowledge of sensible data, a subsequent inference
of our own thinking self?

Here again we should beware of a too literal interpretation
which would distort the style and borrowings which are not
so much genuine derivations as wilful aberrations from
Augustinianism. We should therefore show no mercy to
alleged disciples who have injured rather than propagated
the authentic spirit of St. Augustine. The proof of this contention is the diversity of such abstract borrowings which
result, for the most part, in positive errors.

Thus methodical doubt and the Cartesian *cogito* have been
referred back to St. Augustine, and certain passages in his
writings almost identical with passages in the *Méditations
Métaphysiques*. Descartes declared that he had no knowledge
of them, but, as he was intimately associated with the Orator-
ians, who were brought up on St. Augustine, his indebted-
ness to the Bishop of Hippo has been confidently asserted.
Pascal, however, had already pointed out the great difference
between a mere *obiter dictum* and a statement which becomes
the principle of a whole system of philosophy. The Cartesian
cogito, taken in its prematurely ontological sense, in its artificial isolation and false realism, soon turns turtle and plunges
us into the sea of modern Idealist speculation. Nothing of the
sort, fortunately, is to be found in St. Augustine, who admits
a datum of experience but is exceedingly careful not to
extract from it an entity on which the whole edifice of reality
could not possibly be erected with impunity. Malebranche,
too, has been turned into a great Augustinian. But, as regards
both his theory of knowledge and his theory of the nature of
bodies and spirits, there are considerable discrepancies with
Augustine which might usefully be described and explained.

If we want to see how, as Pascal says, thoughts to all
appearance deriving from the same source, and similar
in form, develop differently in different minds, let us

consider the case of Malebranche. Malebranche, doubly dependent on Augustine and Descartes, might, one would have thought, have been ready to follow, as regards the doctrine of the soul, the reputedly Augustinian Descartes of the *cogito* ; but he separates – and widely – from both. As against his mentor, Descartes, Malebranche, with an acute sense of the richness of the inner life, allows us only an obscure feeling of the existence of the soul, because, if we saw it in its essence, we should be diverted, by the sight of its beauty, from the care of the most necessary interests of our material conservation, and in this opinion he would seem to approximate to Augustine. But he is, on the other hand, ever so far removed from the Augustinian conception which reconciles the certainty of the mystery of the soul, the initial experience which serves as a link for all our investigations, and the increasing possibility of its illumination in the divine light, by the ascending scale of humility and charity. He is also poles apart from Augustine in his geometrical ontology, his absolutely ideological interpretation of divine exemplarism and his abstractly intellectual mysticism. Here again it must be said that the borrowings from Augustine are really misappropriations and forgeries. And this discovery should still further increase our eagerness to pierce the secret of a philosophy which is so organically one that it can suffer none of its constituent elements to be violently detached from it.

In the light of the problems discussed by contemporary psychologists, we can quickly realize what great advantage we can derive from the philosophy of Augustine in settling, in accordance with his spirit, the differences dividing the experimental school, the philosophy of intuition and Idealist speculation, all equally extravagant, whereas in the philosophy of the saint we find in an implicit, but yet most live, form, a synthesis, or rather, a vital unity which allows each of these elements its legitimate share : hereditary fatalities, conscious experiences, rational elaboration, triumphs of the spiritual life, conflicts of the will, the influence of grace ; all in admirable harmony in that stupendous tilting ground which is the soul, and in which all nature, the human will, and divine assistance compete together for the prize.

(v)

Closely connected with the points just touched, and one of the most largely debated questions, is the problem of the relations between knowledge and belief ; and here again an attempt has been made to discover Augustine in contradiction with himself or other doctors ; or, at the least, certain confusions of thought or failures to make the necessary distinctions.

How is the reciprocal causality of the *crede ut intelligas* and the *intellige ut credas* to be understood ?

Does he always sufficiently discriminate between the natural, psychological, moral, supernatural aspects, the faith-belief in past or remote facts, in obscure or inaccessible truths, in tidings from the other world, and the faith-confidence in a Being worthy of our love, whom we cannot suppose to be a deceiver ? Again, how are we to reconcile this alternative priority of sight and faith with the thesis according to which the same truth cannot be known and believed at the same time, the thesis which maintains *nil volitum et amatum nisi praecognitum* ? And yet there is nothing more coherent than the analyses and syntheses of Augustine, who does not confound the genesis of belief with its dissection, and discriminates between formal abstractions and real implications. Dealing presently with the apparent conflict between liberty and grace, we shall have to elucidate an analogous but still more embarrassing difficulty, and the reflection from such light as we may be able to throw on the one will also serve to illuminate the other. To object to the Augustinian doctrine of intelligent faith and the submission of the intellect to a divine authority, the articulations and distinctions, in themselves useful and precise, required by didactic science, is tantamount to the belief that the skeleton is primarily given as a necessary frame-work for the support of the flesh, whereas it has grown, in and by the flesh, as a living thing, and is the basis of motion, not an extrinsic support or manifestation of death. Here again Augustine provides a principle of unity which brings the multifarious aspects of the modern problem of belief into the most spontaneous harmony, without any confusion of the psychological, moral, logical, and supernatural data.

(vi)

If the Augustinian doctrine on the knowledge that thought has of itself has been imperfectly understood and insufficiently made use of, has even been not unfrequently distorted in opposite senses, his theory of the knowledge of God and the ways by which we are led to Him would appear to have suffered the same fate. At one time emphasis was laid on the intuitive, and, so to speak, immediate character of the proofs of *mere glance* which Malebranche borrowed, with the expression itself, from his master. At another, the long and painful journey which Augustine must have made, and which he describes for us, in his pursuit of the last end and the first Love, is put before us in detail. At still another, the subtle analyses which reveal, in all sensible and intellectual data, the presence of a truth, a necessary truth, an eternal and divine truth, a truth which is God Himself, are the object of commendation.

How can one possibly find one's way in such a labyrinth of complications, where commentators have discovered antitheses and, as it were, unconscious recantations, or the

doctrinal inconsistencies of a mind more lyrical than logical?
And, has not the ordered progress of St. Thomas been contrasted with the wanderings of St. Augustine, the straight-
forward, inevitable progress which sets out from visible
things and intellectual principles to lead us by five ways to
God, without apparently allowing any place for proofs based
on intimate experience, on the life of the mind and moral
aspirations ?

Nevertheless, such doubts and conflicts must disappear.
It would be just as much a misconception of the philosophy
of St. Thomas to do away with the secret foundations on
which his five proofs rest, and forget the way in which he
speaks of the unconscious approach of God in the soul as of a
yet unknown Friend, as it would be of the philosophy of St.
Augustine not to harmonize the multiple notes and masterly
orchestration of his theory of the knowledge of God. In this
case also, knowledge, consciousness, intelligence, will, love,
form a concert the beauty and strength of which are not
fully realized if we fail to perceive its unity. It is not for
nothing that Augustine is simultaneously the author of *De
Musica*, a lover of numbers, a born mathematician, the most
subtle reasoner, the most luminous and inexorable dialec-
tician that ever sent piercing shafts of light through the most
opaque difficulties. And that he is also the contemplative
who, transposing Platonic dialectic and Aristotle's *Organon*
into spiritual flights, such as those last conversations with
Monica on the beach at Ostia, teaches us that God, to whom
we can just attain by logical argument, whose existence is
implicit in the whole movement of sensibility and knowledge, can, and should, over and above be welcomed by the
whole soul, obeyed by a purified and submissive will, and
loved under the inspiration of a grace which, although given
us gratuitously, cannot be fruitful without our collaboration.
God is thus sought for, at the extreme confines of space as a
Being most remote and inaccessible and found at hand, as

close to us as possible. *Quaeritur non ambulando, sed amando.*

It is, therefore, a mistake to confront St. Augustine with certain doctrines which were once thought to be in opposition to his, and it is an even greater mistake to attribute to him preferences as, e.g., for Ontologism, Illuminism, and Quietism. He has even been criticized as the father of Pragmatism, Immanentism, and Religious Moralism. The truth is that he satisfies, in advance, the needs exploited by those false doctrines, precisely because the legitimate and salutary elements in such needs had not been adequately distinguished or satisfactorily provided for. Here again the services which St. Augustine can render are of immense value at the present time. Nothing could be more opportune than to point out, in " the recent disputes about Atheism " or " the problem of God," the essential part to be played by rational truths, the implied presence of spontaneous certitudes, the moral rectification of the will, when it is a question of solving the supreme problem of the living God.[1] No one has suggested better than Augustine that below, above, and within critical examinations and intellectual demonstrations there are integrated elements none of which may be omitted with impunity from a philosophy of God fit to serve as a preamble to faith, a foundation for social life, and a support for the individual conscience.

(vii)

We have so far contented ourselves with taking the point of view of spectators, considering the multifarious aspects of his doctrine from without and so doing it less than justice. It is time to get to the centre of the Augustinian perspective,

---

[1] See in the *Bulletin de la Société française de philosophie*, M. Brunschvicg's article on *La Querelle de l'Athéisme* and M. Edouard le Roy's on *Le Problème de Dieu* with the accompanying letters and discussions (Paris, Armand Colin, 1928 and 1930).

to the profound unity without which it is impossible to grasp
his real thought. What, ever since the day of his conversion,
became for Augustine a decisive and never-to-be-forgotten
experience, an imperious and transfiguring conviction, was
that vision and disposition of his whole soul. Man is not a
light unto himself; nothing that we know is luminous.
To seek for light, to tend towards truth, is not to get to know
things, objects, facts of consciousness, rational ideas, trans-
cendentals ; all that, which we imagine to be the first step
in the ascent to God, gives us no enlightenment ; it is what
needs to be enlightened, because it has no truth except that
which comes from God. *Ubi inveni veritatem, inveni Deum.*
There is no more treacherous illusion than the arrogant
belief that we bear within ourselves a principle of enlightenment and explanation, or that the very idea which we conceive of God, so far as it is our own, can be other than an idol.
*Cum de Te cogitabam, non Tu eras, sed vanum phantasma. Et
error meus erat Deus meus.* All such things, no doubt, are useful, but only at second hand. *Foris admonitio, intus magisterium.*
The proper method of approach is, therefore, the reverse
of Rationalism or Empiricism, and, though things may
help to reflect light and reason, may receive the brightness
of the Word, they supply no satisfactory answer to Fénelon's
ironical question, " Reason, Reason, art not thou the God
I seek ? " ; we believe, when we so start out, that we have
something complete, solid, and clear to go upon : what an
illusion ! If we think that we can be at home within ourselves,
it is because we have failed to get to know our very own being.
God is more intimate to us than our own intimacy to ourselves : of God I must say : " *intus est, ego foris.*" Whether I climb
to the summit of my self or sink to the lowest depth, I find
only a void in what is peculiarly myself, and that void was
made, and can only be filled, for and by God.

Now we see how this inversion of the usual perspectives
renews every successive step in the investigation, how it is

linked up with spiritual conversion, how it implies the purification of the senses, intellectual humility, a docile and loving welcome to a God who has ceased to be a concept, and
come to life. And does not such a doctrine strike even those
who have given it but lip service, as a complete novelty, seeing that its consequences have been so frequently misunderstood ? All the recent controversies on Immanence and
Extrinsicism, considered from this point of view, appear to be
so many misconceptions, because aspects which were put in
abstract opposition become united, without being confounded, in this Augustinian philosophy emancipated from
the tyranny of antithetical images and concepts. We should
bear this liberating view in mind until we perceive, in a
similar and complementary perspective, the salutary alliance
of liberty and grace.

(viii)

It has been said that the Augustinian conception of human
nature remains ambiguous or confused, and that the whole of
Jansenism was engrafted on this ambiguity. There is nothing
more essential than to elucidate this capital point ; and we
shall see that, whilst exonerating Augustine from all com-
plicity in the past, we are on the way to derive the greatest
advantage for which we can be indebted to his genius.

How does this conflict, so often unsuspected, present itself
to us, a conflict all the more dangerous for the fact that no
particular care has always been taken to guard against the
dangerous hazards to be encountered on the perilous
journey ?

Many commentators have rightly remarked that, under
the inspiration of his own sinful experience and the victorious
grace of his conversion, Augustine insists on the consequences
of the original fall and the efficacy of redemption, as though
the benefit of gratuitous justification consisted in giving us

back, if not our primitive integrity, at least our essential nature. It may then appear, from this concrete and, as it were, experimental point of view, that the primitive nature of man had been established in a state of grace without Augustine's making any radical distinction between what is a gift naturally incorporated in the first man and what is supernatural, absolutely reserved to an entirely gratuitous addition on the part of God, because this new gift is not to be found in a state of nature in any creature whatsoever.

No such distinction would ever seem to have been explicitly drawn by St. Augustine ; yet there is no doubt that, implicitly, he was unacquainted with, and would have been hostile to, the abstract use and misleading deductions which Jansenism drew from that very ambiguity. For Jansenism, exaggerating the native strength of human nature and the original will, exaggerated also the destructive effects of the first sin, and, so doing, attributed to concupiscence an absolute domination which could only be overcome by an opposite and more powerful concupiscence, namely, the concupiscence of grace which proceeds to save a few chosen souls from that mass of perdition – the human race : man is merely the theatre of this battle between two concupiscences, and the whole drama consists in the conflict between two contrary predestinations. Not only are the varied and moving writings of Augustine a protest against such an abstract system, but his whole soul, his generous heart, and his whole conception of charity, also exclaim against it. It was certainly necessary to define exactly what he seemed to leave ambiguous ; and this is the incomparable service which St. Thomas rendered by studying the conception of the absolute supernatural, so anticipating all possibility of error and confusion. But it is not sufficient merely to draw distinctions ; there must be unity : nature and grace must be made to co-operate, and it is at this point that St. Augustine reappears to stimulate a science of inner dynamism.

It has often been observed that periods of concentration
and tightening-up in the life of the Church, have, by their
very rigour and the precision of their definitions, prepared
the way for a new expansion, a possibility of enlargement
thenceforth unattended by any danger. Now that is, more
than any other, the kind of help that we are entitled to
require from the inspiration of St. Augustine in attempting to
solve the most agonizing, the most urgent problems perplex-
ing the Christian conscience. If the supernatural gift had
been subsequently imposed on a nature in full possession of
itself and capable of ensuring its self-sufficiency, would it not
seem that such an addition had been made quite arbitrarily,
and was an intrusion, as it were, apt rather to impress the
nature with terror of a powerful God and the law of fear
than to manifest infinite charity and the new law of love?
And all the more so, inasmuch as the supernatural gift is
not an optional offer made to man, even though it appears
entirely gratuitous on the part of God. To reunite these
various aspects, St. Augustine keeps suggesting to us the
idea of an inner presence which makes the command that
resounds from without, possible, acceptable, and infinitely
gracious : the elevation, then, to which we are compulsorily
invited is not a creation *ex nihilo*, or an additional burthen
upon the obligations of our own human conscience, or a
right to be asserted, or a simple choice left to our own whim ;
the demands of charity are a mere translation of that
intimate stimulus by which God loves Himself and desires
Himself in us, owing to the adoption which places in man
the very spirit of the Heavenly Father, the life of the Son
who was made flesh for us, and the sanctifying action of the
Spirit.

The apparent objections, ambiguities, and contradictions
which disturb so many contemporary souls immediately
cease. They now find it possible to harmonize the indispensable transcendence of the supernatural order with the

possibility of explaining how it becomes immanent in us and answers a twofold aspiration – a vague aspiration of the rational nature which tends to know God without being capable of determining under what form and to what extent ; and an aspiration resulting from infused grace prevenient in every man ; for Christ died for all, and all may answer in various ways the challenge of His death by putting to use such graces as they have which may so prepare the way for, and the reign of, habitual and sanctifying grace. The most disparate and, at times, most disconcerting passages in St. Augustine, so considered, harmonize, cast light upon each other, and lead us to a more and more exact conception of the supernatural itself. The revival of Thomism makes the revival of Augustinianism still more desirable, less dangerous, and more beneficent.

(ix)

Of the many obstacles which have arisen between modern philosophy and Christianity, none seems more formidable than the bare idea, the very mention of, the supernatural, a scarecrow from which many people, in the end, avert their gaze. Again, even of those who retain this essential idea, how few succeed in clearly defining its form and content ! How many employ the word imperfectly, at one time vaguely, at another in derivative senses or otherwise inaccurately. Some consider the supernatural as a form of opposition to nature which cannot be preserved in the purity of its definition and function except by avoiding the least admixture with the natural and rational. Others go very near to confusing it with the extraordinary occurrences which had better be described by the name of preternatural. Others, again, who cleave to a more exalted and purer conception, and agree with Dechamps that nothing is supernatural but what proceeds to union with God through the grace of transforming charity, are nevertheless often confused by an ambiguity as to the nature of this union. Is it a question of making the transfigured man by such an assimilation a copy, a mirror, an extrinsic vision which would reveal the metaphysical secrets of the Infinite Being ? Or is it rather some effective participation, some vital assimilation which, without compromising the necessary distinction between the Creator and His creature, incorporates us in the life of the Trinity by a sort of intus-susception ? And is it not the second hypothesis which makes the first conceivable, by taking most account of the texts of Scripture ?

Now St. Augustine provides, no doubt implicitly, but none the less convincingly, the solution of this problem. He clearly perceived that every intelligence congenitally tends to know and possess the God of Truth from whom all light derives, of the sensible, rational, esthetic, and moral, no less than the religious order ; but he also realized that such truth could not be grasped, and was not, in fact, grasped by mere metaphysical curiosity, or the removal of some material or intellectual obstacle. What was apparent to him, what he ceaselessly calls attention to, is this, that union between God and man, however desired it may be, remains impossible, if the only standpoint adopted is that of essences and natures. The mysterious wedding between the soul and God takes place, therefore, in the order of the will and of love, by the gift of the Holy Spirit, by the help of a grace that could not be incorporated in any nature ; so that man, without losing his limitations and personality, has become the friend, the adopted son of God, and may be described as *consors naturæ divinæ*. What would otherwise be chimerical, or even absurd, as Aristotle said, who considered the excessive love of God and man out of place, is realized by the discovery of a charity which does not need to do away with the abyss in order to cross over it.

It has been alleged that the fruitfulness of Christian metaphysics has been exhausted or, as it were, destroyed by the
lofty speculation of modern metaphysicians ; we see that, on
the contrary, St. Augustine opens hitherto untrodden paths
to this metaphysic which unites the intellect with charity.

(x)

To explain the gravest difficulty presented by Augustianism, we must not fail to touch on the problems of sin, grace,
and liberty : for this aspect of his philosophy gives the
greatest offence to most admirers of the author of the
Confessions.

The reader might make that an objection against our
whole attempt to interpret Augustinian doctrine as a marvellous unity, a harmony between reason, the sense of the
moral life, and the pure love required by our supernatural
vocation.

How, the question may arise, can the sombre theory of
humanity as a mass of perdition, and of concupiscence as an
overwhelming tyrant preventing our will from carrying out
even the good which the intellect has perceived and which
we would like to accomplish without being in the least capable of producing and effectively achieving it, be reconciled
with the idea of a God of charity, with the greatness attributed to the spirit which enlightens the very brightness of the
Word, and with the reiterated statement of our liberty ? For
(and this is what disconcerts our modern ideas) where we see
a conflict between a powerlessness to accomplish the good
and our own free will to pursue it, Augustine seems to find no
embarrassment at all. The answer is then that he adopts a
different standpoint from ours and that we have not yet
attained that implicit unity towards which we are tending.

Let it be observed in the first place, that, as opposed to the
abstract and exclusive theses which the Jansenists derived

from certain isolated and, therefore, misunderstood propositions, Augustine always maintained the truth of free will and
the part played by the will ; the inference is that the original
fall is not the radical corruption of nature, any more than
nature, before the fall, was a sovereign power, conferred on
man as his absolute property (and as connatural to him) in
order to attain to God and realize his supernatural destiny.
If there were any contradiction, Augustine would certainly
have seen it : are we not then on the road to a discovery
likely to lead us into the inmost recesses of his secret observ-
atory ? What Augustine had experienced, what he saw with
a convincing certainty and unwavering clarity is this, and it
is the capital point : that, in order to attain the divine end
which, in the concrete order wherein we are historically
constituted, is nothing less than a participation in the life of
God Himself, nothing, absolutely nothing simply human,
purely moral, could possibly be sufficient, and that every
natural, rational and deliberate presumption, so far from
beginning the work of salvation and deification, would be
not so much a help and preparation as a hindrance and an
obstacle, an indication of that sacrilegious insolence of which
the Greeks had a presentiment when they had such ὕβρις
chastised by the divine νέμεσις. Even when we catch a
glimpse of, and, above all, when we perceive this sublime
destiny, all we can do is but confess our weakness, our
nothingness, which made us liable to sin and which sin has
transformed into positive evil, a humanly incurable defect.

Now surely we see the obscurity gradually disappear, the
apparent contradiction on our path resolved ? But it is also
important to anticipate an objection which will enable us to
penetrate still farther into this Augustinian angle of vision.

Why, the question will be asked, does Augustine speak
only of sin and grace, as though grace had happened only
after sin, and as though he had had no conception of an
ordeal before the fall, as a condition of attaining divine

beatitude ? St. Paul also, perhaps, suggests the solution of the riddle : " But the Scripture hath concluded all under sin "[1] – under this more affecting aspect, something more than simple reparation must be involved. Neither man, in the state of innocence, endowed with all his natural or preter-natural gifts, nor, according to tradition, even the angels themselves, were dispensed from this fundamental mortifica-tion, to which Augustine, who has insisted on it so strongly, gives the name of humility and sacrifice. Which comes to this – that, to secure the precious pearl of the divine life, the first gifts granted to spiritual beings had to be in some way repudiated by an act of loving submission and abnegation, in order that a second, and infinitely superior, gift might be received and acquired at such a price.

Some interpreters of the Augustinian metaphysic of charity have at times been inclined to refer the second of those gifts back to the first, or, rather, to see only one unique original gift which would have had only to expand in souls faithful to the discipline of a human and religious morality, as though to mitigate the demands made by asceticism and expiation were a manner of magnifying the divine goodness. This is, however, merely a deviation from, and a diminution of, Augustine's sentiment of the Christian ideal. No one felt more strongly than he not only the bondage of sin and the urgency of reparatory grace, but also the congenital duty of a mortified humility and the gratuitous, transcendent, and indispensable character of prevenient, auxiliary, and elevat-ing grace. In describing this complex history of every deifying vocation, whether we begin with the state of sin, which has become the common law, or, by hypothesis, with the state of innocence, there is always a victory to be gained over self, a hatred of egoism, and, according to his formula, a love of God carried to the extent of despising self, otherwise guilty self-love is exalted to contempt for God. There is no middle

[1] *Conclusit Scriptura omnia sub peccato. Gal.* iii, 22.

course, no other destiny than salvation or damnation. Man
has not the power to content himself by remaining simply
man : either, with the help of grace, he ascends to where his
reason and will tended, even unconsciously, or, by the
abuse of grace, he sinks below himself, without the possibility
of there being any separate wisdom closed to those divine
horizons. How can God be born in man, if man does not
begin by making room for God within himself and dying to
himself?

The theses we are now trying to analyse are not, in the
philosophy of St. Augustine, ideas in the air, speculations of
the study; they are the expression of his own most vivid, un-
questionable, personal experience. We see, then, the luminous
centre which irradiates and purifies his whole existence. But
if it has been said of Maine de Biran that he became a
philosopher through perceiving in the peculiarities of his
individual psychology truths of a general order and metaphysical import of which they were the vehicle, how much
more ought we not to recognize in Augustine's experience of
his conversion and Christian practice a science of universal
character, an explanation valid and communicable everywhere and at all times, a unity capable of explaining all the
springs of thought, the whole dynamism of the spiritual life,
every incident in the drama that is being played for all
eternity in the depths of the individual conscience, as in the
whole history of the human race and the world ?

(xi)

But the objection may be raised, is Augustine not being
credited with intentions far surpassing his own and explicit
doctrines flatly contradicting his principal views ? Is he not
expressly the doctor of sin, conversion, and grace, and did
not the ardour of his most charitable zeal turn into rigorism

and a doctrine of predestination of which so many of his
fervent disciples were interpreters, and have they not been
so interpreted in the course of history, more particularly in
the sixteenth and seventeenth centuries ? Is he not, above all,
the adversary of Pelagius ?

Here, again, we are bound to protest against any uni-
lateralism, if we are not to misinterpret the spirit underlying
the letter, and mutilate the philosophy of Augustine. The
precision of his doctrine is not a mere matter of rigid abstraction and logic : his strength and originality lie in his having
associated feeling and idea, idea and will, will and love ; all
these avenues converge towards a common centre, from
which radiate the light, warmth, and charm which start
everything going, make all things clear, in a philosophy
whose unity is not impaired by any discursive analysis whatsoever. Hence his profound conception of time and eternity.
He places himself at a standpoint where duration appears as
the form under which our psychological and moral life
develops, but not as a physical reality ; where we deceive
ourselves is in frittering away our minds, our lives, and our
affections in that dust of phenomena so far as they succeed
one another in multiplicity and succession : in such a case
we should be, as it were, dissociated and lost in all things :
*distenti per omnia, tumultuosis varietatibus dilaniuntur cogitationes
meæ.* True vision, on the contrary, the true attitude, is to
embrace all those subordinate things which are the means
of realizing a superior end ; in that end we once more find,
and dominate, the whole visible and invisible universe by
becoming in a way co-extensive with the divine order, so
making ourselves like unto God Himself in that eternal life
which is promised to us and which we can begin beneath the
veils of Time : *extentus per omnia, solidabor in Te, forma mea,
Deus.*

Augustine brings together and unifies all things in such a
conception of eternity : thence derives also his magnificent

conception of the Catholic Church, which, in her successive
phases, forms but one and the same being. She appears to us
at different stages ; we have to believe in her unity and per-
petuity. The Apostles saw Christ and believed in the mystic
body of the Church that was yet to be ; we see the body of
the Church and have now to believe in the historic, invisible,
eternal Christ. Permeated by this truth of a tradition containing within itself at any given moment the whole deposit,
Augustine repeats that it is this very universality, and the
word Catholic, which express the integrity which keeps
him in the bosom of the Church. Therefore we once again
find everywhere, in the secret of consciences no less than in
the whole life of the Church, this sense of unity, of unity and
simplicity, by no means abstract, but in which everything
has an implication and in which the various aspects, instead
of becoming reconciled with difficulty, as so many originally
isolated data, call out to each other, and secure a feeling of
complete satisfaction, intelligibility, and, to adopt a word of
Augustine's, of solidity, or consolidation. Many philosophical
systems are like drafts of plane geometry on which the lines
intersect and which the eye cannot but consider in an invari-
able way in spite of the illusions produced by an artificial
perspective. In the case of solids, however, the spectator can
shift his position and there is no end to the unforeseen aspects
he can discover : the forms are as inexhaustible as the forms
of living natures. Can any more actual philosophy be conceived than the one under consideration : a philosophy which,
as we have here attempted to show, combines within itself
diversity and unity, each performing its peculiar function in
terms of the other ?

(xii)

And yet, even so, we have not said enough : it is not sufficient, so powerful is his social sense, his feeling for unity, to

350 A MONUMENT TO ST. AUGUSTINE

show that his horizon stretches away to eternity and the universality of beings ; it must also be shown that, in his view, the totality of life, like the Word itself, finds expression in mystic but none the less real fashion in the conscience of every man, and that the individual history of every soul is capable of containing, so to speak, the metaphysical and supernatural world. Newman used to say : " The soul alone, face to face with God alone " ; a profoundly true and salutary idea. But such solitude is, at the same time, pure and universal union with the whole of creation understood and loved in God.

Many commentators have confined themselves to noting the duality of an absolutely impersonal and timeless speculation and a psychology fully alive to the most intimate personal details. Augustine at one time speculates on truth, divine exemplarism, and interior illumination as though he took no interest whatever in the individual life of each of us : at another time it is the history of his soul, and, in his soul, the history of every human soul, which seems to be the special theme of his meditations, the supreme stake of his effort, the goal of his journey towards beatitude, distinguished, as always, by the most consummate psychological acumen and the most unsparing moral analyses. This alleged duality will now cease to cause us any surprise, and we are now ready to understand the reason for this complexity when we reflect that, for him, there is no spirit but contains the universal, incarnates, each by itself and in communion with all the rest, the history of creation, redemption, and the last judgement. It is, therefore, a genesis, a philosophy of history, an eschatology, that he discovers in every human being, and this dramatic conception gives his immense work the moving unity summarily expressed in the diptych of the two Cities. From the little to the great, with symbolism, or the greatest possible realism, Augustine describes the combats, the changing fortunes, the alternations of triumph and disaster, which combine to make the apparently confused but, to his eyes, luminous web of our inner life, of the conflict of powers warring with themselves, until the time comes when chaos shall be reduced to order in sight of the divine justice. So far, then, from leaving the various parts of the Augustinian work in the state of an erratic block, we should, for the better understanding of it and to make it more fruitful, climb to a position from which the prospects radiate in all directions from a single centre. Augustine is at once the master of the inner life in its most secret recesses and the doctor of history embracing in a glance the whole scheme of Providence so as to make goodness, even in its most exacting demands, intelligible.

When, on August 28th, 430, Augustine, old and enfeebled, lay dying at Hippo, which the Vandals threatened to raze to the ground, could he, could anyone, have foreseen the prodigious influence and ever-youthful vitality of his doctrine, or, rather, of his soul, destined to produce so many religious families, so many spiritual renovations, so many conversions and sanctifications? Alone, or perhaps with Paul Orosius and a few rare spirits, Salvian, a priest of Marseilles, contemplating the ruins which had accumulated everywhere, had a presentiment that the fall of the Roman Empire would not be the end of civilization, that the turn of the Barbarians had come, and that from those ruins a new world would arise for the future of Christendom. History repeats itself after the lapse of centuries. We too are taking part in transformations which seem to be overthrowing all the old spiritual values : the invasion of an anti-Christian philosophy, of a materialistic science ; the invasion of the pseudo-civilized and of young nations forced to suffer, without the leaven of Christianity, the contamination of ancient cultures. If, at the dawn of the Middle Ages, and in the greatest centuries of religious history, Augustine served as a torch to rekindle philosophical speculation, religious fervour, and Christian metaphysics, we may hope, now more than ever, on this 1,500th anniversary of his death, that his day has once more returned, and that his message has lost none of its novelty and power.

Many partial statements of his, taken literally, many figurative interpretations, are, no doubt, now out of date, or convicted of error : for the materials on which Augustine worked as exegete, historian, or psychologist gave him but frail support ; the spirit, however, which he brought to bear on such imperfect tools remains intact because his work was something more than a mere scholar's, more than a mere system of ideas : it acquired unity from a form of contemplation transcending the occasions which may have given rise to it. Other philosophers, no doubt, have constructed an apparently more technical and really more explicit metaphysic ; others, again, have been granted wisdom no less supernatural ; but none, perhaps, has been to the same extent such a philosophic critic of thought, such an experienced master of the inner life. Doctor of sin, conversion, grace, and justification, master of the mystic ways, philosopher of interior illumination, herald of charity, the Eucharist, Tradition, and the Catholic Church : so many aspects are united in him without confusion that he escapes all definition, all special classification.

And now, perhaps, the statement with which we began may seem less paradoxical : St. Augustine has more to give us than he has yet done. The fragmentary borrowings which have been made from him have not unfrequently rather distorted than adequately conveyed his philosophical value ; and if, in the spiritual order, innumerable souls have drawn inspiration from his true spirit, the lessons he teaches, in the speculative order, still need to be more fully understood, the manner in which method and doctrine, the path of speculation and the path of charity, unite in him, more clearly perceived. Alone, perhaps, of all philosophers, Augustine boldly

faced the concrete and complete state of man as he is in the
unity of his destiny and *transnatural*[1] state, for our real state
is not, of itself, either a state of pure nature or, at once, a
supernatural one. Every doctrine, therefore, based on the
study of either of these states, runs the risk of misinterpreting
the authentic datum from which alone a philosophy spon-
taneously corresponding to historic reality, moral experience,
the designs of Providence, and the demands of the Christian
religion, can proceed. Justin the Philosopher, Origen, and
some others no doubt had already had a presentiment of
such a vital unity leaving the incommensurability of the two
orders – the natural and supernatural – intact, and so
Tertullian's famous phrase – " the naturally Christian
soul " – should be interpreted. But Augustine, more
than any other, opened up, and travelled the full extent
of, this path, which is the path of philosophy and salvation
alike. Doctrines straying from that path, despite the precious
truths they may contain, end either in a separate philosophy
or a factitious and precarious concordance, and from such
points of view a Christian philosophy appears somewhat
hybrid. The Augustinian outlook alone allows not only *the*
Catholic philosophy, but also the fully human one. If this
has not yet been fully realised, the reason is that the future
reserves for the doctrine of St. Augustine a fruitful activity
far surpassing all the influence it has exercised in the past.

[1] See this word in *Le Vocabulaire technique et critique de la philosophie*, by Lalande.
(Paris, Librairie Alcan, 1926.)

YA

Afterword

St. Augustine and the Twentieth-Century Renaissance in Catholic Thought and Culture

A MONUMENT TO SAINT *Augustine* was published in 1930 in order to mark and celebrate the fifteenth centenary of the saint's death. Returning to it now, more than eighty-five years after its first publication, readers will see that *Monument* bore witness not only to the lasting power of Augustine's thought, but also to a remarkable interwar renaissance in Catholic thought and culture that was then underway in England, France, and much of the world. Far too often eclipsed by the vocal move away from neo-scholasticism in the work of Rahner, Schillebeeckx, Ratzinger, and the *ressourcement* theologians, the earlier Catholic revival of the 1920s and 1930s can itself be read as a time of great ferment, of philosophical, theological, and cultural creativity, and of genuine continuing importance.

Such a claim may strike some as counterintuitive, even bewildering. Many of us have been taught to read the drama of twentieth-century Catholic theology as a story of the overcoming and surpassing of neo-scholasticism.[1] We are told that the Leonine revival, especially as codified in Pope Leo's own *Aeterni Patris* (1879),

1. Thus Walter Kasper's famous declaration, "There is no doubt that the outstanding event in Catholic theology of our century is the surmounting of neoscholasticism." Kasper, *Theology and Church*, 1; quoted in Kerr, *Twentieth-Century Catholic Theologians*, vii.

355

Pope St. Pius X's *Doctoris Angelici* (1914), and the manualist tradition, created an atmosphere of retreat in which Catholic thinkers, rejecting the temptations of modernity, sheltered themselves in a propositional and deracinated appropriation of the Thomistic tradition. The basic theses of official Thomism, especially as synthesized by Aquinas's sixteenth-century interpreters, were to be taken as the foundation of Catholic doctrine and were thus held to be beyond debate. Aquinas's authority and the putatively comprehensive scope of his achievement, moreover, all but obviated the need for critical and constructive appropriation of the great figures of the past. For all of their historical importance, whatever Augustine and Anselm rightly taught us to believe had later been taught more clearly, systematically, and authoritatively by the Angelic Doctor. In the face of this "Thomistic triumphalism," as Norris Clarke has called it, returning to the sources of theology could seem only an invitation to muddy the waters. Thus, in a strange sort of theological burlesque, the desire to return to the great founts of theological tradition appeared either as a sort of dilettantish move or even a kind of dangerous progressivism. Inured in such an approach, so the story goes, early twentieth-century Catholic theology was more reactionary than creative, more insular than evangelical, and thus in desperate need of the new openness that Vatican II would finally bring. On this telling, the popularity of figures like Etienne Gilson, Jacques Maritain, E. I. Watkin, and Christopher Dawson in the decades *before* Vatican II—combined with their later skepticism about post-conciliar developments—only justifies our ignoring them *in the wake of* Vatican II. After all, don't they represent precisely what Catholic theology succeeded in overcoming?

As a matter of fact, no, not really. There is something to the above critique, versions of which have been told and retold for more than fifty years now, but it is vastly overstated. To begin with, it willfully ignores the diversity and creativity of Catholic and even neo-scholastic thought in the pre-conciliar period. For example, while one can discern a reactionary element in the reinvigoration of scholasticism under Pius IX and especially in response to the

Syllabus of Errors, this invocation of scholasticism as a replacement for or inoculation against modernism is arguably quite different from Leo XIII's later plea for the rediscovery and renewal of the thought of Thomas Aquinas in order that theology might be given a philosophical framework able to address the intellectual challenges of the nineteenth century. One can read Leo's encyclicals less as a circling of the wagons or dismissal of modernity *tout court* and more as a series of interventions intended to provide the Church with a means to dialogue with and, indeed, to reshape modernity. Thus, for example, Pope Leo's own creative challenge to the modern world is evident in *Rerum Novarum*, rightly identified as the *Magna Carta* of Catholic Social Teaching and arguably the most important papal encyclical in centuries. Nor should it be forgotten that in the same year Leo promulgated *Aeterni Patris* he elevated the decisively Augustinian and Romantic John Henry Newman to the office of Cardinal. All of which makes the acknowledged swing back to a kind of reactionary antimodernism during the reign of Pius X all the more striking. In order to make sense of this history, we need to beware of telling potted but popular stories about the overcoming of neo-scholasticism and certain types of Thomism. As Russell Hittinger notes, neo-scholasticism was never a monolithic movement but was from the very outset characterized by a variety of competing interpretations, motivations, and challenges. "At times, a reactionary, legislative, and disciplinary form of Thomism was deployed, directed inward at members of the Church, chiefly about uses of philosophy in the study of sacred doctrine. At other times, Thomism was allowed to play a more constructive, synthetic, and open role, directed outward to the world, chiefly on questions of social and political order."[2]

Now, to be sure, a "legislative, disciplinary, and reactionary" form of Thomism did exert significant influence over Catholic thought and culture, not least through its reiteration in the scholastic manuals studied by nearly all seminarians of the period. Still, this influence should not be exaggerated. The manuals

2. Hittinger, "Two Thomisms, Two Modernities," 33.

presented a kind of digested Aquinas anachronistically deployed as a bulwark against *modernism*, the latter ascription having become shorthand for the the desultory introduction of historical methods into the study of the Bible and theology (i.e., higher criticism), on the one hand, and the philosophical claim that doctrines were not perennially established truths but culturally particular symbolic expressions of anthropological drives (e.g., Feuerbach, Marx, Durkheim), on the other. But we should be careful neither to confuse the manuals with neo-scholasticism itself nor to treat neo-scholasticism as a single movement rather than an internally diversified tradition. Moreover, while one may indeed object to the arid combination of propositionalism and moralism in much neo-scholasticism—the "rupture between theology and life," as Jean Danielou has said[3]—it is also the case that leading neo-scholastic theologians such as Matthias Scheeben, Pierre Rousselot, and even Garrigou-Lagrange himself understood that spirituality and theology could not finally be divorced, that indeed the mystical life was the end of every genuine life of faith and reason. Outside of the theological faculties where Garrigou-Lagrange-style Thomism "of strict observance" enjoyed almost hegemonic influence, even more alternatives flourished. During the first three decades of the twentieth century, for example, Maurice Blondel, Etienne Gilson, Jacques and Raissa Maritain, and Eric Przywara all diversely championed more dynamic, plurivocal, imaginative, and historically robust visions not only of Aquinas but also of the broader Catholic intellectual tradition.

Across the channel, a great English Catholic renaissance in art and culture was also underway. In the decades preceding and especially during the interwar period, English Catholicism was marked by the extraordinary flourishing of a generation of singularly gifted Catholic writers, artists, and scholars, most of them converts from high-church Anglo-Catholicism. Arguably, this Anglo-Catholic heritage bequeathed to the movement its

---

3. On the response of Danielou and the *nouvelle théologie* to this perceived "rupture," see Boersma, *Nouvelle Théologie and Sacramental Ontology*, 1–34.

peculiarly literary quality and its striking feeling for the theological importance of beauty, both of which were anticipated by the Oxford Movement. One thinks, in this regard, of Newman, Hopkins, and Chesterton, but also David Jones, Eric Gill, Evelyn Waugh, and J. R. R. Tolkien. High-church Anglicans such as C. S. Lewis, Charles Williams, T. S. Eliot, and Dorothy Sayers might be seen as fellow travelers participating in a similar cultural and theological moment. And although they are less remembered now than the luminaries I have just listed, the Anglophone writers collected in this volume were also key figures in this interwar British Catholic cultural renaissance.

So who indeed is it that we meet in the pages of this book? *Monument* was compiled by Thomas ("Tom") Ferrier Burns, then an editor at the newly founded Catholic publishing house, Sheed & Ward, and the volume reflects the particularly vibrant Catholic literary circle that used to meet regularly in Burns's Chelsea apartment. Throughout the last years of the 1920s, Burns's apartment was the site of a "never-ending party" including figures such as Christopher Dawson, Fr. Martin D'Arcy, David Jones, Robert Speaight, Alexander Dru, Maisie Ward, and others—appearances were also made by Eric Gill, W. H. Auden and once Jacques Maritain—all told, a kind of who's who of (mostly) younger British Catholic intellectuals spurring one another on in their quest for the renewal of art and culture. In this, they were not alone. In the first decades of the twentieth century, and especially in the aftermath of World War I, literary circles abounded as artists and intellectuals sought not only to make sense of a world that seemed to have come apart but also to discover ways of repairing a world whose violence and dissolution seemed only temporarily quelled. Perhaps the most famous of these literary circles was the Bloomsbury Group, that loose collective of writers and scholars including E. M. Forster, Virginia Woolf, John Maynard Keynes, Duncan Grant, and others. The Bloomsbury Set was modernist in style, recherché, deliberately difficult, and fiercely secular in orientation (hearing of T. S. Eliot's conversion, Virginia Woolf was "shocked" and pronounced Eliot "dead to us all from this day forward").[4] The other great literary circle from this interwar period was arguably as culturally important as the Bloomsbury Set, though almost diametrically opposed in style and orientation. This group, the Oxford Inklings, who wouldn't formally begin their meetings in C. S. Lewis's Magdalene College chambers until the early 1930s, were unapologetically Christian, ecumenical, and possessed of literary tastes decisively outside the high modernist mainstream.

The writers and thinkers who gathered in Burns's Chelsea apartment had something of both groups in them. On the one hand, like Bloomsbury, they were sympathetic to the aesthetics of modernism, innovative in style, and revolutionary in ambition. On the other hand, they were as convinced of the salutary cultural power and truth of Catholicism as the Bloomsbury circle was of atheism. They styled themselves, accordingly, as a kind of Catholic avant-garde, both radical and orthodox, rooted in tradition but progressive and creative in vision. These two seemingly disparate sides can be seen in the first literary production of the group: the short-lived but fascinating journal *Order: An Occasional Catholic Review*. The first issue of the journal debuted spectacularly in May 1928, its initial run of two thousand copies selling out within two weeks.[5] The journal was experimental in nature; contributions contained no attribution, anonymity fortifying the impression of collective movement rather than individual genius. There were, of course, individual geniuses among them, not least the historian Christopher Dawson, the philosopher Fr. Martin D'Arcy, and the engraver, poet, and artist David Jones. Dawson and Fr. D'Arcy were the elders of the group, though both were barely out of their thirties. Nevertheless, Dawson's writings and his first book had already earned him a stunning reputation, and Fr. D'Arcy was well known for leading many of the most illustrious converts of the day into the Catholic Church.[6] In large measure animated by the vision

4. Quoted in Eliot, *Letters of T. S. Eliot*, 3:39.

5. Burns, *Use of Memory*, 41.

6. Harp, "A Conjuror at the Xmas Party."

Maritain had presented in *Art and Scholasticism*, these Catholic intellectuals sought to champion the power of beauty, goodness, and truth in the face of an age increasingly consumed by the pale rationalism of utility, efficiency, and bureaucracy. These were writers and thinkers who witnessed firsthand the nihilistic devastation of modernity's first Great War and then found themselves in its bureaucratic aftermath as the centralized war effort transformed itself into the pseudo-rationalistic, aesthetically desultory, and ecologically destructive central planning of peacetime efforts. Too often, the Church was not an exception but a willing participant in these trends, and so the journal critiqued "ecclesiastical materialism" and "the hideous aesthetic expressions of modern religion" wherever it found them.[7]

For all of this, however, the spirit animating both the Chelsea discussions and their literary publications was not reactionary but creative and constructive. The journal took its name from the opening line of Thomas Aquinas's *Summa contra Gentiles*: "According to established popular usage, which the Philosopher considers should be our guide in the naming of things, those are called wise who put things into their right *order* and control them well."[8] To put things in their right order requires that we see things as they really are in the fullness of their dignity and relations. Modernity, however, in the eyes of the *Order* writers, had largely lost the ability to see the goodness and beauty of things. "The Break," as they called it, had taken place.[9] Whether the precipitating cause was the Reformation, the Industrial Revolution, the decadence of

7. Burns, *Use of Memory*, 44–45.

8. *Summa contra Gentiles* I.1

9. In the preface to his long poem *Anathemata,* David Jones explains, "In the late nineteen-twenties and early thirties among my most immediate friends there used to be discussed something that we christened 'The Break.' We did not discover the phenomenon so described; it had been evident in various ways to various people for perhaps a century; it is now, I suppose, apparent to most. Or at least most now see that in the nineteenth century, Western Man moved across a rubicon which, if as unseen as the 38th Parallel, seems to have been as definitive as the Styx."

late scholasticism, or some more complex and diffuse process, the result was the same: modern men and women found themselves increasingly alienated from the sacral roots of their own cultures, and thus increasingly blind to the way that sign and sacrament might reveal the diaphaneity of creatures, things, and persons. The modern world presented itself as opaque and prosaic, but it also bore within itself subversive traces of something grander. As David Jones puts it, "The Break" represents the crossing of a cultural Rubicon, but "it was not the memory-effacing Lethe that was crossed; and consequently, although man has found much to his liking, advantage, and considerable wonderment [in modernity], he has still retained ineradicable longings for, as it were, the farther shore."[10] The argument of the *Order* writers, then, following Maritain, Newman, and finally Augustine, was that this ineradicable, restless longing for the divine might still teach us that all things find their place and dignity only when properly ordered to God from whom alone all things come. Nor was this presented as an elective affinity for Catholics alone. Rejecting the anti-democratic separatism championed by an older generation of English Catholics, most notably Hillaire Belloc, the writers, thinkers, and artists who met in Burns's apartment sought a deeply incarnational, sacramental, and transformative vision of Christian cultural engagement.[11] Although theirs was an engagement in culture, art, and religion more than politics, in all of it they sought not to leave but rather to transfigure the surrounding culture through presence and witness.

Through the efforts of Tom Burns, these young, gifted British Catholic humanists eventually made contact with the currents of Catholic renewal throughout Europe: among others, Etienne Gilson, Jacques Maritain, George Bernanos, Nicholas Berdyaev, Erich Pryzwara, and Maurice Blondel. *Order* only ran for four issues and it went defunct before the 1920s were through, but the movement

10. Ibid.

11. On which see Lothian, *The Making and Unmaking of the English Catholic Intellectual Community, 1910–1950*.

theme for this inaugural volume is telling. Augustine also wrote at a hinge point in history—the "Break," in his case, being the tidal shock of the fall of Rome. He was, in a certain sense, a theologian of crisis, but the grandeur of Augustine's thought lies in the way he refused to indulge in pessimism and reactionary formulations. Instead, on perhaps the greatest scale possible, he reimagined the world in light of movements far deeper and passions far more enduring than those issuing in the surface calamities of his time. Moreover, Augustine's great project of understanding the world in the light of faith was undertaken in a time like ours, a time of extraordinary religious pluralism and cultural ferment. For all of these reasons and more, Augustine's life and writings seemed to commend themselves in 1930—as, arguably, they still do now—to the creative project of rethinking and renewing culture in the wake of modernity's own "Break."

A Monument to Saint Augustine, now happily reprinted by Wipf and Stock, gathers all of the diverse strands we have been considering together within its pages: the creative transformation of neo-scholasticism through a kind *ressourcement*, the Catholic literary intellectual renaissance in Europe and Britain, the focus upon the renewal of Christian humanism in the face of modernity's proliferating dangers, the Augustinian turn as a resource for

12. We can gauge something of the influence of the thinkers associated with *Order* by attending to one who was not explicitly of their number. In *The Golden String*, Bede Griffiths, a gifted Oxford student of C. S. Lewis's, recalls the story of his conversion first to Christianity and then to Catholicism, and of his subsequent entry to the Benedictines at Prinknash Abbey. Griffiths mentions five authors as having had an unparalleled influence upon his formation as a young Catholic convert and monastic novice: Thomas Aquinas, of course, but also Etienne Gilson, Jacques Maritain, E. I. Watkin, and especially Christopher Dawson—in other words, the authors associated with *Order*, all of them collected later in the pages of *A Monument to Saint Augustine*. See Griffiths, *Golden String*, 168–69.

the theology of crisis, and so forth. Were it to do nothing else, this volume would be of extraordinary historical importance insofar as it makes clear how central the legacy of St. Augustine was to the interwar renaissance in Catholic thought and culture, not only to Burns, Dawson, and the British Catholics but also to the great figures of the Continent: Blondel, Gilson, Maritain, and Przywara. But the volume does much more. The contributions themselves are of real, substantive, and lasting value.

The essays contained in this volume are not in theology per se—though theology, especially the doctrine of creation and theological anthropology, lies ever just beneath the surface. Rather, they treat Augustine from the perspective of philosophy, history, religious studies, and the humanities more generally. A few words about each essay may be in order. The chapters may be divided into two sets of five. The first five chapters were penned by British authors, all of them associated in some way with the circle that met in Burns's Chelsea salon; the second five were all commissioned from the Continent and translated for publication here. The long two-part opening essay by Dawson may be the most powerful and eloquent of the Anglophone contributions to *Monument*. Choosing as his theme "St. Augustine and His Age," Dawson presents an erudite and historically compelling case for taking seriously what scholars now call late antiquity, a period overwhelmingly neglected by historians in Dawson's time. It is easy to imagine the urgency behind Dawson's essay. Having seen the conflagrations, violence, and dissolution of the early twentieth century, might one learn from what happened in the age of Augustine when the Roman Empire itself began to fall? Augustine asked himself nearly the same questions Dawson now poses. Dawson, taking his cues from the African bishop, implicitly argues that the possibility of our own cultural renewal lies open if only we return to the sources of life itself. As Dawson writes,

> To neglect or despise the religious achievement of the age
> [i.e., late antiquity] is as fatal to any true understanding of
> it as a complete disregard of the economic factor would be

in the case of nineteenth-century Europe. For the real interest and importance of that age are essentially religious.
It marks the failure of the greatest experiment in secular
civilization that the world had ever seen, and the return
of society to spiritual principles. It was at once an age of
material loss and of spiritual recovery, when amidst the
ruins of a bankrupt order men strove slowly and painfully
to rebuild the house of life on eternal foundations. (42)

Dawson reads Augustine as the founder of the Christian philosophy of history and, indeed, the "first man in the world to discover
the meaning of time" (95). For Augustine, time is meaningful
precisely insofar as it refuses to make itself absolute. When time,
history, and our transient adventures in becoming are all there is,
time itself threatens to become meaningless; it buckles under a
weight it was never designed to shoulder. Paradoxically, by attending so fully to the love of a transcendent good, Augustine discovers the extraordinary meaning and value of our immanent human
efforts toward finite moral ends. As Dawson summarizes Augustine's teaching in the last twelve books of *The City of God,* "That
which is begun in time is consummated in eternity. Hence time is
not a perpetually revolving image of eternity; it is an irreversible
process moving in a definite direction" (95). The consequences for
individual persons and whole societies are vast. By cleansing the
state of its presumed divinity, by demythologizing the immanent
politics of history, Augustine allows one to discover the order of
the polis within finite human wills. Accordingly, the Augustinian
vision of transcendence, far from oppressing individuals in their
self-expression or societies in their flourishing, bestows upon both
the individual and her society the inextirpable and irreducible
dignity of being co-laborers with Christ, drawn by the love of God
to work toward a spiritual peace and a spiritual kingdom, the city
whose builder and maker is God.

The following four chapters all run variations on this theme.
In chapter 2, an essay perhaps too brief to do its subject justice, the
eminent Jesuit and Christian humanist C. C. Martindale provides

an account highlighting the way the desire for God shaped Augustine's life and character. Subsequently, in chapter 3, Dawson's longtime friend, the polymath E. I. Watkin, treats Augustine as a kind of archetypal embodiment of mysticism, itself defined as the soul's quest for the Absolute Good.[13] Perhaps the least known of the authors in this volume, the Dominican John-Baptist Reeves, reflects in chapter 4 upon the legacy of Saint Augustine for the long tradition of Christian humanism, as important an issue today as it was in the beginning of the last century. Echoing some of the themes sounded in Dawson's opening essay, Reeves sketches an argument for taking Augustine's prodigious assimilation of the empire's great learning and his reproduction of it in the service of Christ and Church both as the historical source for the preservation of humanistic learning throughout the Middle Ages and as the preeminent model for Christian engagement with culture. For all of his rumored dualism and otherworldliness, with Augustine it is never a case of bifurcating church and culture, Christian and pagan, or theology and liberal learning. Instead, as Augustine argues in *De doctrina Christiana*, the pagan or, rather, humanistic learning of the classical traditions is preserved, caught up, and transfigured in the Christian calling to know God through Word and sacrament. Because God has chosen to speak with us through human instruments and human languages—and most thoroughly through his incarnation in the man Christ Jesus—human learning is accorded an ineluctable dignity. As Reeves writes,

> [Augustine] was much more than a literary humanist
> and the father of literary humanism. For his own and all

13. It needs to be said that Watkin's chapter, which draws upon some of the material he presented in his earlier study, *The Philosophy of Mysticism*, is occasionally marked by some of the anachronisms that characterize so many discussions of mysticism from the first decades of the twentieth century—a tendency to treat "mysticism" as a kind of perennial religious fact, rather than an historically and socially conditioned possibility, for instance. Nevertheless, there is still much in the essay of continuing interest, especially the way his treatment of Augustine's mysticism coheres with the vision of Christian humanism treated by other authors in this volume.

succeeding ages he solved, both in theory and practice, the attitude to be adopted by Christians towards those things which in their origin are human and not peculiarly Christian. Before his day, in the West at any rate, there was no such example of Christian humanism so complete as this. (154–55)

Finally, in chapter 5, Fr. Martin D'Arcy—who was later to author *The Mind and Heart of Love*, a philosophical study of *eros* and *agape*—turns his attention to the philosophy of St. Augustine, essentially reading Augustine as the preeminent philosopher of Christian love. The genitive is both objective and subjective, for D'Arcy argues that Augustine's philosophy is not only about love and desire—the love of God for us and the desire for God that drives us—but is also itself marked by an awareness of the limitations of human rationality and, therefore, of the need for philosophy to be suffused, ordered, and transfigured by the workings of love. Accordingly, Augustine "refuses to allow natural reason the whole field in philosophy" (181), a move that upsets the chaste distinctions between philosophy and theology upon which a certain type of scholasticism and a certain type of secularism equally insist. Reason is neither secular nor wholly ordered toward immanence; reason itself has an adorative vocation, its weight and direction provided by a divine love—*pondus meus, amor meum* (*Conf.* 13.9.10)—its consummation nothing less than the exchange of love in the vision of the Triune God.

The second set of essays issue from Catholic thinkers across the Channel, four from France and Przywara's from Germany. All five of them deal in one manner or another with the question of Christian philosophy, whether it is possible and, if so, how. Though Augustine remains the subject of these final chapters, Aquinas and the neo-scholasticism of the nineteenth and early twentieth centuries are constant presences, implicitly in the essays by Roland-Gosselin and Przywara, explicitly in the pieces by Maritain, Gilson, and Blondel. Because the latter three chapters deal with such similar themes, I'll treat them together, skipping Maritain for the moment and turning now to chapter 7. In this chapter, Roland-Gosselin, condensing many of the arguments from his 1925 volume *La morale de saint Augustin*, presents us with what he calls Augustine's "system of morals." Roland-Gosselin argues that the greatness of Augustine's moral philosophy may be seen, first, in his overcoming of materialism as a principle of happiness, and then, secondly, in his realization that even the cultivation of the soul alone cannot deliver true beatitude. As Roland-Gosselin argues, Augustine came to see that the teachings of the Stoics and the Greco-Roman moralists were profoundly inhuman precisely because the paths they prescribed were "superhuman" (257). The effort to rid one's soul of desire, fear, joy, and sorrow, to achieve complete equanimity or impassibility—such an effort was finally self-destructive, for these are natural qualities of the soul and not merely habits of the body alone. Moreover, Roland-Gosselin argues, Augustine's greatness as a moral thinker lies in the way he went decisively beyond the moral philosophers of antiquity by showing how the anthropological observation—"We tend naturally to seek for God"—might be turned into a normative claim: "We are bound to seek God." How can one legitimately travel from this *is* to an *ought*? "Nature," says Gosselin, "can only express a wish, an optative; it can never utter an imperative" (260). Augustine, however, is able to surpass the naturalistic metaethical constraints of the ancients precisely by drawing upon a robust theology of creation, for in creation God makes things to be what they in fact *are* and declares them *good*. Thus, for Augustine, the whole of our moral obligation, and the whole of the law, stems from the injunction "Give to each his due, to God, to self, to others; and do this for the love of God" (261).

Erich Przywara's chapter, "St. Augustine and the Modern World," is another of the most enduring and consequential pieces within *Monument*. Pryzwara was an extraordinary figure: a Jesuit priest and leading Catholic intellectual, he served on the editorial team of *Stimmen der Zeit* (*Voices of the Times*), an important German monthly dedicated to a vigorous Christian engagement with modernity. This put Przywara at the center of many of the currents within the Catholic intellectual renaissance discussed above. Equally adept in philosophy and theology, Przywara was among the first to bring Catholic philosophy into a creative dialogue with phenomenologists such as Husserl, Scheler, and Heidegger, on the one hand, and with leading Protestant theologians such as Karl Barth, on the other.[14] Augustine and Newman stood at the heart of much of Przywara's work: when *Monument* was published, Przywara was in the process of editing an important anthology of the writings of Saint Augustine while also translating into German the work of John Henry Newman (whom he called *Augustine redivivus*). Both figures play prominent roles in this chapter, which takes as its starting point the oft-repeated claim that modernity is a kind of outworking of Augustine's thought.[15] Przywara claims, by contrast, that modernity derives not so much from Augustine as from the irreconcilable tension between competing pseudo-Augustinian distortions of the African bishop's legacy: "The modern world is indeed the advent of Augustine, but an advent to overcome it from within" (278). Przywara argues that the modern pseudo-Augustinian turn to the subject—anticipated in the Reformation's desire for subjective knowledge of the assurance of salvation, and philosophically actualized in Descartes's quest for epistemological certainty—was inherently unstable. By locating the quest for certainty in the rational powers of the self, modernity simultaneously inflated the self beyond its station and paved the way for the shadow of this inflated and thus unsustainable self-regard to return in the form of skepticism and nihilism. Przywara sees this conflict played out in a series of later philosophical polarities: notably, in the tension between the rationalist optimism of Malebranche and

14. For more on Pryzwara, see John R. Betz, "Metaphysics and Theology: An Introduction to Erich Przywara's *Analogia Entis*," in Przywara, *Analogia Entis*, 1–115.

15. Recent iterations of the claim that Augustine lies behind the genealogy of modernity can be found in Charles Taylor, *Sources of the Self*, and Phillip Cary, *Augustine's Invention of the Inner Self*. For strong counterarguments against this narrative, see Michael Hanby, *Augustine and Modernity*, and Lydia Schumacher, *Divine Illumination*.

the epistemological Jansenism of Pascal, on the one hand, and then especially in the Hegelian divinization of thought as the Absolute, and the ironic, anti-philosophical, Kierkegaardian unmasking of reason's pretensions to find room for religion. Accordingly, Przywara sees modernity caught in an aporetic shuttle swinging from the "comprehended Hegelian God, Who is therefore not God" to "the unattainable God of Kierkegaard, of Whom therefore man must despair" (305). The distorted legacy of Augustine thus runs through Descartes into the bifurcations of modern consciousness. Are we condemned to live or go mad in the tension between these irreconcilable positions, stuck in what Gregory Bateson might have described as a kind of modern "double bind"? No, argues Przywara, our way out lies, as it were, in a step back, a return to the genuinely Augustinian position that Descartes forfeited in his embrace of pseudo-Augustinian extremes. What we need is the recuperation of an Augustine, writes Przywara "who decisively overcomes the Augstinianism of modernity—it should be obvious where alone in this modern age his spirit finds its perfect reincarnation: in Newman." What Newman especially receives from Augustine is a vision of transcendence as the superlative mode of immanence, God's genuine otherness as the source of a nearness beyond that of any created thing, "the unity of the 'God Who is at once without and within'" (305).

Chapters 6, 9, and 10, by Maritain, Gilson, and Blondel respectively, deal directly with the very idea of Christian philosophy. Indeed, this triptych of chapters arguably launched the controversy over Christian philosophy that occupied the attention of so many Catholic intellectuals throughout much of the 1930s.[16] Is the notion of Christian philosophy a coherent one? Does it make sense to talk about a Christian philosophy as, say, something distinct from secular philosophy or Christian theology? It is fitting that writings commemorating the fifteenth centenary of the death of Augustine should spark such a controversy, for Augustine's way of reconciling philosophy and theology—often expressed in his phrase

16. Sadler, *Reason Fulfilled by Revelation*, 34.

credo ut intelligam—might justifiably be seen as the leitmotif of any philosophy claiming to be genuinely Christian. In response to the essays included here, as well as to a number of publications elsewhere, a great debate about whether Christian philosophy was desirable or even possible ensued and brought to the fore a series of questions about the relationship of faith and reason, theology and history, doctrine and demonstration, the natural and the supernatural, the connection of reason to will and desire, and the very nature of philosophy and theology themselves.

In chapter 6, Maritain attempts to show how one might reconcile the diverse approaches of Augustine and Aquinas. Essentially, Maritain argues that the two approaches and their diverse metaphysics most differ in the way in which they primarily understand *wisdom*. For the Christian, Maritain argues, wisdom can either refer to a gift of the Holy Spirit, that is, the *infused wisdom* that leads finally to beatitude, or to theological wisdom, in other words, a theological and philosophical systematization of knowledge. This latter road is the path taken by Maritain's Aquinas and, while the living faith of Augustine's spiritual wisdom must always remain the lifeblood of the concrete Christian person, Aquinas's method points to the importance of an inquiry that proceeds not by one's own disposition and sentiments but rather according to the intellectual constraints of the essences and ideas one seeks to know. Maritain takes Augustine's Neo-Platonism to be an "incontestably deficient" metaphysic (203), but this hardly matters for Augustine's theology erupts from the vitality of his spiritual life and not from ratiocination. Augustine's Christian philosophy, such as it is, is more of a metaphysical intuition descended from a higher wisdom than it is a philosophy or a system of metaphysics (236), but for all that it never rationally reconstructs the paths through which someone unacquainted with such religious experiences might come to believe. Thus, for Maritain, Aquinas's way offers something our own age especially needs, a genuinely philosophical and not merely theological or spiritual approach to matters of faith:

Put a scientist before St. Augustine's doctrine and he is
confronted with a world of religious wisdom with which
his own intelligible universe cannot establish a living
connection. If, as a believer, he accepts this teaching, his
thought is cut in twain. The marvel of Thomist wisdom,
the metaphysic of being and causes, of theology as a science, is that such knowledge, placed at the topmost peak
of human reason, conscious of its inferiority to infused
wisdom, superior to all others, and distinguishing only
to unite, establishes in the human soul, without altering
or diminishing by an iota, a rigorous coherence and vital
solidarity between such spiritual activities as touch the
heavens and such as touch the earth. (240)

Maritain's proposed reconciliation of Augustine and Aquinas
essentially commends a division of labor, one not at all out of place
in the milieu of early twentieth-century neo-scholasticism: let us,
he seems to say, cultivate Thomistic minds and Augustinian hearts.
Gilson's approach, in chapter 9, by contrast, signals a greater break
with neo-scholasticism precisely to the degree that it contemplates
a vital future not only for Augustinian theology and spirituality
but also for Augustinian philosophy and metaphysics. Gilson begins, as he had a couple of years earlier in his magisterial volume
The Christian Philosophy of Saint Augustine, by insisting upon this
point: Augustinianism is not only a "Christian philosophy," it is, in
one sense, the paradigm of Christian philosophy precisely insofar
as it makes faith the catalyst for thought (334). Augustine was fond
of quoting Isaiah 7:9 (LXX), "Nisi credideritis, non intelligetis"—
unless you believe, you will not understand. This maxim, says
Gilson, "is and will always remain the charter of every Christian
philosophy. It is what distinguishes a Christian system not only
from anti-Christian systems, but even from systems merely compatible with Christianity" (316). Nevertheless, Gilson recognizes
that neo-scholastic thinkers have been particularly skittish about
Augustine's philosophical contributions, a concern that Gilson
traces largely to problems of reception history. The fragmentary
and occasional nature of Augustine's texts—arguably, a correlate of

their attention to concrete human life and subjectivity—rendered Augustine's writings particularly susceptible to distortion and mis-understanding. The metaphysical straitjackets of Cartesianism and the mystical intuitions of ontologism and German Idealism, for example, imagine themselves to be following in an Augustinian line, but in fact deeply disfigure the thought of Augustine him-self. The remedy for these distortions is not the marginalization of Augustine and his philosophical legacy, but rather an Augustin-ian *ressourcement*, a return to the texts and thought of the saint himself.

What do we find when we return to Augustine's texts in search of his Christian philosophy? We find that, far from being the precur-sor of rationalism or idealism, Augustine never begins with mere ideas, but rather always begins with facts, especially the facts of concrete human experience. By recuperating Augustine's "radical empiricism," Gilson argues, one is able to see that Augustine and Aquinas differ, not as theology to philosophy, but rather as two philosophical approaches rooted in two different starting points. Where Thomas begins with the cosmos and with the essences of created beings, Augustine begins with the soul and its powers (336). The structure of their arguments are remarkably similar; it is only in their departure points that they differ. Both Augustine and Thomas seek to find their way to God through the traces that God has left of himself in the contingencies of creation. For Augustine, this con-tingency is especially seen in the precarious fact that our intellect finds itself capable of making true judgments while nevertheless not being itself the sufficient cause of the truth of our judgments. But if not from us, then from where does the truth of our judgments come? Gilson's exposition is worth quoting at length:

> It is in no case possible for man to start from God to
> deduce from Him the creature; on the contrary, he must
> mount from the creature to God. The course recom-
> mended by St. Augustine—and herein lies his personal
> contribution to the treasure of tradition—is the path to
> God, leading through this particular creature which is

man, and in man, thought, and in thought, truth. But this means, quite beyond speculations about the nature of truth and its metaphysical conditions, a sort of moral dialectic that, taking as object of its search the search itself by man of God, endeavors to show the presence in the heart of man of a contingency much more tragic and disturbing than that of the universe, because it is the contingency of our own beatitude. Even when we know how and why we are capable of truths, we still need to know why we are capable of the desire of truth; we need to understand the presence in us of an appeal by God who, working in our soul, creates in us a fruitful restlessness, moves, stirs our soul, and leaves it no rest until it has finally put itself into His hands. (338)

At end, Gilson concludes, Augustinianism and Thomism are not at odds with one another, nor is one intrinsically to be preferred to the other; rather, they must both be seen as complementary but distinct metaphysical paths, two Christian philosophies, one proceeding by an inner way, the other walking the great outdoors, but both capable of lending their impressive strength to the ongoing tasks of Christian theology and culture.

The final chapter of *Monument* is given to Maurice Blondel, known affectionately as the philosopher of Aix-en-Provence. Like Dawson, Blondel is far too little remembered and appreciated today despite his having been a towering intellectual figure in the early decades of the twentieth century and perhaps the single most important *provacateur* in the controversy over Christian philosophy. His first great work, *L'Action*, set off a firestorm of controversy when it sought to establish the right relationship between purely philosophical inquiry and the great mysteries of the Christian faith. Infuriating secularists and neo-scholastics alike, Blondel had argued, and would continue to argue throughout his life, that reason itself inherently raised questions and sought ends that only a supernatural religion could provide. Eventually, Blondel came to see that Augustine was the great pioneer of such an approach. Blondel's contribution to *Monument*, "The Latent Resources in

St. Augustine's Thought," was the fruit of nearly ten years spent teaching and meditating upon Augustine. It was also the first of Blondel's works to be published in English.

As far as Blondel is concerned, the future belongs to Saint Augustine in a far more radical way than nearly any of Blondel's contemporaries had yet acknowledged. Although there is much to commend in Gilson's winsome and evocative reconstruction of Augustine's thought, Blondel held that Gilson's reconciliation of Augustine and Aquinas was still too partial and abstract. Gilson allowed Augustine his place as a philosopher, but still split Christian philosophy into two competing paths, the inner and the outer, both salutary and commendable, but each finally irreconcilable to the other. For Blondel, by contrast, Augstine's thought was something far richer than one philosophical option among others. Rather, Augustine's work offered contemporary readers "a unity of thought and life, a novel superior kind of philosophy in close relation to the aspirations and needs of many contemporary minds . . ." (345). Not even a philosophy for Christian peoples alone, Augustinianism presents modern men and women with "a truly integral philosophy . . . susceptible of unlimited adaptations and developments" (348).

Indeed, the path Augustine offers us is one that restores the grandeur of philosophy by reuniting the paths of speculation and adoration, "of philosophy and salvation alike" (379). The metaphysical discomfort of the human mind and heart is what gives rise to philosophy. However, insofar as philosophy fails to find a rational solution to its perplexity, this very failure successfully opens reason to the deliverances of a superior order (356). It is not that philosophy might be provoked to new insight under the impress of revelation, but philosophy itself becomes, for Blondel following Augustine, a moment in the integral experience of Christian life and faith. Moreover, Blondel contends that this is not only Augustine's path but also, however much some of his interpreters may protest, the path of Thomas Aquinas. Those neo-scholastics who claim to discover in Aquinas a strict demarcation of philosophy from theology and nature from grace are wrong both speculatively and historically, not least because Augustine and Aquinas equally recognized a natural desire for the supernatural in the heart of created existence (356–57). Aquinas, to be sure, clarified certain aspects Augustine's teaching left obscure—and provided powerful tools for thinking about the relations of the natural and the supernatural—but in doing so Aquinas was animated by Augustine's own spirit and was, indeed, acting as perhaps Augustine's most faithful disciple. To ignore this relationship is to distort both saints. Indeed, "[t]he revival of Thomism makes the revival of Augustinianism still more desirable, less dangerous, and more beneficent" (368).

Nearly a century later, Blondel's contributions—along with most of those in the other chapters collected in *A Monument to Saint Augustine*—read as remarkably prescient. The renewed attention to Augstine by thinkers in France, Britain, and elsewhere served as one of the key catalysts for overcoming the hegemony of a narrowly rationalist and arguably hypermodern form of neo-scholasticism. The spirit of Saint Augustine that so animated both the discussions in Frank Burns's Chelsea salons and the intellectual controversies over Christian philosophy in Europe is one that unites the mystical and the speculative, the head and the heart, the feeling intellect and the thoughtful passions. The impact of this Augustinianism is hard to overstate. The work of the *ressourcement* theologians—Henri de Lubac, Hans Urs von Balthasar, Jean Danielou, and many others—drew mightily upon the thought of Augustine, and often upon many of the writers collected in this volume, in order to complement the interwar renaissance in Catholic thought and culture with a new spring in Catholic theology, one whose deep influence upon Vatican II remains visible, if nevertheless controversial, to this day.

Today, the issues explored in this volume appear as salient as ever. John Milbank has argued that, now that the heyday of liberal Prostestant theology seems to have passed, the new divide in twenty-first-century theology is one that pits a kind of romantic orthodoxy against a "classical" neo-scholasticism. The advocates of the former—followers of Augustine, Newman, and Blondel, but also figures such as Coleridge, Ruskin, and David Jones—believe that the legitimacy crises of our postmodern moment may be traced to the hiatus modernity interjected between reason and the higher eros to which a more integral Christian intellection is always ordered.[17] By contrast, a putatively "classical" orthodoxy repeats the claims of earlier neo-scholastics and holds that our modern problems stem for the most part from a series of rational mistakes, errors that a tighter, more analytic, and secure use of reason might fix. Accordingly, for the classically orthodox, what we need are new, more demonstratively powerful iterations of natural theology and natural law theory rooted in the strict demarcations of nature and grace. For the romantically orthodox, by contrast, what we need is really a renewed integral Augustinianism, a conversion of the feeling intellect, such that we become as attentive to the probative power of beauty and love as to the spiritual elevation of dialectic and arugment. For those of us who live on the farther side of "The Break," it is not enough for us to hear new arguments; we must be initiated into new worlds, new cosmic and social imaginaries always being converted and reshaped by the love of God in Christ. This is not in any way to minimize the importance of truth or formal argument, but rather to recognize that fidelity and access to the truth involves more than cognitive assent; it requires metanoia, the transformation of our intellect by the renewing of our minds in fellowship with the one who is the way, the truth, and the life.[18]

17. Milbank, "The New Divide: Romantic versus Classical Orthodoxy."

18. It is important to note that the Augustianism of this volume, and the romantically orthodox recuperation of Augustine in our own day, is worlds apart from the way that the terms "Augustinianism" and "neo-Augustinian" serve as terms of opprobrium in many post-Vatican II polemics. Massimo Faggioli, for example, has described the post-conciliar situation as a debate between "neo-Augustinian" and a "post-Vatican II [neo-]Thomist" schools. Faggioli argues that the neo-Augustinian approach sees the church and world not as interspersed, but rather as rivals. This supposedly Augustinian vision sees the world as so beset by sin and death that it always merits the Church's distrust and caution. On the other side, Faggioli identifies a "progressive" group of revisionary Thomists who hold "that twentieth-century theology

At the heart of Augustine's life and theology is the paradox of our ineluctable aspiration toward the divine, on the one hand, and our equally prevalent tendency to turn from God, on the other. Because we seek and we turn with both our minds and our hearts, our remedy must be equally holistic. As any reader of the *Confessions* knows, the concrete tension of this vital situation is dramatic and palpable. "You have made us for yourself, O Lord, and our hearts are restless until they rest in you." Restless, yes, but also inconstant, and prone to error. "You were inside me and I was without." What Augustine explores through his own biography in the *Confessions* he portrays through (a certain) world history in the *City of God*: the theodrama of our inextirpable longing for God and our inevitable failure to know and love him. The tension is overwhelming and it is only relieved—whether for persons and their lives, for societies in history, or for the cosmos itself—through the complete reconciliation of divinity and humanity in the incarnate face of Christ. In other words, as Gilson notes in his contribution to this volume, while we begin our inquiries from the concrete fact of our own created *eros* for the divine goodness, truth, and beauty, we do not rest our inquiry upon the subjective fact of our longing but rather upon God's always prior quest for us. We love him because he first loved us, as the apostle says (1 John 4:19).

The personal, historical, and cosmic centrality of the incarnation for Augustine's thought renders it a perpetual font both for a true Christian humanism and for a truly Christian philosophy. For Augustine, in his own way, as much as for Aquinas, grace does not destroy nature but surprises and perfects it.[19] This is something completely different from, say, the Cartesian conceptualist

should do with modern philosophy and social sciences what Thomas had done with Aristotle in the thirteenth century, but now based on a new view of the relationship between faith and history . . ." Permit me only to note how odd it would seem to Dawson, Gilson, D'Arcy, or Blondel to see Augustine identified with this kind of reactionary anti-historicism and cultural pessimism. See Faggioli, *Vatican II*, 66–91.

19. For a defense of this reading of Augustine, especially as against extrincisist construals of illumination, see Schumacher, *Divine Illumination*.

deformation of Augustine's interior quest, the Lutheran quasi-Augustinian opposition of the gift of faith and our essentially desultory human reason, or from Theodore Beza's monstrous disfigurement of Augustinianism in the doctrine of "double predestination." Augustine is too great and too important a figure to be handed over to such pseudo-Augustainain parodies. Far better for us to consider the theological, cultural, and artistic rediscovery of Augustine by the authors in this anthology and by those they influenced. When we do so we will meet an Augustine sobered by our limitations but consumed with the cosmic sweep and unfathomable scope of the workings of grace upon all human endeavors, even our human failings. In these pages we are reintroduced to an Augustine who remains historically distant and yet is nevertheless our peer, and not only our peer but perhaps, as Dawson, Gilson, Blondel, and Przywara all intimate, our future as well.

Bibliography

Boersma, Hans. *Nouvelle théologie and Sacramental Ontology: A Return to Mystery*. Oxford: Oxford University Press, 2009.

Burns, Tom. *The Use of Memory: Publishing and Further Pursuits*. London: Sheed & Ward, 1993.

Cary, Phillip. *Augustine's Invention of the Inner Self: The Legacy of a Christian Platonist*. New York: Oxford University Press, 2000.

Eliot, T. S. *The Letters of T. S. Eliot*. Edited by Valerie Eliot, Hugh Haughton, and John Haffenden. Vol. 3. New Haven: Yale University Press, 2011.

Faggioli, Massimo. *Vatican II : The Battle for Meaning*. New York: Paulist, 2012.

Griffiths, Bede. *The Golden String*. Springfield, IL: Templgate, 1980 [1954].

Hanby, Michael. *Augustine and Modernity*. Radical Orthodoxy. London: Routledge, 2003.

Harp, Richard. "A Conjuror at the Xmas Party." *Times Literary Supplement*, December 11, 2009, 13–15.

Hittinger, Russel. "Two Thomisms, Two Modernities." *First Things* 184 (2008) 33–38.

Kasper, Walter. *Theology and Church*. New York: Crossroad, 1989.

Kerr, Fergus. *Twentieth-Century Catholic Theologians: From Neoscholasticism to Nuptial Mysticism*. Malden, MA: Blackwell, 2007.

Lothian, James R. *The Making and Unmaking of the English Catholic Intellectual Community, 1910–1950*. Notre Dame: University of Notre Dame Press, 2009.

Milbank, John. "The New Divide: Romantic versus Classical Orthodoxy." *Modern Theology* 26 (2010) 26–38.

Przywara, Erich. *Analogia Entis: Metaphysics: Original Structure and Universal Rhythm*. Translated by John R. Betz and David Bentley Hart. Grand Rapids: Eerdmans, 2014.

Sadler, Gregory B. *Reason Fulfilled by Revelation: The 1930s Christian Philosophy Debates in France*. Washington, DC: Catholic University of America Press, 2011.

Schumacher, Lydia. *Divine Illumination: The History and Future of Augustine's Theory of Knowledge*. Challenges in Contemporary Theology. Malden, MA: Wiley-Blackwell, 2011.

Taylor, Charles. *Sources of the Self: The Making of the Modern Identity*. Cambridge: Harvard University Press, 1989.

Watkin, E. I. *The Philosophy of Mysticism*. London: G. Richards, 1920.

INDEX

INDEX

(*Note.* Subject-matter is not always referred to in the actual words used in the text. The nearest or most convenient equivalent has been made to represent the varying words or phrases used by different authors.

Points relating personally to Saint Augustine are grouped with some attempt at system under his name, and usually omitted elsewhere.)

394

CPSIA information can be obtained
at www.ICGtesting.com
Printed in the USA
LVHW081319220819
628587LV00016B/406/P

9 781532 613586